THE ARMY OF ONE

The Army of One

A Christian's Guide to Spiritual Warfare

Jon Cody

© 2025 Jon Cody. All rights reserved.

No portion of this book may be reproduced in any form without written permission from the publisher or author, except as permitted by U.S. copyright law.

Scripture quotations marked *(ESV)* are taken from The Holy Bible, English Standard Version®, ESV®), copyright © 2001 by Crossway, a publishing ministry of Good News Publishers. Used by permission. All rights reserved.

Scripture quotations marked NIV are taken from The Holy Bible, New International Version®, NIV®. Copyright © 1973, 1978, 1984, 2011 by Biblica, Inc.™ Used by permission of Zondervan. All rights reserved worldwide. www.zondervan.com

ISBN:979-8-9924966-0-4
Library of Congress Control Number: 2025901564

Published by: JCC Publishing

Cover Verse: *1 Corinthians 12:27 NIV*

This book is dedicated to all who have supported me on my Christian walk

TABLE OF CONTENTS

Acknowledgment 1
Prayer 3

1 Life Before Christ   6
The Missing Link 8
The Good and the Bad 10
Being Slaves to Sin 14
The Inability to Do Things on Our Own 15

2 The Calling   32
Hearing the Call 33
Picking a Path 36
Accepting the Call 38

3 The Recruitment   44
What's Your Story? 48
How Do I Join? 52
What Is Jesus's Significance? 53

4 The Journey Begins   58
Wanted Dead or Alive 61
A New Life 64
What Is Your Life Source? 67

5 Out with the Old   70
Why We Must Be Broken 72
We Will Be Challenged 76
Accepting Forgiveness and Forgiving Others 77

6 Recognize Your Place   82
You Are Trying Too Hard 87
God Is in Control 91

7 Discovering Who You Are   94
Why Are You Here? 99
What Defines You? 102
What Is Your Purpose? 105

8 Becoming United   112
No Dream Team 117
Building Each Other Up in Christ 121
Learn How to Love 124

9 Graduation Day — 130
- Your Daily Workout — 135
- Humble Yourself — 136
- No Place to Judge — 140

10 Knowing Your Leader — 150
- The Father — 153
- The Son — 155
- The Holy Spirit — 159

11 The Armor of God — 164
- Belt of Truth — 166
- Breastplate of Righteousness — 170
- Footgear of Readiness — 172
- Shield of Faith — 174
- Helmet of Salvation — 178
- Sword of the Spirit — 180
- Power of Prayer — 185

12 Knowing Your Enemy — 188
- The Roaming Lion — 192
- You Can't Always Count On Friends — 193
- Quick to Listen, Slow to Speak — 194
- A Testing of Faith — 195
- No Power Is Greater Than God's — 198

13 Types of War — 202
- Biological Warfare — 203
- Cyber Warfare — 208
- Trench Warfare — 213

14 Battle Wounds — 224
- Rest and Healing — 226
- Addressing the Wounds — 230
- Finding Victory — 234

15 Undeserved Grace — 240
- The Life-Changing Choice — 246
- Wavering Belief — 248
- Overcoming Doubt — 255
- Share the Gospel — 256
- Service to God — 256

16 The War Is Won — 256
- What Is Praise and Worship? — 256
- Celebrating Victory — 256

Sinner's Prayer — 256
Verse Index — 253

ACKNOWLEDGMENT

To every preacher, teacher, friend, or foe; to every family member, acquaintance, or stranger alike; to anyone who has a part in my life, big or small, I thank you for your inspiration and lessons taught on my life's journey. Every encounter is a learning opportunity that has helped shape my views and made me a stronger person. To everyone who continued to believe in me despite my struggles—thank you for sticking with me.

PRAYER

Father God,

Thank you for the mission to write this book and the words to fill it. I pray that you will bless it and reach hundreds and thousands of readers who will benefit from the truths presented, as I have, Lord. I pray that if I am wrong or have a different opinion from that of my readers, they will not let that distract them from the truth. I pray for everyone who picks up this book to strengthen their calling to be soldiers for you. Bless every one of them in Christ's name.

Amen.

PART 1
THE BROKEN

1

LIFE BEFORE CHRIST

On your mark!

Get set!

Go!

Go on—start running.

Oh, I didn't tell you where you are going?

Just go. You will figure it out.

How often do you feel as if this is your life? From the day you were born, people expected you to get up and go. But you did not know where you were going or why. You knew you had to go, as there must have been a reason for your being here. Yet the destination remained unknown.

We have entered a race unlike any other. No other race can compare to this one, with the obstacles, challenges, and skills involved in this race. There is no set starting line or a single winner, but we are all in the race until the end.

Imagine this race as an expansive jungle where we were all given the same task—to get ourselves to the finish line. When we first entered the jungle, none of us had any idea where to go or what to do, and we became scared. Many obstacles and dangers surrounded us, creating a sense of urgency to find safety.

Luckily, we were not alone. Our parents or loved ones cared for most of us as we took on this race. But as life went on, something still felt missing. We sought friends and family or got involved in different activities to distract us from the feeling that something was wrong. Some of us gave up and settled for whatever we found, never venturing out again to find that missing something. Others persisted and wandered around, looking for things to guide us or to give us the answers we sought.

Over time we got used to the surrounding dangers. The struggles we faced became a part of our existence as we began to wonder about the purpose of it all. But then we noticed that the jungle was not only big and scary but also beautiful. The beauty of the creations before us became a mystery everywhere we looked.

Who was responsible for this creation? Was there more? Why was it so challenging? The race, the jungle, and the challenges all pointed to something bigger than we could ever imagine. Our journey starts now.

* * *

We all have struggles, but how we deal with them differs greatly between individuals. How do you deal with your struggles? Can you overcome them? Or do you let them sit, working away at your life until you can't handle them anymore? What makes the difference?

As you know by now, life is full of struggles. You can often overcome minor struggles quickly. But others can be intense and may last years or even your entire lifetime. What happens when you cannot overcome a struggle on your own? Who do you turn to? Where do you go? Do you ever feel stuck in a never-ending battle, wishing you could break free but finding that you can't?

Most, if not all, of our struggles are consequences of sin, either directly or indirectly. Thankfully, Jesus has the answer.

He said, **"If you abide in my word, you are truly my disciples, and you will know the truth, and the truth will set you free."** *(John 8:31–32 ESV)*.

I have had many battles like these in my life. Some I have conquered, while others I am still fighting, but I am no longer stuck. God's truth has released me from the chains that held me back. I may repeatedly fail in my newfound freedom as I work through the lessons God is trying to teach me through individual battles, but with God's grace, I will achieve the ultimate victory.

This book consists of lessons almost every Christian must experience in their walk with God. I invite you to take the journey with me as we learn what it means to fight in the Army of One. Together we will fight, and together we will win.

The Missing Link

Have you ever sat down and thought about your purpose for living? Many people aim to be happy, live life to the fullest, and have fun while they can. These are not exactly wrong answers, but there is something more. Many may appear to others to be living happy and productive lives. But how often do we remain unsatisfied inside? Not having the answer, we may try to fill this hole with more material possessions, relationships, or work. These things may serve our short-term needs, but our long-term happiness tends to remain unfulfilled.

We may spend our entire lives seeking that fulfillment, moving from one thing to another, trying desperately to fill the void in our hearts. Sometimes we think we have found the solution only to become disappointed later. Other times we grow used to the feeling of emptiness and push it aside, trying to continue with our lives, hoping that the pain will one day disappear.

However, as anyone who has ever experienced a physical injury would know, ignoring pain can often make things worse. Treating injuries with the wrong treatment also does nothing to fix our problems. So why do people do such things with the emptiness and pain they feel in their hearts?

Solomon experienced much of this trouble himself in the book of Ecclesiastes. Because of his great wealth, he did and had what many of us could only dream of. Whatever he wanted, he got. But in verse 2:11 he writes, **"Then I considered all that my hands had done and the toil I had expended in doing it, and** behold, all was vanity and a striving after wind, and there was nothing to be gained under the sun." *(Ecclesiastes 2:11 ESV)*.

Now, therefore, thus says the **LORD** of hosts: **Consider your ways. You have sown much and harvested little. You eat, but you never have enough; you drink, but you never have your fill. You clothe yourselves, but no one is warm. And he who earns wages does so to put them into a bag with holes.** *(Haggai 1:5–6 ESV)*.

What purpose do our daily activities serve? Are we going through the motions with little long-term gain for our actions, or are we serving a power beyond our own? No matter how busy we may be in our daily lives, if we end each day feeling that we have accomplished nothing of significance, we may be trying to serve ourselves and not God.

The good news is that God can fix our broken spirit. It doesn't matter what we did in the past or what we do now. We can learn to accept our weaknesses and give them to God. Then, we can turn everything we have done or had done to us for good.

"Come, everyone who thirsts, come to the waters; and he who has no money, come, buy and eat! Come, buy wine and milk without money and without price. Why do you spend your money for that which is not bread, and your labor for that which does not satisfy? Listen diligently to me, and eat what is good, and delight yourselves in rich food." *(Isaiah 55:1–2 ESV)*.

"Seek the LORD while he may be found; call upon him while he is near; let the wicked forsake his way, and the unrighteous man his thoughts; let him return to the LORD, that he may have compassion on him, and to our God, for he will abundantly pardon." *(Isaiah 55:6–7 ESV)*.

The Good and the Bad

Growing up, each one of us lived a different life. Some of us may have lived lives similar to others, but deep inside, each person has experienced the world differently. Everyone has unique

Life Before Christ

experiences, thoughts, beliefs, challenges, or circumstances that have shaped how we view the world in which we live. But we also have one thing in common—we all start our lives as slaves to sin.

Jesus answered them, "Truly, truly, I say to you, everyone who practices sin is a slave to sin." *(John 8:34 ESV).*

It does not matter if we grew up in a "Christian home" or in a home in the "wrong part of town" without a single bit of religious morals to guide us. Everyone who entered this world was born a sinner. Often this sinful nature becomes so engraved in our lives that we do not even know we are doing it, or if we do, we do not care.

For we ourselves were once foolish, disobedient, led astray, slaves to various passions and pleasures, passing our days in malice and envy, hated by others and hating one another. *(Titus 3:3 ESV).*

Sometimes, this sinful nature causes us to doubt our usefulness to God or the world. We believe that our past circumstances are so horrendous that God would never want to use us. In turn, we may avoid the church out of fear of being "found out."

"You don't know what I did" or "I don't deserve to be loved by God" are common phrases that people often use as they struggle in the chains that bind them to the very things they want to avoid. But there is hope! God's love is unconditional. He can and will empower anyone and everyone who comes to Him for freedom.

"I will remember their sins and their lawless deeds no more." *(Hebrews 10:17 ESV).*

Let us look at some examples in the Bible of people like us whom God used to do great things. See if you can find someone to whom you can relate:

> Merely a shepherd, this short-stature man was the youngest of eight. Still in his youth, God appointed him to become the next king of Israel. Against all odds and with a single stone, he single-handedly defeated the most

prominent member of the Philistine army, which had held the rest of the Israeli army at bay for over a month. His faith in God from the beginning brought him this victory and many others that followed as he waited to become king and during his reign over Israel. Like many other men, he fell into lustful temptations and slept with a married woman. He then tried to cover it up by having her husband killed in battle. Despite this, he was still described as a man after God's heart. This man, who had faith from the beginning, was King David. *(See 1 Samuel 17)*.

As a Pharisee, the strictest and most law-abiding sect of Judaism, this man took great pride in persecuting Christians for their belief in Jesus. He not only sent many Christ followers to prison; he even took the lives of many who no longer followed the Jewish laws. This highly educated man came from a highly respected tribe of Israel, but God had other plans. In the middle of a journey to bring more Christians to prison, God blinded him and commissioned him to proclaim the name of Jesus. This man, once Saul, now Paul, became one of the greatest teachers of the Christian faith. *(See Acts 9 and much of the New Testament)*.

Ignored by most and feared by many, this demon-possessed man also had a place in God's army. Jesus showed the man grace and cast out his demons. He could then share that grace with all he knew. Although this character was not named in the Bible, God used this man despite his physical and relational handicaps. *(See Mark 5)*.

As a prostitute by trade, this woman lived a life disrespected by those of the law. When two spies of Israel entered her house, she had every reason to report them to the guards of Jericho. Instead, she hid them in her home, for she knew they were for the Lord. Due to her faith in God, God spared her from the destruction coming to Jericho. This person of great faith, named Rahab, risked her own life to protect members of God's chosen people. *(See Joshua 2).*

Left for dead by his brothers, sold into slavery, and falsely accused and sentenced to two years in prison, this man soon became second in command in a land destined for poverty. Equipped by God with a spiritual gift that was not yet matured, this man found his faith tested by God through a series of trials that prepared him to secure the land of Egypt for God. Through the ultimate test of faith and forgiveness against those who wronged him, Joseph protected the family line that ultimately led to Jesus's birth. *(See Genesis 37–50).*

Considering himself slow in speech and tongue, this man doubted his ability to do as God asked. But God made him a decisive leader who stood up to Pharaoh and led his people, the Israelites, out of Egypt. He communicated directly with God and was responsible for recording and teaching the laws that God directed His people to follow. He was not perfect and made plenty of mistakes of his own, including the murder of an Egyptian. Even so, God used him to lead his people to the Promised Land. God loved Moses, who made it his life to serve with the direction and help of God, who called upon him. *(See Exodus 3).*

In addition, God used many other people in the Bible with more familiar, or in one case, crazy backgrounds.

Abraham thought he was too old to have children, yet he became the father of many nations. *(See Genesis 17).*

Job lost everything—his servants, livestock, family, and health—yet never gave up his faith in God. *(See the Book of Job).*

Jonah was unwilling to fulfill the task God had entrusted to him and ended up being swallowed by a large fish as he attempted to run away. But God used him for the task anyway, despite Jonah's unwillingness to serve. *(See the book of Jonah).*

Isaiah preached naked for three years as commanded by God and was a major Hebrew prophet who taught the supremacy of the God of Israel. *(See Isaiah 20).*[1]

There are many more examples, but I am sure you can now see that God used people of many backgrounds to carry out His will. Perhaps your lifestyle is like that of one of these characters. It does not matter what you have done in the past or if you believe you have nothing to offer, such as education or wealth. It does not matter if you struggle to talk to people or are otherwise disabled. And it does not matter if you have ever set foot in a church or opened a Bible.

You do not have to have your life figured out, nor do you have to be completely free of any addictions or bad habits. You do not have to completely understand what God wants you to do right away. If God calls to you, you should only say, "Here I am," and then listen and obey. God will then work in you in ways you may not have thought possible. You do not have to be perfect before God can use you. God could never use us if that were the case. All you must do is believe and follow where God leads you through His Son, Jesus.

Being Slaves to Sin

"No one can serve two masters, for either he will hate the one and love the other, or he will be devoted to the one

---

[1] This act was a command from God to send a specific message to a specific set of leaders as a sign of Egypt's defeat by Assyria. He was likely partially covered by a small rag. The symbolism was a representation of the prisoners who would soon be free after the conquest.

Life Before Christ

and despise the other. You cannot serve God and money." *(Matthew 6:24 ESV).*

As mentioned earlier, we are bound from birth by the destructive force called sin. Anything that falls short of God's glory is sin. In today's terms it is like breaking the law, but it encompasses much more than we can understand from a worldly perspective.

Everyone who makes a practice of sinning also practices lawlessness; sin is lawlessness. ... Whoever makes a practice of sinning is of the devil, for the devil has been sinning from the beginning. The reason the Son of God appeared was to destroy the works of the devil. *(1 John 3:4, 8 ESV).*

For example, let us say you have a younger brother who continues getting on your nerves by refusing to leave you alone to do something you enjoy. One day you have enough, and you snap at him, maybe calling him a few names and telling him you want him out of your life. Your brother only wants to spend time with you but has now gone away feeling rejected and unloved.

The example I provided would not get you arrested by today's laws and may or may not cause a lasting impact on your brother's life, but it may still be sinful in the eyes of God because of the simple lack of love. Your actions focused on yourself, your words caused emotional destruction, and God did not glorify that interaction with your brother.

Imagine if Jesus lashed out at the people persecuting Him by calling them names or condemning them to hell. He had every right to be mad at being wrongfully prosecuted. Yet He chose to remain silent for much of the trial, and His last words were **"Forgive them, for they do not know what they do."** *(Luke 23:34 ESV).* Jesus continued loving even those who turned on Him, just as He taught us, as anything less would make His entire ministry meaningless.

You may think that eternal punishment in hell for wanting a bit of peace for yourself is extreme. God will understand and not count that against you, right? Unfortunately, that is not the case.

Whoever keeps the whole law but fails in one point has become guilty of all of it. *(James 2:10 ESV).*

Whoever does not practice righteousness is not of God, nor is the one who does not love his brother. *(1 John 3:10 ESV).*

If your whole life were perfect and this was the only bad thing you did, you would still be outside the absolute perfection that God requires to be with Him. He knew it would be impossible for us to come close to the perfection He desires, so He provided a way out with Jesus. Many of us try, thinking of God's requirements as a set of dos and don'ts we must follow, but we often fail to see the bigger picture. Our lives become more about saving ourselves through our actions and less about bringing God the glory by trusting Him to free us from destruction.

Now to the one who works, his wages are not counted as a gift but as his due. And to the one who does not work but believes in him who justifies the ungodly, his faith is counted as righteousness. *(Romans 4:4–5 ESV).*

The Inability to Do Things on Our Own

"Whoever would save his life will lose it, but whoever loses his life for my sake and the gospel's will save it. For what does it profit a man to gain the whole world and forfeit his soul?" *(Mark 8:35–36 ESV).*

In America when convicted of a crime, we are considered innocent until proven guilty beyond a reasonable doubt. Concerning God, we are guilty until declared justified. We do not get a jury because God has already seen our actions. Pleading our case will not help because God always knows our true motives. So then, how do we prove our innocence?

The truth is that we can't. The world's most behaved and law-abiding citizen is just as guilty of sin as the most ruthless, criminally minded individual known to man. Sure, on earth these two individuals would experience drastically different outcomes for their actions, but to the ultimate judge, sin is sin. There are no levels of sin and no way to rectify the sin we have committed by our actions.

"The wages of sin is death" *(Romans 6:23 ESV)*, and there is nothing we can do about it without Jesus.

David also speaks of the blessing of the one to whom God counts righteousness apart from works: **"Blessed are those whose lawless deeds are forgiven, and whose sins are covered; blessed is the man against whom the Lord will not count his sin."** *(Romans 4:6–8 ESV).*

We require help from someone so pure in his ways that Jesus became the only person who could truly fill the emptiness of our hearts and rectify our sinful behavior just by knowing and believing in Him. He clearly states this in John 14:6: **"I am the way, and the truth, and the life. No one comes to the Father except through me."**

Although we were all given free will to live and make our own decisions as we spend our short lives here on earth, we can't earn our way into heaven. Many people think that God will favor them because they obey all the laws or do good things, but that is a false assumption—first, because that is not how you get to heaven, and second, because most people break more of God's laws than they think according to His Word.

Let us look at the Ten Commandments, found in Exodus 20:1-17. Do you know what they are? How many do you think you have managed to avoid breaking?

Please note that some of the examples I am about to give may seem very legalistic and, in our society, would likely go unnoticed or unpunished. However, God sees things differently than the world and judges many actions we would never consider sin. Many of my examples are here to illustrate a point.

First Commandment: You shall have no other gods before me.

Is your love for God first in your life? Is your love for Him more significant than your love for your children, your spouse, your parents, or yourself? How often do you suggest to God, "I've got this; I don't need your help"? Do you think you have more power than God over your life? Would you have the faith to offer your very own son as a living sacrifice if God told you to do so as He did with Abraham in Genesis 22—the son whom Abraham did not receive until he was 100 years old, the son who was supposed to lead many nations?

How often do you hear God telling you to do something, only for you to do the complete opposite because you think you know better or cannot comprehend God's reasoning? Or perhaps you think you hear God, but it's just your own desires. Chances are—you do this regularly. We all do; we cannot help it. When we do, we put ourselves, or those we love, above God. You may not call them God or worship them as you would a god, but you treat that person or thing as more important than Him and thus break commandment one. Are you willing to trust in God entirely and **"to put off your old self, which is being corrupted by its deceitful desires?"** *(Ephesians 4:22 NIV)*.

Jesus expects us to **"Make every effort to enter through the narrow door, because many, I tell you, will try to enter and will not be able to."** *(Luke 13:24 NIV)*.

When we try to achieve salvation through our good deeds or self–righteousness, it does not matter how much we may know about God. We risk being shut out of His kingdom if our salvation does not come from Him alone.

Life Before Christ

Second Commandment: You Shall Not Make for Yourself an Idol.

The second commandment may be the most recognized failing point of most people. Of course, you probably do not have a golden calf near your bedside that you pray to every night before bed, but what is near your bed? Is it your Bible so you can get into the Word of God, or is it a magazine to catch up on your favorite celebrity gossip, sports, or technological breakthroughs? Perhaps it is your phone. People these days spend so much time on their phones browsing social media or doing other tasks that they miss out on the rest of the world around them. Do you consume large amounts of time learning facts about people or popular trends that have little to no direct impact on your life? Sometimes, you may know more about others than you know about yourself—and more importantly, than what you know about God.

Now, some may argue that idols are only thing that represent a god or an object of worship. But 1 John 2:15-17 *(ESV)* has this to say:

Do not love the world or the things in the world. If anyone loves the world, the love of the Father is not in him. For all that is in the world—the desires of the flesh and the desires of the eyes and pride of life—is not from the Father but is from the world. And the world is passing away along with its desires, but whoever does the will of God abides forever.

The more time you spend thinking about a particular person or thing, the less time you spend with God. Thus, you consider that person or object more important than the God you serve. Jeremiah 16:19–20 *(NIV)* says about idols, **"Our ancestors possessed nothing but false gods, worthless idols that did them no good. Do people make their own gods? Yes, but they are not gods!"**

Galatians 4:8 *(NIV)* states, **"Formerly, when you did not know God, you were slaves to those who, by nature, are not gods."**

Having interests outside the Bible is okay, but they should not dominate your time or distract you from your fellowship with God. When you start putting work, entertainment, or other things above getting to know your God, it may be time to reexamine your life and bring your focus back to Him. Even "Christian things" such as worship services or ministry obligations can become idols if you forget why you are doing these things.

Third Commandment: Do Not Use the Lord's Name in Vain.

Most people think this commandment is the easiest one to avoid breaking. Just limit your cussing or use substitute expressions such as "Dang it" or "Gosh, darn it," and everything will be okay. Although this may be one possibility to the meaning of the law, and indeed a good practice to follow even if not the true meaning, I will propose that there is more to it than just cussing. This is especially true because God's Word applies to more than only the English language in which those phrases are used and because the sin is often due to the intent behind the words and not the words themselves. Substitution words are just as bad if the attitude behind them remains the same.

To understand this better, let us explore what vain means. According to Webster's dictionary, vain means "having no real value" or "having or showing an undue or excessive pride in one's appearance or achievements."

When you choose to follow Christ, you take on His name. That is where we get the designation "Christian." When you take on that name, you represent what it stands for. Just as when a woman marries a man and changes her last name to that of the man, she represents that family and what it stands for. When people look at you as a Christian, they should know that you represent who God is and what He stands for. If you claim one thing but do another, your words have no value and thus devalue the Lord's name. We must consciously ensure our actions match our words and reflect the God we claim to represent. Every time we knowingly disobey God's plan for us, we are essentially taking His name in vain. We must be God's ambassadors, seeking to reconcile with God and proclaim His name. *(2 Corinthians 5:20).*

It is also worth noting Matthew 23, which refers to scribes and Pharisees who teach one thing and do another—otherwise known as hypocrites. A Christian is not one who simply teaches or hears the Word but one who strives to obey it.

Fourth Commandment: Keep the Sabbath

Out of all the commandments, this may be one of the most often ignored. There is no alternate way of looking at it, as there was with the previous and subsequent commandments, though there is some debate as to the actual day of the Sabbath. Either we keep it, or we don't, but why is it important?

Keeping the Sabbath is the midpoint between laws geared toward loving God and those meant to love others, as summarized in the two greatest commandments mentioned in Matthew 22:37–40. Often in the gospels, Jesus performed work on the Sabbath only to be criticized by the Pharisees. But Jesus had to remind them of the purpose of the Sabbath. He said, **"The Sabbath was made for man, not man for the Sabbath. So the Son of Man is Lord even of the Sabbath."** *(Mark 2:27–28 ESV)*.

Then, in Matthew 12:6–8 *(ESV)*, He said, **"I tell you, something greater than the temple is here. And if you had known what this means, 'I desire mercy, and not sacrifice,' you would not have condemned the guiltless. For the Son of Man is lord of the Sabbath."**

God gave us the Sabbath so we could rest from life's tasks that may distract us from our time with Him. Instead, it became more ceremonial, with its own set of rules enforced by the Pharisees, instead of a means of remembering the things God did for His church.

Hebrews 4:9–11 *(ESV)* says, **"So then, there remains a Sabbath rest for the people of God, for whoever has entered God's rest has also rested from his works as God did from his. Let us therefore strive to enter that rest, so that no one may fall by the same sort of disobedience."**

Whether you celebrate the Sabbath on Saturday, Sunday, or any other day, the point should be to honor the Lord. Romans 14:5–6 *(ESV)* states, **"One person esteems one day as better than another, while another esteems all days alike. Each one should be fully convinced in his own mind. The one who observes the day, observes it in honor of the Lord."**

Isaiah 56:2 *(ESV)* also states, **"Blessed is the man who does this, and the son of man who holds it fast, who keeps the Sabbath, not profaning it, and keeps his hand from doing any evil."** There is a point and benefit to the Sabbath, but ultimately, it is up to the individual's convictions about the day in question. If you were a Jew before Christ came, you might have been punished for your various chores and errands on this day as there were many man-made laws that dictated what was considered work, but Jesus replaced the Mosaic covenant and, therefore, left the Sabbath day open to personal convictions.

Therefore do not let anyone judge you by what you eat or drink, or with regard to a religious festival, a New Moon celebration or a Sabbath day. These are a shadow of the things that were to come; the reality, however, is found in Christ. *(Colossians 2:16–17 NIV)*.

Fifth Commandment: Honor Your Parents

The fifth commandment is another one that many people claim they obey well. Do what your parents tell you when they tell you, and you are good, right? I agree with that conclusion if you are still a child living under your parents' roof. However, this also means following their rules when you're not around them. It

Life Before Christ

does not mean you can push your limits as much as possible when you know your parents likely would disapprove.

My son, keep your father's commandment, and forsake not your mother's teaching. Bind them on your heart always; tie them around your neck. When you walk, they will lead you; when you lie down, they will watch over you; and when you awake, they will talk with you. *(Proverbs 6:20–22 ESV).*

When you move out, do you continue to honor your parents' values, or do you suddenly experiment with everything you were not allowed to do under your parents' supervision? Once you become an adult, you might be free to make your own decisions, but you should still avoid disgracing your parents by respecting at least the fundamental values and morals placed by them. If they did not have good values or morals to begin with, I would suggest honoring them with your own positive values. In addition, you should honor your parents by being willing to take care of them in their old age as they cared for you when you were young.

But why is this important? It teaches us to respect and honor authority and, more importantly, how to honor our heavenly Father. Malachi 1:6 *(ESV)* states, **"A son honors his father, and a servant his master. If then I am a father, where is my honor? And if I am a master, where is my fear? says the LORD of hosts to you."**

In a perfect world, parents are supposed to be the teachers of proper morals and other life lessons. Unfortunately, this is not always the case, but the rule still applies. By honoring your parents' authority, you will also learn to honor the authority of other leaders in your life.

Sometimes, parents fail to teach their children properly. This often results in kids learning the hard way in school, the workplace, or, in the worst cases, jail or prison. Those who learn to respect the authority that God has provided each of us will benefit from the only commandment with a promise, **"that you may live long in the land the LORD your God is giving you."** *(Exodus 20:12 NIV).*

Sixth Commandment: Do Not Murder

If we were to do a poll on which commandment people have broken the least, I bet this one would be the winner unless we polled a high-security prison. Most of us do not go around killing people. So, can we put a star next to our names on this one? Not so fast. As with the commandment below, thoughts count just as much as actions in the eyes of God. Have you ever been so angry with someone that if you knew you could get away with it, you might have inflicted severe harm or death on them? Maybe you are strong enough not to go through with it, but Jesus condemns even the thought. Any anger toward someone never brings life to that person. Matthew 5:22 *(ESV)* says, **"But I say to you that everyone who is angry with his brother will be liable to judgment; whoever insults his brother will be liable to the council; and whoever says, 'You fool!' will be liable to the hell of fire."** This verse says that even the act of insulting someone with words is punishable by God.

When we put someone down with our words, we do not bring the person life. Instead, we demoralize that person, which may cause mental or emotional pain and suffering. First John 3:15 *(NIV)* states, **"Anyone who hates a brother or sister is a murderer, and you know that no murderer has eternal life residing in him."** This is not what God desires for us. He calls us to bring life and to love one another as He has loved us. The next verse explains what it means to love: **"This is how we know what love is: Jesus Christ laid down his life for us. And we ought to lay down our lives for our brothers and sisters."** *(1 John 3:16 NIV).*

One note about this commandment. This is only about people and not of animals, nor does it refer to acts of punishment, self–defense, war by those designated to do so, or accidental death from another. In both the Hebrew culture and our laws in America today, murder is defined as "the intentional, premeditated killing of another person with malice." Killing, on the other hand, might be justifiable except in the case of accidents. In this case, it must be determined if the accident was caused by a punishable offense other than the charge of murder. But I am neither a lawyer nor god, so try to avoid all the above. Those things might not be defined as murder, but other factors are likely at play that may still be sin.

Seventh Commandment: Do Not Commit Adultery

Adultery is defined as a married person having sexual relations with someone who is not his or her spouse. You would think that staying faithful to your spouse is all that is needed, and you either do so or you don't. Unfortunately, as with all the other commandments, there is more to it in the eyes of God. Even if you have remained faithful physically, this simple commandment could fail in two ways. The first is through lust. Jesus said in Matthew 5:28 *(NIV)*, **"Anyone who looks at a woman lustfully has already committed adultery with her in his heart."** This goes for both men and women, but since men are more visually stimulated, they are more likely to fail this way.

What if you are not married; can you still commit adultery? Even if you are the unmarried one in an adulterous relationship, then you are still in sin, even if the worldly consequences may be less. If neither party is married, you are still not home-free. Although it may not be considered adultery in this case, this action is still a sin called fornication. Not to mention that this act probably started with lust, which we found out is equivalent to adultery in the heart. Despite the view that is becoming more acceptable today, a man is supposed to be with one woman and a woman with one man unless the two are separated by death. The surviving partner is then free to marry again. By choosing to have sex with others before marriage, you take away that special bond between a partner and their future spouse. **"Let marriage be held in honor among all, and let the marriage bed be undefiled, for God will judge the sexually immoral and adulterous."** *(Hebrews 13:4 ESV)*.

Eighth Commandment: Do Not Steal

When your parents teach you well, "Do not steal," seems like an easy rule to follow. Always pay for what you want from the store, and you will avoid getting in trouble with the police or, worse yet, your parents when they find out. Well, as usual there is more. Let us just look at a few examples of other ways you may steal without realizing it.

First, let us visit your place of work. Your employers pay you, expecting you to spend all your time working — but how many of us can say you do this 100 percent? Often, we stop work to catch up with coworkers about our personal lives, or we sit at a computer playing games or doing personal research instead of completing our given work. Then there are those of us who make a daily habit of catching up on the latest gossip at the water cooler or, these days, on social media. These things are all stealing time from the employer paying you. Similarly, employers who hold back wages from their employees who rightfully earned those wages are also stealing.

Look! The wages you failed to pay the workers who mowed your fields are crying out against you. The cries of the harvesters have reached the ears of the Lord Almighty. *(James 5:4 NIV).*

Gossip is another form of stealing that many of us do not consider. Gossiping or talking about someone behind their back steals the person's privacy and can rob them of their dignity and reputation, especially when the gossip is based on lies.

"It is not what goes into the mouth that defiles a person, but what comes out of the mouth; this defiles a person." *(Matthew 15:11 ESV).*

To avoid going on too long with examples, the final way of stealing I will mention is stealing from God directly. We do this primarily by denying God what belongs to Him anyway. God blesses us each with what we need to live, sometimes much more, but it comes with a simple request—that is, to recognize His blessings by returning at least ten percent of your possessions (usually as money) to God and His church to be used to further His kingdom and bless you in ways you cannot imagine. *(See Malachi 3:6–12.)*

Ephesians 4:28 *(NIV)* explains what we should do instead of stealing: **"Anyone who has been stealing must steal no longer, but must work, doing something useful with their own hands, that they may have something to share with those in need."**

Ninth Commandment: Do Not Be a False Witness

What does being a false witness mean? It means to be someone who lies about a person or situation or withholds the truth by not saying anything. Although this commandment generally refers to your testimony for or against another person, it can also apply to your testament of yourself. So why does this commandment matter? If we know the truth but fail to provide it for an innocent person, we are causing harm to that person by allowing him or her to suffer unjust punishment. By lying to protect a guilty person, we become guilty ourselves by aiding in the offense. Similarly, Leviticus 5:1 *(NIV)* states, **"If anyone sins because they do not speak up when they hear a public charge to testify regarding something they have seen or learned about, they will be held responsible."**

Regarding false witness against yourself, you may avoid punishment for your actions here on earth, but you will never escape the eyes of God. On Earth, the truth often gets revealed and actions are punished. Judge for yourself if your words and actions portray the whole truth and nothing but the truth.

Before I move on to the last commandment, I would like to mention that this verse also applies to false teachings or testimonies regarding God's Word. Whether intentionally or not, the manipulation or misuse of scripture to promote a meaning other than one that corresponds with the rest of God's Word is a false witness against that Word. Be careful telling people that

"God told me to do XYZ." Unless XYZ's actions can be backed up with scripture in the proper context, claiming it is from God is giving false testimony to His Word and power.

If anyone teaches otherwise and does not agree to the sound instruction of our Lord Jesus Christ and to godly teaching, they are conceited and understand nothing. They have an unhealthy interest in controversies and quarrels about words that result in envy, strife, malicious talk, evil suspicions and constant friction between people of corrupt mind, who have been robbed of the truth and who think that godliness is a means to financial gain. *(1 Timothy 6:3–5 NIV).*

Guard what has been entrusted to your care. Turn away from godless chatter and the opposing ideas of what is falsely called knowledge, which some have professed and in so doing have departed from the faith.

Grace be with you all. *(1 Timothy 6:20–21 NIV).*

Tenth Commandment: Do Not Covet

The final commandment is harder to recognize on the outside, as it is more about your inner thoughts. To covet means to desire something that is not yours. You may ask, what is wrong with wanting something someone else has? Well, let us look at the rest of the verse. The whole verse states, **"You shall not covet your neighbor's house. You shall not covet your neighbor's wife, or his male or female servant, his ox or donkey, or anything that belongs to your neighbor."** *(Exodus 20:17 NIV).*

What happens when we covet such things? The most obvious answer is that those thoughts may eventually lead to breaking some of the previous commandments. These include the commandments against making idols, stealing, committing adultery, and in severe cases, murder. Each of those actions begins with the desire to have something that is not yours.

Life Before Christ

Second, when we covet, we think that we deserve more than what God has provided for us. This leads us to believe we are above God, and our actions will be for ourselves instead of for God.

First Timothy 6:6–10 *(NIV)* states, **"Godliness with contentment is great gain. For we brought nothing into the world, and we can take nothing out of it. But if we have food and clothing, we will be content with that. Those who want to get rich fall into temptation and a trap and into many foolish and harmful desires that plunge people into ruin and destruction. For the love of money is a root of all kinds of evil. Some people, eager for money, have wandered from the faith and pierced themselves with many griefs."** Coveting takes us further from God, which is the last thing we want.

"Watch out! Be on your guard against all kinds of greed; life does not consist in an abundance of possessions." *(Luke 12:15 NIV).*

Keep your lives free from the love of money and be content with what you have, because God has said, **"Never will I leave you; never will I forsake you."** *(Hebrews 13:5 NIV).*

* * *

The reason for writing this is not to make you feel that you are a horrible person but to make you realize that you cannot possibly obey all that is required to enter heaven on your own. The Ten Commandments are just 10 of 613 laws found in the Old Testament, yet we cannot get those correct. Making Christianity a list of dos and don'ts is the perfect way to ensure failure.

Even if you are "the perfect angel" and have somehow managed to break only one of these laws, that is enough to deny you access to heaven. Thankfully, many of the 613 laws in the Old Testament were not meant for us to begin with, as they were written for the Jewish population of the time in accordance with their culture and way of living. Even those that can be applied to our lives today are difficult if not impossible to keep, but there is still a reason for them.

Why then the law? It was added because of transgressions, until the offspring should come to whom the promise had been made, and it was put in place through angels by an intermediary. *(Galatians 3:19 ESV)*.

God knew we could not keep the laws, but He gave them for two reasons. The first was to provide a basis for living. Without laws there would be no order, as people would do whatever they pleased. Since we are prone to sin, doing what we please will eventually lead to widespread disaster.

What then? Are we to sin because we are not under the law but under grace? By no means! Do you not know that if you present yourselves to anyone as obedient slaves, you are slaves of the one whom you obey, either of sin, which leads to death, or of obedience, which leads to righteousness? *(Romans 6:15–16 ESV)*.

Whoever knows the right thing to do and fails to do it, for him it is sin. *(James 4:17 ESV)*.

The second reason was to demonstrate that we cannot achieve a perfect record without help, no matter how hard we try. Proverbs 16:2 *(NIV)* shows us that even our best intentions are not safe. **"All a person's ways seem pure to them, but motives are weighed by the LORD."** Similar verses can be found in Proverbs 12:15; 21:2; and 30:12.

The only way to achieve salvation would be by accepting the grace of God, who gave us His Son so that we may live. Read Acts 13:38–39 *(NIV)*: **"I want you to know that through Jesus, the forgiveness of sins is proclaimed to you. Through him, everyone who believes is set free from every sin, a justification you were not able to obtain under the law of Moses."**

This does not mean we are free to do whatever we want without consequence if we believe in Jesus. The Scriptures still have a purpose for general living. Second Timothy 3:16–17 *(NIV)* states,

Life Before Christ

"All Scripture is God-breathed and is useful for teaching, rebuking, correcting and training in righteousness, so that the servant of God may be thoroughly equipped for every good work." Sin still has consequences and can affect our lives and the lives of others if left unchecked.

For those who are self-seeking and do not obey the truth, but obey unrighteousness, there will be wrath and fury. There will be tribulation and distress for every human being who does evil, the Jew first and also the Greek. *(Romans 2:8–9 ESV).*

God does not want us to suffer the burdens of sin. He wants to set us free. God will not prevent us from sinning, but He will give us the freedom and ability to step away if we choose to do so. He wants to help us live our lives to the fullest they can be, but we must first understand that we cannot do it alone. We will not succeed.

No temptation has overtaken you except what is common to mankind. And God is faithful; he will not let you be tempted beyond what you can bear. But when you are tempted, he will also provide a way out so that you can endure it. *(1 Corinthians 10:13 NIV).*

God calls us to do great things, but we must first answer that call. There is a long journey ahead, and I promise you it will not be easy, but if we put our trust in God to get us through, it will be the most rewarding thing we have ever experienced.

You were called to freedom, brothers. Only do not use your freedom as an opportunity for the flesh, but through love serve one another. For the whole law is fulfilled in one word: "You shall love your neighbor as yourself." *(Galatians 5:13–14 ESV).*

2

The Calling

The following is a mini-story that will appear throughout the rest of the book.

"We want you! Seeking good men and women with a desire to serve," one sign read as I continued walking down the road after another long, hard day at work.

"Let us change your life," read another sign.

Like they can change my life. I bet they don't know about all the stuff I have to put up with, I thought as I continued walking home without considering the message's meaning.

You see, everything seemed to be going against me. The managers at my job treat me horribly, and the job hardly pays the bills. My health and relationships are in ruins, and every time I try to get ahead, I seem to get knocked down repeatedly.

Little did I know, I was already beginning my training for an even greater task than I could ever imagine. I was being called to help save the world.

How often are we stuck in our ways and miss the signs laid out right in front of us? Many people go about living their lives not aware of their true calling. They may go to work or school or try to raise a family, repeating the same old routines daily. Often, these people find themselves unaware of their purpose. They feel stuck in a never-ending cycle, leading to more conflict and stress.

Others follow a different path. To the outside world and maybe even themselves, they seem to have it all figured out. They appear happy and give people the impression that they have everything they want. Many would classify them as successful. However, a good number of those people also have their share of struggles. They may have everything, yet something is still missing in their hearts, so they spend most of their lives trying to find it.

Although these assumptions are broad and may not cover everyone, the common thing is that no matter who we are and how we live, we all have needs and struggles. We think we deserve more, so we continuously strive to find a purpose and make our short life on this planet meaningful and happy.

But for who or what are we living? Are we living for ourselves, our family, our friends, or for a higher being?

Do not be ashamed of the testimony about our Lord, nor of me his prisoner, but share in suffering for the gospel by the power of God, who saved us and called us to a holy calling, not because of our works but because of his own purpose and grace, which he gave us in Christ Jesus before the ages began, and which now has been manifested through the appearing of our Savior Christ Jesus, who abolished death and brought life and immortality to light through the gospel. *(2 Timothy 1:8-10 ESV).*

Hearing the Call

What would you do if you saw a sign promising to change your life? Would you ignore it, knowing that many such claims exist? Would you at least be curious and want to know what the sign's owner is offering?

Most people fall into one of two camps. Those who ignore it have probably seen such claims before and investigated, only to be disappointed by the results. They may now be full of doubt, not wanting to be taken advantage of or hurt by false promises. Or perhaps they are already happy with their lives and do not need someone to "change their lives."

Hope deferred makes the heart sick, but a desire fulfilled is a tree of life. *(Proverbs 13:12 ESV).*

The curious folks are the seekers. They are unhappy with at least one aspect of their lives, and they will entertain any idea that may improve it. Some of these people may just be greedy and never satisfied with what they have, so they want more. Others recognize something missing in their lives and want to find that one thing to fill that hole they have been harboring for far too long.

"I love those who love me, and those who seek me diligently find me." *(Proverbs 8:17 ESV).*

God rarely gives us literal signs recruiting us to be with Him, but He often puts us in circumstances designed to help us realize we need Him. Each sign or circumstance is hand-tailored for each individual and designed to capture our attention. Some of us recognize that call, and others remain stubborn and insist on figuring things out for ourselves. Some may have tried to trust God but gave up before God could complete His work. They did not know that God's solution might not always be quick and easy.

How is God calling you?

One way He calls us is through other people. They may be people we love or know or strangers trying to share God's love. Often the effectiveness of these people depends on your current life circumstances. If you are a seeker, as described above, these people may provide the answer you have been looking for. If everything is going well in your eyes or you think you have it under control, people approaching you with the news of Jesus may irritate you.

My brothers, if anyone among you wanders from the truth and someone brings him back, let him know that whoever brings back a sinner from his wandering will save his soul from death and will cover a multitude of sins. *(James 5:19–20 ESV).*

Another way God calls us is through our circumstances. Perhaps you lived your life a particular way only to see it fall apart around you. Your choices of going to parties, getting drunk, doing drugs, or anything else you felt inclined to do just did not provide the fulfillment you had hoped they would. You felt that you had reached a new low. When you did not know where else to go, you sought after God.

Therefore, since Christ suffered in his body, arm yourselves also with the same attitude, because whoever suffers in the body

is done with sin. As a result, they do not live the rest of their earthly lives for evil human desires, but rather for the will of God. For you have spent enough time in the past doing what pagans choose to do—living in debauchery, lust, drunkenness, orgies, carousing and detestable idolatry. They are surprised that you do not join them in their reckless, wild living, and they heap abuse on you. But they will have to give account to him who is ready to judge the living and the dead. For this is the reason the gospel was preached even to those who are now dead, so that they might be judged according to human standards in regard to the body, but live according to God in regard to the spirit.

(1 Peter 4:1–6 NIV).

Maybe you were not involved in the things mentioned above, but suddenly you lost or almost lost someone you loved in an accident, or perhaps you were in an accident yourself. This realization made you realize how short life is and became the turning point in your life.

His days are determined, and the number of his months is with you, and you have appointed his limits that he cannot pass. *(Job 14:5 ESV).*

O LORD, make me know my end and what is the measure of my days; let me know how fleeting I am! Behold, you have made my days a few handbreadths, and my lifetime is as nothing before you. Surely all mankind stands as a mere breath! Surely a man goes about as a shadow! *(Psalm 39:4–6 ESV).*

Less dramatic circumstances could result from time spent outside observing the creations that God provided for us to enjoy. Maybe you have seen the same scenery thousands of times, but one day it clicked for you, and you fell in love with the one who created the beauty before you. You may not have known much about Him, but you sought an answer.

How many are your works, LORD! In wisdom you made them all; the earth is full of your creatures. There is the sea, vast

and spacious, teeming with creatures beyond number— living things both large and small. *(Psalm 104:24–25 NIV)*.

The heavens declare the glory of God, and the sky above proclaims his handiwork. Day to day pours out speech, and night to night reveals knowledge. *(Psalm 19:1–2 ESV)*.

God may also call you directly, as He did with many biblical characters. You may not be presented with a burning bush or a pillar of fire as in the Bible, but a direct calling these days may come in the form of a dream or something you read that connected with you. Some people experience what they describe as a faint whisper calling out to them. These callings are often hard to hear if we are not ready to receive them, but it can be a life-changing experience when you learn to hear God's voice.

The LORD said, "Go out and stand on the mountain in the presence of the LORD, for the LORD is about to pass by."

Then a great and powerful wind tore the mountains apart and shattered the rocks before the LORD, but the LORD was not in the wind. After the wind there was an earthquake, but the Lord was not in the earthquake. After the earthquake came a fire, but the LORD was not in the fire. And after the fire came a gentle whisper. *(1 Kings 19:11–12 NIV)*.

Picking a Path

"Enter through the narrow gate. For wide is the gate and broad is the road that leads to destruction, and many enter through it. But small is the gate and narrow the road that leads to life, and only a few find it." *(Matthew 7:13–14 NIV)*.

In the Matthew 7 verse above, I like to picture two trails up the side of a mountain with views unlike anything you have ever seen if you reach the top. Trail one is the trail traveled by most. This trail is a well-worn, man-made path with little resistance other than the mountain's length and a gradual incline. Along the way, it offers short glimpses of the full beauty in store for those who reach the top.

For many these glimpses are enough to satisfy them. They continue up and down the path, thinking they have seen all the mountain offers. They become comfortable traveling on the path that so many have traveled before them. They are comfortable doing it independently, with little support from others.

Some, however, realize that there is something more to be sought, and they spend considerable time trying to find it, but there are many paths along the way. Most of these paths lead not to the top of the mountain but to other distractions that look great but still do not compare to the treasure awaiting those who reach the top. Unfortunately, many of these seekers become satisfied with these newfound "treasures" and discontinue their search for the path that leads to the top.

They will throw their silver into the streets, and their gold will be treated as a thing unclean. Their silver and gold will not be able to deliver them in the day of the Lord's wrath. It will not satisfy their hunger or fill their stomachs, for it has caused them to stumble into sin. *(Ezekiel 7:19 NIV).*

A small percentage of the people traveling on this mountain know there is still a greater treasure to discover. They spend the time necessary to find the one correct path that leads to the top, crying, **"Show me your ways, LORD, teach me your paths."** *(Psalm 25:4 NIV).* When they find it, they realize it is no walk in the park. There are many obstacles along the way that would make the weak turn back and settle for one of the other treasures of the mountain. But for those who persist and call on God for help through the struggles they face, they reach the top. They achieve their goal and are blown away by the ultimate treasure that awaits them. Nothing that the mountain offers below compares to the experience of pure beauty you experience as you stand and relish all that the mountain offers at the top of your climb.

The Calling

You make known to me the path of life; you will fill me with joy in your presence, with eternal pleasures at your right hand. *(Psalm 16:11 NIV).*

This is how it is when we choose to follow Christ. Many do not realize how much more life has to offer by accepting our position in God's army. For those who are called and accept what God offers, there is a heaven beyond what I can begin to describe in this book. It may be a difficult road ahead, but as you will see through the rest of the book, you are about to become a part of something much more significant. Your journey will not be undertaken alone. You will have the help of all those who have gone before you and those making the journey with you. You will be led by the ultimate guide, Jesus, who knows exactly where to go and how to get there.

Accepting the Call

When you accept God's call, your whole life changes. **As for you, you were dead in your transgressions and sins, in which you used to live when you followed the ways of this world and of the ruler of the kingdom of the air, the spirit who is now at work in those who are disobedient. All of us also lived among them at one time, gratifying the cravings of our flesh and following its desires and thoughts. Like the rest, we were by nature deserving of wrath.** *(Ephesians 2:1–3 NIV).*

Because of a loving Father's desire to see His children live in peace, the ways of our past have been made right through His Son.

Praise be to the God and Father of our Lord Jesus Christ, who has blessed us in the heavenly realms with every spiritual blessing in Christ. For he chose us in him before the creation of the world to be holy and blameless in his sight. In love he predestined us for adoption to sonship through Jesus Christ, in accordance with his pleasure and will— to the praise of his glorious grace, which he has freely given us in the One he loves.

In him we have redemption through his blood, the forgiveness of sins, in accordance with the riches of God's grace that he lavished on us. With all wisdom and understanding, he made known to us the mystery of his will according to his good pleasure, which he purposed in Christ, to be put into effect when the times reach their fulfillment—to bring unity to all things in heaven and on earth under Christ. *(Ephesians 1:3–10 NIV).*

When God calls you, you can be sure He loves you and has a place for you in His kingdom. God has called every one of us to join His kingdom. It is not an exclusive, invitation-only club. John 3:16 says, **"God so loved the world…"** It does not say, "God so loved [insert your nationality, religion, or social status here]." Jesus died to save the world and everyone in it who believes in Him.

The saying is trustworthy and deserving of full acceptance, that Christ Jesus came into the world to save sinners, of whom I am the foremost. But I received mercy for this reason, that in me, as the foremost, Jesus Christ might display his perfect patience as an example to those who were to believe in him for eternal life. *(1 Timothy 1:15–16 ESV).*

It is pleasing in the sight of God our Savior, who desires all people to be saved and to come to the knowledge of the truth. For there is one God, and there is one mediator between God and men, the man Christ Jesus, who gave himself as a ransom for all, which is the testimony given at the proper time. *(1 Timothy 2:3–6 ESV).*

God sends out a personal invitation to everyone, but many people do not answer that call, as they are too busy with their own lives to hear God calling. Revelation 3:20 *(NIV)* says, **"Here I am! I stand at the door and knock. If anyone hears my voice and opens the door, I will come in and eat with that person, and they with me."**

To accept the Father's call and receive the blessings of salvation, we must be willing to humble ourselves. This means turning from our old ways that bring destruction and acting again like a child eager to learn the ways of his or her Father in heaven. Without the Father's help, direction, and resources, our purpose in life will never advance to its full potential.

"Truly, I say to you, unless you turn and become like children, you will never enter the kingdom of heaven. Whoever humbles himself like this child is the greatest in the kingdom of heaven." *(Matthew 18:3–4 ESV).*

First Peter 2:1–3 *(ESV)* instructs us to **"put away all malice and all deceit and hypocrisy and envy and all slander. Like newborn infants, long for the pure spiritual milk, that by it you may grow up into salvation— if indeed you have tasted that the Lord is good."**

Some of us have accepted Christ long ago but still have not been taught the basics of Christianity and are missing out on the life-changing blessings of God.

Though by this time you ought to be teachers, you need someone to teach you again the basic principles of the oracles of God. You need milk, not solid food, for everyone who lives on milk is unskilled in the word of righteousness, since he is a child. But solid food is for the mature, for those who have their powers of discernment trained by constant practice to distinguish good from evil.

Therefore, let us leave the elementary doctrine of Christ and go on to maturity, not laying again a foundation of repentance from dead works and of faith toward God, and of instruction about washings, the laying on of hands, the resurrection of the dead, and eternal judgment. *(Hebrews 5:12–6:2 ESV).*

Brothers and sisters, I could not address you as people who live by the Spirit but as people who are still worldly—mere infants in Christ. I gave you milk, not solid food, for you were not yet ready for it. Indeed, you are still not ready. You are still worldly. For since there is jealousy and quarreling among you, are you not worldly? Are you not acting like mere humans? *(1 Corinthians 3:1–3 NIV).*

Our fleshly desires have kept many people, both Christians and non-Christians alike, from receiving and sharing the fruit of God's love.

So I say, walk by the Spirit, and you will not gratify the desires of the flesh. For the flesh desires what is contrary to the Spirit, and the Spirit what is contrary to the flesh. They are in conflict with each other, so that you are not to do whatever you want. But if you are led by the Spirit, you are not under the law.

The acts of the flesh are obvious: sexual immorality, impurity and debauchery; idolatry and witchcraft; hatred, discord, jealousy, fits of rage, selfish ambition, dissensions, factions and envy; drunkenness, orgies, and the like. I warn you, as I did before, that those who live like this will not inherit the kingdom of God. *(Galatians 5:16–21 NIV).*

By becoming children of God, we receive the fruit of the Spirit. Notice it is a singular fruit and not plural, which implies that we receive a comprehensive all-in-one package when we allow the Spirit to work.

The fruit of the Spirit is love, joy, peace, patience, kindness, goodness, faithfulness, gentleness, self-control; against such things there is no law. *(Galatians 5:22–23 ESV).*

Let us break down the significance of the fruit of the spirit to better understand it. First, you get love *(1 Corinthians 13)*, and God is love *(1 John 4:8)*, so you get all of who God is. Then you receive joy, the joy of knowing you have been saved not just from a few sins of the flesh but from all sins *(Jude 24)*.

Next comes the peace in knowing you are no longer an enemy of God but a friend *(John 15:15; Romans 5:1)*. Patience to follow God's timing instead of our own comes next *(Hebrew 6:12; Colossians 1:9–14)*, followed by kindness and forgiveness toward others *(Romans 2:3–4; Ephesians 4:32)*. Similarly, goodness implies our generosity toward others, both in the church and outside the church. Faithfulness also comes with the integrity to stick to your word — doing what you say you will do. Gentleness relates to people who are not easily provoked or may be nurturing. And finally, we receive the discipline and power to resist the temptations of the flesh through self-control *(1 Corinthians 10:13)*.

Receiving Christ and the fruit of the Spirit should never make one have a "holier than thou" attitude toward nonbelievers, because the reality is that until Jesus's return, we will continue struggling with the desires of the flesh just like nonbelievers. We must learn to turn from the world's temptations and seek after God with everything we have. In Galatians 1:10–12 *(ESV)*, Paul writes, **"Am I now seeking the approval of man, or of God? Or am I trying to please man? If I were still trying to please man, I would not be a servant of Christ. For I would have you know, brothers, that the gospel that was preached by me is not man's gospel. For I did not receive it from any man, nor was I taught it, but I received it through a revelation of Jesus Christ."**

You see, we have been delivered by becoming like children, learning the ways of the Father and receiving the fruit of the Spirit. **"He has delivered us from the domain of darkness and transformed us to the kingdom of His beloved Son, in whom we have redemption, the forgiveness of sins."** *(Colossians 1:13–14 ESV)*.

And now, dear children, continue in him, so that when he appears we may be confident and unashamed before him at his coming.

If you know that he is righteous, you know that everyone who does what is right has been born of him. See what great love the Father has lavished on us, that we should be called children of God! And that is what we are! The reason the world does not know us is that it did not know him. Dear friends, now we are children of God, and what we will be has not yet been made known. But we know that when Christ appears, we shall be like him, for we shall see him as he is. All who have this hope in him purify themselves, just as he is pure. *(1 John 2:28 – 3:3 NIV)*.

3

The Recruitment

The next day I was doing errands because it was my day off. I was walking around town when I passed the tiny office with those signs I saw the day before.

I stopped and peered into the dimly lit room that was empty except for a man behind a large desk and a couple of cushioned chairs placed before the desk.

Curious, I walked in to see what was being offered.

"Hi," I said as I walked in toward the figure sitting at the desk. "I was walking by and noticed the signs out front saying you could change my life."

"That's correct," the man said as he stood up and approached me. "What is your name?"

I told him my name was Allen and met him near the desk to shake his hand.

"Pleased to meet you, Allen; you've come to the right place. Please have a seat and tell me a little about yourself. Oh, and you can call me JC."

I took a seat as he returned to his desk and sat down with his hands clasped in front of him on the desk.

"Well, what do you want to know?" I looked around the room again with a puzzled look on my face. "I'm not even sure what this place is."

"Oh, well, you can think of me as a recruiter. And let us start with 'How is your desire to serve?'"

"Oh, like an army recruiter? If you are an army recruiter, where are all the flags, your uniform, and all that good stuff? As far as my desire to serve, um, I guess it is all right. I work at the big retail store down the road, and I like helping customers and all, but I wish I could do more to use my talents better. The management does not seem to take me seriously there. I'm thinking about getting a new job."

JC leaned back in his chair with his hands folded behind his head and answered, "Well, that's a good start, but there is room for improvement. And yes, you could think of me as an army recruiter, just not the army you are thinking of. I follow a commander higher

The Army of One

than any earthly powers. My leader can and will change your life beyond what you could imagine and can provide you with everything you would ever need. But it requires a lot of work and a lot of faith."

"That sounds like a great deal. I mean getting everything I've ever wanted. I could sure use more money and a car—and a girlfriend, but what is the catch? You said it requires a lot of work. What kind of work? It's not illegal, is it?"

Chuckling, JC replied, "No, you heard me wrong. I didn't say He will give you everything you want. I said He would provide everything you need. This means that when it seems like everything is going wrong, He will provide a way out. He will not let you get into any circumstance you cannot handle on your own, and He will provide what your heart desires if it is according to His will for your life. All you have to do is trust in Him completely and obey His commands, and everything will be given to you according to His will."

"Okay, you lost me," I said as I leaned forward in my chair with a confused look on my face. "So, I don't get a ton of money or my car or anything else on my wish list? Instead, I get a bodyguard who gives me stuff, but only if he wants to? But to do that, I must do everything he says and trust in him, though I don't have a clue who he is?"

"Well, sort of. Think of Him more like a father who loves you more than anyone else ever has. He wants to see you grow and become a great man, but He does not want to control your life. Instead, He will let you go and learn on your own. He wants you to experience life for yourself, hoping that you will come to Him for advice when you are struggling, to be a friend when you are lonely, or simply someone who will give you the encouragement you need during your day-to-day trials. He has his expectations, but if you break them, He is also very forgiving if you recognize your mistakes and strive to do better by following His instructions. He knows what you need better than you do and will provide only that. If He knows you need a car, money, or a girlfriend to do His will, He will give you that, but only if it is for His will, not your own. He won't give you something that will hurt you in the long run, even if you believe it will solve all your problems in the short run."

Leaning back again and pausing for a few moments to consider all that was said, I finally responded. "Okay, how do I get all that? I really could use someone in my life to look up to for advice and encouragement like that. I am up for a change if he can do it. Where do I sign up?"

The Recruitment

"There's no 'signing up,'" JC said as he walked around the desk to sit next to me. "And. of course, He can do it—, He can do anything. There are only three requirements to join this army and to get the most from it. First, you must confess that you are a sinner and that you need help and forgiveness, as you are weak and unable to conquer your sins on your own. Second, you must ask my leader, God, to be your leader, to guide you through your struggles, and to be your provider and protector. Third, you must believe in and accept the sacrifice He made so that you may be free from the chains that keep you from being with Him. It also helps to accept that He is the ruler of your life and has your best interests in mind. When you do that, you will be a part of the greatest army in the world, and you will begin experiencing changes in your life that will greatly support the army you serve. It will not be easy, but the reward gained will far outweigh any problems you encounter along the way. Are you ready for this commitment?"

"Yes, I am. Let's do it!"

Why do people join the military? Some join to serve their country or prove bravery and strength. Others join because of family tradition, which they are expected to be a part of. Some might join only because they have nowhere else to go. Maybe they are by themselves or running away from something or someone. Perhaps they are trying to find a new sense of belonging, a new family, or a new home. It could also be that they feel that they messed up so badly that they should have to fight in a war to regain a sense of respect for themselves and from others. In the worst case, maybe they feel so bad about themselves or what they have done that they believe they have nothing else to live for, so they join, expecting to die in combat.

There are other reasons people join the military, but have you ever considered that the reasons mentioned are also some of the same reasons people seek religion in their lives? The Christian body is made up of people from many different backgrounds. A good number of people become Christians because that is all they know. One or both of their parents were Christians, and they would force their kids to get up and go to church every Sunday.

The Army of One

This is how I started my Christian walk. As a kid, I hated getting up early in the morning and sitting through a long, boring service, not knowing what was happening. The weekend was supposed to be my time to sleep in and play. Going to church was just another thing I "had to do." Eventually it became a habit for me to go, but then there was a point at which I understood what I was learning, and the church became somewhere I wanted to go.

I was eight years old when I decided I wanted to "follow God," but even then I still did not get why. Though I went through the routines of attending church and Sunday school and did all that stuff "good kids" do, I may not have been a Christian until several years later when I moved with my family and found a new church. My new church was where I discovered the meaning and power of knowing God on my own. It was the first time I felt that my peers wanted to be there and were not forced to be there. As a result, I also wanted to be there.

What's Your Story?

I imagine many of you reading this have had similar circumstances of growing up Christian, though you did not understand all of it until later. I also believe there are just as many of you out there who did not grow up Christian. Some of you may come from broken homes or maybe lived with parents who did not go to church or were part of another religion. Some of you may have started trying to discover yourselves through various activities. Some may have gotten in trouble from their actions, and some may have just continued piling on activity after activity, trying to find a purpose until they could not take it anymore and God was introduced into their lives.

Below are a few examples of ways people may have come to Christ.

Family Tradition

As I mentioned earlier, many people fall into this category of how they started their journey into the Christian faith. Unfortunately, this scenario also comes with a warning. Some people think that just because they grew up practicing Christian traditions, they are guaranteed a place in heaven. This is not the case. Jesus warns us of that fact in Matthew 7:21–23 *(NIV)*:

"Not everyone who says to me, 'Lord, Lord,' will enter the kingdom of heaven, but only the one who does the will of my Father who is in heaven. Many will say to me on that day, 'Lord, Lord, did we not prophesy in your name and in your name drive out demons and in your name perform many miracles?' Then I will tell them plainly, 'I never knew you. Away from me, you evildoers!'"

To illustrate this, let us go back to the military theme. Perhaps you spent your whole life as a military brat; one or both parents were in the military. Perhaps your parents raised you as if you were in the military, keeping strict rules, expecting military-like perfection, and more. You may appear to be a part of the military based on your actions, attitude, or appearance to the outsider. You may have extensive knowledge of military principles and ways of life or participated in ROTC, but that alone does not mean you are in the military. You will be considered a soldier only when you consciously decide to walk into the recruiter's office and enlist.

This is the same for the Christian faith. You could practice all the moves, read all the books, or attend all the church or Christian events you want, but you are not a member of His army until you approach God in prayer and accept Him personally as your God.

Growing up in a Christian environment may make it easier to accept, but it also makes it easy for people to think they are saved when they are not. If there is any doubt, pray a prayer of salvation right now to confirm your place in heaven. A prayer will be provided at the end of the book, or you can find a Christian friend or pastor to help you. If you are still doubt, keep praying until you believe. The words aren't what saves you but rather your belief in Christ.

Discovering Your Purpose

Another popular scenario that brings people to Christ is the fact that they started as seekers. Many knew there was something more to their lives, but they could not figure out what. People who share this story probably did not have Christian relationships with their family or friends growing up, but God still reached them. Some people spent significant time studying many religions while others tried various activities. All this was to find the one thing they could connect with to make themselves feel complete. At some point in these people's lives, either through personal study or through a random encounter with someone who shared the gospel with them, these people found the answer they were looking for and accepted God.

Hitting Rock Bottom

People in this category may also have been seekers, though they probably were not seeking any religion. At some point in their lives, through circumstance or personal choice, these people reached a point at which things could not get any worse. Often people in these categories share stories of drugs, alcohol, sex, or other addictions. For some, being workaholics also proved detrimental. They wanted to have fun, be recognized, or be loved. Instead, their actions led them down a path that would prove extremely difficult to leave alone.

Relationships and reputations may have been ruined, self-worth was non-existent, finances may have fallen to the wayside, and depression may have kicked in. Everything was falling apart around them, they thought. They had nothing more to live for.

Some sought help and were fortunate enough to have God revealed to them in their times of trouble. God found these people at their worst and invited them to be with Him.

Tragic Circumstance

"Life is short" is an expression you may commonly hear from people who share this story. Through a near-death experience of their own, or from the loss or near-loss of someone they were close to, these people realized that life was not all about fun and games. They took life more seriously as they learned how short it could be. Many eliminated any activities that had the potential to put them back into similar adverse circumstances. They sought a way to improve their lives by being more productive, strengthening relationships that may have fallen short, and just figuring out how to live their lives to the fullest. They realized they were given a second chance, and they changed. This tragic or near–tragic event in their lives became enough to bring focus to their life, and they sought God.

These short generalizations represent only some of the more common themes in testimonies I have heard over the years. The truth is that God can and will work in many ways. I can't imagine all the ways that God may have brought someone to Christ. Every story told is a miracle of God's work in that person's life.

No matter how you come to faith in Christ, your story is never complete. God continues working in you every day, sometimes needing to knock you onto your butt a few times to get your attention. As you continue growing, you will learn new things as your rank in His army increases. Each time, you must consciously acknowledge the new truths that God will teach you throughout your journey. It is a long road ahead, but the trip will always be worth it.

Every person has a different story of how they became Christian. Some stories are more "exciting" than others, but all are works of one God and His Son, Jesus Christ. Every story is a miracle, of a life reborn to God's saving grace. If you are not yet Christian—you are reading this book, so there might be a spark in your heart. Maybe one day you too will let God into your life.

How Do I Join?

We saw some of how people were influenced to find Jesus, but what must happen for this decision to be made official?

Do you have to have a perfect record? No.

Do you have to build up many good deeds before you can be saved? No.

Do you have to understand the whole Bible or basic biblical principles completely? No.

Do you have to talk to someone else to get in? No, but you should tell someone after you have decided so they can celebrate with you and help you on your journey.

The point is that the gift of salvation is accessible to everyone who accepts it. There are no requirements to be freed from the chains that bind you to sin. Jesus is the key. Take that key and believe that it will free you.

In the previous chapter I mentioned the first half of the famous verse John 3:16 *(ESV)*: **"For God so loved the world,"** but the rest makes this relationship so impactful. **"He gave his only Son, that whoever believes in him should not perish but have eternal life."**

"Whoever believes"—that is it. Romans 10:9 *(ESV)* expands on this by saying, **"If you confess with your mouth that Jesus is Lord and believe in your heart that God raised him from the dead, you will be saved."**

This seems so easy, yet people often try to reach heaven on their terms. Jesus states in John 14:6 *(ESV)*, **"I am the way, and the truth, and the life. No one comes to the Father except through me."**

It does not matter how good you have been or how long you have been a Christian. Even people who have been to jail or received the death penalty can accept Jesus into their hearts if they believe and accept what Jesus did for them.

What Is Jesus's Significance?

Since death came through a man, the resurrection of the dead comes also through a man. For as in Adam all die, so in Christ all will be made alive. *(1 Corinthians 15:21–22 NIV).*

God made him who had no sin to be sin for us, so that in him we might become the righteousness of God. *(2 Corinthians 5:21 NIV).*

Jesus suffered the punishment for all sins, from the first sin committed by Adam and Eve to every daily sin that followed, including all the sins that our future generations will commit in their lifetimes.

"The wages of sin is death," according to Romans 6:23, and someone had to fulfill the punishment. Jesus did not get off easy because He was the Son of God. He was whipped within inches of death and had a ring of thorns pushed hard into His head. He was ridiculed, spat on, and tormented. He was then required to travel about half a mile with a wooden cross attached to His back to the crucifixion site. Once there, He was hung on the cross with nails in His wrists and ankles, all while the guards mocked Him and gambled for His clothes. He was poked, prodded, and left to die in one of the most humiliating ways. *(See Matthew 27:24–56).*

That was just earthly suffering, nothing compared to the hell He was about to face. He paid the ultimate punishment for every lie, lustful thought, selfish desire, and hurtful remark. He paid for every cheat, every addict, every adulterer, and for everyone who ever robbed, wounded, or murdered someone. He also paid for the sins of the people who put Him on that cross. Every single sin, whether great or small, was fully paid for by someone who is perfectly flawless in His very nature. He deserved none of these punishments—we did, but He suffered through them for us. He did this before you and I ever had the choice to accept Him. He did this knowing that some people still would not accept the sacrifice He made for us.

For what I received I passed on to you as of first importance: that Christ died for our sins according to the Scriptures, that he was buried, that he was raised on the third day according to the Scriptures, and that he appeared to Cephas, and then to the Twelve. After that, he appeared to more than five hundred of the brothers and sisters at the same time, most of whom are still living, though some have fallen asleep. Then he appeared to James, then to all the apostles. *(1 Corinthians 15:3–7 NIV)*.

But if it is preached that Christ has been raised from the dead, how can some of you say that there is no resurrection of the dead? If there is no resurrection of the dead, then not even Christ has been raised. And if Christ has not been raised, our preaching is useless and so is your faith. More than that, we are then found to be false witnesses about God, for we have testified about God that he raised Christ from the dead. But he did not raise him if in fact the dead are not raised. For if the dead are not raised, then Christ has not been raised either. And if Christ has not been raised, your faith is futile; you are still in your sins. Then those also who have fallen asleep in Christ are lost. If only for this life we have hope in Christ, we are of all people most to be pitied.

But Christ has indeed been raised from the dead, the firstfruits of those who have fallen asleep. For since death came through a man, the resurrection of the dead comes also through a man. For as in Adam all die, so in Christ all will be made alive. But each in turn: Christ, the firstfruits; then, when he comes, those who belong to him. *(1 Corinthians 15:12–23 NIV)*.

We know that Christ, being raised from the dead, will never die again; death no longer has dominion over him. For the death he died, he died to sin once for all, but the life he lives he lives to God. So, you also must consider yourselves dead to sin and alive to God in Christ Jesus. *(Romans 6:9–11 ESV).*

Without Jesus, our bodies would be in total separation from God. If you are not a Christian, you may not understand why this is a big deal and may rejoice at the chance to be separated from any reference to God. This is because God still allows you to experience some of who He is, whether through love, wisdom, or any other way He shares His power.

When your life is finished and you are declared guilty by God because you choose not to accept Jesus's sacrifice for you, every bit of love you have ever known will be taken away. Any freedom you think you have now will be gone. There will be no friends in hell as friendship requires love. Hell will not merely be an extension of the current worldly lifestyle you may be living. It does not matter how rich, how bright, how successful, or how good a person you may have been here on earth. Without the acceptance of Jesus, everything you have ever worked for will disappear. There will be only an afterlife full of agony, extreme loneliness, and pain.

People gnawed their tongues in anguish and cursed the God of heaven for their pain and sores. *(Revelation 16:10–11 ESV).*

They will be tormented day and night forever and ever. *(Revelation 20:10 ESV).*

Some may think they have it bad now and that it could not be any worse, but it can. Multiply whatever level of suffering you believe you have now by 100, and you probably have not scratched the surface of knowing what it is to be totally separated from God.

They will be punished with everlasting destruction and shut out from the presence of the Lord and from the glory of his might. *(2 Thessalonians 1:9 NIV).*

Jesus frees us of all this pain and suffering if we accept the gift He has given us. Once we are free, it does not mean we will immediately be immune to sin while we are still here on earth. But once we enter the kingdom of heaven, all sin and pain will be removed. We will experience love in ways we could never imagine here on Earth. We will be wiser, and we will finally feel complete. There will be no more suffering or conflict of any kind. We will be brought back to the state God intended us to be before the fall of Adam and Eve.

He will wipe away every tear from their eyes, and death shall be no more, neither shall there be mourning, nor crying, nor pain anymore, for the former things have passed away. *(Revelation 21:4 ESV).*

The Journey Begins

I left the recruiter's office extremely excited about what was to come. I was ready for a change that would finally make a difference in my life.

The next day I woke up with the sudden realization that life as I knew it was about to be changed entirely. This is the day I start my training. This is the day I will be transformed into a soldier in the army of God.

The road I was about to take was bumpy and full of roadside distractions trying to get me to pull over and delay the process of change I was about to undergo. One thing I knew for sure—someone out there didn't want to make it easy for those making the journey.

As I began the journey to my training camp, doubts flowed in. Would I be strong enough? Would I understand everything the instructors wanted me to do? What if I tried and failed miserably?

I worried if my decision was the right one. Would I have to give up relationships with old friends? Would I be required to stop doing things I enjoyed? What if this was not a fun lifestyle? Would people be proud of me for choosing to serve in this army, or would I be ridiculed by those I care about?

"It doesn't matter now," I thought out loud after driving a while. "I made a commitment, and I will stick to it no matter what the cost."

"Besides, JC told me that God would be my leader and protector. I'm sure He will know what I should do."

With that last thought, I continued driving on, knowing in my heart that the choice I made was the right one.

As I approached the gates of the training camp, I could not help but notice how beautiful it was. Every square inch was covered in precious metals and stones.

As I pulled closer, I witnessed the gate open, and a figure stepped out to greet me. It was JC again! "He must be everywhere," I thought.

I pulled my car into the closest parking space and began to unload my belongings as JC approached.

The Army of One

"Leave everything and follow me!" he commanded in a firm but gentle manner.

"But I need to get my stuff, don't I?" I asked and immediately regretted it as JC turned around and got right up in my face.

"Are you already questioning my commands?" he asked with a hint of sarcastic amusement. "Didn't I tell you in the office we would provide everything you need? Leave your past behind you and follow me." With that, he turned around again and proceeded to walk back toward the gate with me following quickly behind, wondering if I should be scared or excited about what was to come.

To start this section, I would like to share an illustration I heard a while back about a bear in captivity inside a zoo. The zoo was small, and bears are dangerous animals, so this bear was always chained up. Every day at the same time, the zookeeper would put some meat out for the bear to eat. The bear would get up, walk the length of his chain of about fifteen feet, and then go back to his spot to sleep. This routine repeated for years. The bear would get up, eat its food, and then return to his place to spend the rest of his time sleeping. He knew nothing else.

One day, the zookeepers experimented. While the bear was subdued, they removed his chain. When it was again time to eat, the food was placed in the usual spot, and as usual the bear got up, walked the fifteen feet to his food, and returned to his place. After a few days of this, the zookeepers changed the conditions. They moved the food thirty feet away to see if the bear would explore the other areas of his enclosure. But the bear got up, walked fifteen feet, and when he did not find his food, he returned to his spot to sleep, missing out on the dinner only slightly farther away.

Seeing this behavior repeated a few times, the zookeepers changed the circumstances again. They removed the enclosures completely. Now the bear was free and could go anywhere he wished; nothing held him back.

The Journey Begins

As previously observed, the bear got up and walked his fifteen feet to where his food should have been and then walked back to his spot, slowly dying as he became weaker with each passing day.

Although that story is just an illustration, this is the sad reality that most of us face when we become Christians. We have become so used to the sins that have held us in bondage for so long that even when we have been set free, we continue to stick with what we know or try to take it with us. We get so stuck in the patterns of past living that it is difficult for most of us to escape and live in our newfound freedom. Complete life healing could be mere steps away, but so many of us continue staying right where we were, slowly withering away as if we were never set free to begin with.

So let us say you have been set free; now what? Where do you go from here?

For freedom, Christ has set us free; stand firm therefore, and do not submit again to a yoke of slavery. *(Galatians 5:1 ESV).*

Living as a Christian takes work. You must learn how to live your new life all over again. Mistakes will be made, and lessons will be learned, but with the help of our loving God, you will overcome the challenges that lie in your path.

From here on out you are at war with a great enemy determined to keep you locked up under his control. He knows you have been freed, but he will do everything in his power to convince you otherwise and to prevent you from freeing others.

How the rest of your life plays out directly correlates to the amount of power you let the enemy have over you. Only when you learn how to fight and stand firm in your beliefs as a Christian will you see what it means to be free.

Wanted Dead or Alive

I declare to you, brothers and sisters, that flesh and blood cannot inherit the kingdom of God, nor does the perishable inherit the imperishable. *(1 Corinthians 15:50 NIV).*

I have good news and bad news. The good news is that whether Christian or not, you are wanted. The bad news is that one side of the spiritual war for your life wants you dead. The enemy knows how powerful a force you are when you are alive under the power of God and will attempt every trick in the book to prevent you from reaching that point.

My enemies say of me in malice, "When will he die and his name perish?" *(Psalm 41:5 NIV).*

When we were born, we were all born dead spiritually. The sins we are plagued with as humans slowly eat away at our souls until we become nothing more than a walking carcass with no real long-term worth beyond that made up in our minds. Now, I know this sounds harsh, but let me explain. When God created us, He created us to have a relationship with Him. Colossians 1:16 *(ESV)* states, **"All things have been created through Him and for Him."**

God wants to see you have the life He designed for you. **"Jesus said to [Martha], 'I am the resurrection and the life. The one who believes in me will live, even though they die; and whoever lives by believing in me will never die. Do you believe this?'"** *(John 11:25–26 NIV).*

He has a perfect plan for your life that if followed would maximize your relationship with Him. This is the ultimate treasure. The problem is that we have the option not to follow that plan. Instead of following a plan for life, you end up following the enemy's plan, which leads you right down a road of pain and suffering and eventually spiritual death, with no real chance of rescue without Jesus.

"I have said these things to you, that in me you may have peace. In the world you will have tribulation. But take heart; I have overcome the world." *(John 16:33 ESV).*

The enemy takes joy when you attempt to do things without God's backing. He wants you to think that the good things you accomplish result from your efforts. You may wonder why this would be a big deal, and the answer is simple and can be found in Jesus's words in John 15:1–6 *(NIV):*

"I am the true vine, and my Father is the gardener. He cuts off every branch in me that bears no fruit, while every branch that does bear fruit he prunes so that it will be even more fruitful. You are already clean because of the word I have spoken to you. Remain in me, as I also remain in you. No branch can bear fruit by itself; it must remain in the vine. Neither can you bear fruit unless you remain in me.

"I am the vine; you are the branches. If you remain in me and I in you, you will bear much fruit; apart from me you can do nothing. If you do not remain in me, you are like a branch that is thrown away and withers; such branches are picked up, thrown into the fire and burned."

A branch that bears no fruit despite all that the gardener may do to help it along is of no use to the whole of the plant. If God is the life source for your true purpose of bearing fruit (helping others believe), then choosing to separate yourself from that source of life results in your being cut off and left to wither and be burned. At most, we become like a weed. A weed may grow plentiful, but it only hinders the growth of the fruit-bearing plants and must be removed to allow their development. *(See Matthew 13:24– 30, 36–43.)*

Thankfully, if you have fallen from the vine and have withered close to death, you can still be reattached to the vine. The technical term for this is grafting— a complex method of taking a fallen branch and carefully attaching it back into the main vine or trunk. When done correctly, that withering branch has a new chance at life as it becomes connected to a new water source—its source of life.

The process is not as easy as it may sound. You cannot just tape a branch onto a tree anywhere and expect it to survive. It must be carefully cut in such a way that when the detached branch fits in with the main plant, it becomes compatible. If the detached branch remains incompatible and resists making the changes needed to join the host plant, it will die within an inch of its source of new life. *(See Romans 11:11–24.)*

A New Life

So is it with the resurrection of the dead. What is sown is perishable; what is raised is imperishable. It is sown in dishonor; it is raised in glory. It is sown in weakness; it is raised in power. It is sown a natural body; it is raised a spiritual body. If there is a natural body, there is also a spiritual body. *(1 Corinthians 15:42–44 ESV)*.

We must know the complexities involved with grafting in our own lives. If you decide to reunite with the true source of life, changes must be made. Jesus instructs us of these changes in Matthew 16:24–25 *(NIV)*:

"Whoever wants to be my disciple must deny themselves and take up their cross and follow me. For whoever wants to save their life will lose it, but whoever loses their life for me will find it."

When we choose to be a follower of God, we are committing to a new life. We switch sides in the spiritual war for our lives. Instead of letting the enemy continue to starve us of the riches God has in place for us, we are now fighting to maintain those riches. We are now serving a master whose goal is to give us life.

Matthew 6:24 *(ESV)* clarifies that **"No one can serve two masters, for either he will hate the one and love the other, or he will be devoted to the one and despise the other. You cannot serve God and money."**

The Journey Begins

This particular passage is about storing up treasures in heaven (making idols), but it can be equally applied here. Everything we do apart from God is serving another master. There are no double agents in the spiritual battle for our lives. Either we serve one side or we serve the other.

But how does this work?

To grow as Christians, God calls us to die to ourselves and begin a new life following Him. This means we must stop being a weed that hinders the growth of God's fruit and instead choose to live a new life that increases the harvest. Our old ways of doing things are no longer acceptable. God calls us to a higher standard.

When people choose to follow Christ, they do not get off scot-free. We are still responsible for the sin we do and must share the burden of that sin. The punishment we may experience here on earth will be far less painful than the punishment Jesus had to endure to protect us from an eternity in hell, but it must still be done.

Many people will try to keep their worldly goods or way of life to preserve the good life here on earth. By doing so and choosing not to follow God, they give up their chance for a new life. The people who can offer up their worldly possessions and allow God to change them will be the ones who experience the rebirth into the way God intended us to be.

This passage does not always mean we must give up everything we have or know to be called a Christian. God has blessed us all with the ability to create great things and great wealth, and I doubt He would deny us that opportunity to enjoy it. But the question is—are we using these gifts and abilities to better serve God and His kingdom, or are they turning into idols or hindrances in our lives? Are we taking the time to thank Him for what He has given us?

Command those who are rich in this present world not to be arrogant nor to put their hope in wealth, which is so uncertain, but to put their hope in God, who richly provides us with

everything for our enjoyment. **Command them to do good, to be rich in good deeds, and to be generous and willing to share. In this way they will lay up treasure for themselves as a firm foundation for the coming age, so that they may take hold of the life that is truly life.** *(1 Timothy 6:17–19 NIV).*

As in everything, there will be a struggle to give everything up to God, especially right away. Many people hold on to sinful ways long after accepting God into their lives, but there should at least be a conviction present in your heart if you genuinely believe. You should recognize that what you are doing is against the will of God and that you will eventually be paying the price for those actions. This does not mean you are not a faithful Christian if you continue to struggle with various sins, but it does mean you should be praying for God to change your heart to draw you closer to Him.

What Is Your Life Source?

If you have been around for a while, you have probably heard that humans cannot go without water for more than three to five days in ideal conditions. In less-than-ideal conditions, such as extreme heat or after strenuous physical activity, the time you could survive without water would be much less.

In civilized nations water is a seemingly plentiful source. You turn on the faucet in your house or go to the store to purchase water from another source. Sometimes, if you want something a bit more special, you can get water infused with blends of vitamins and minerals or artificial flavoring.

In less civilized nations water is much harder to come by. Sometimes villagers of various tribes must travel several hours to and from a contaminated water source with only a small drum or bucket to carry it in. Depending on the number of people and animals they must provide for, they may have to make this trip several times a day. Their primary purpose of living becomes retrieving water so that others may live.

In biblical times people did not have indoor plumbing in which you could get your water, nor did they have a grocery store to stock up for those days they did not feel like going. In those days if they wanted to drink, they had to get water from a well or river daily, as I described earlier.

One day a Samaritan woman went to draw her water for the day. While there, she came upon a stranger who happened to be Jesus. He was thirsty but had no way to draw water from the well.

After some debate about why He was talking to her since Jews never associated with Samaritans, Jesus responded by offering her a different kind of water: living water (not available at your local supermarket).

This water offered significant benefits to those who drank it. Jesus promised that through this water, one would never thirst again. In today's times this would probably sound like some marketing scheme, but Jesus explained:

"Everyone who drinks of this water will be thirsty again, but whoever drinks of the water that I will give him will never be thirsty again. The water that I will give him will become in him a spring of water welling up to eternal life." *(John 4:13–14 ESV)*.

In John 7:37-38 *(NIV)* Jesus shouts to those around Him (no longer with the Samaritan woman), **"Let anyone who is thirsty come to me and drink. Whoever believes in me, as Scripture has said, rivers of living water will flow from within them."** As believers in Jesus, you are now connected to a never-ending spring of living water. When this living water—the Spirit of the living God—enters you, He will never leave. Once grafted back onto the vine with the grace of God, you will never again be without your source of life.

Because this is a flowing spring you are connected to and not just a stagnant bucket, the water you receive is not just for you. It is now your responsibility to help ensure that others have their

The Army of One

water source as well. If their well keeps drying up due to unbelief, we must continue offering them water until God decides they are beyond the point of being reconnected to the vine of life.

God will tell you when your watering efforts fall into the infertile soil. Do not worry too much if your attempts to "water" (share the Holy Spirit) fail. God is the master gardener and will replant His seeds as often as necessary for His children to grow according to His will. All you can do is share what God has given you and let God do the rest.

Part 2
Boot Camp

5

Out with the Old

As we reached the gate, JC stopped again and turned toward me. "Are you ready?" he asked, putting his hand on my shoulder. I nodded my head. With a comforting smile, he said, "Great! Let us go in."

With that, he opened the heavy gate and motioned for me to enter. I looked him in the eye and nodded to say, 'Thank you,' then stepped through the open gate. As soon as my foot hit the ground, the world as I knew it seemed to change. Everywhere I looked was full of people tackling seemingly impossible tasks. People worked together to help each other, and everything seemed ...different.

Suddenly my concentration on everything around me was broken as JC once again got in my face and began questioning why I deserved to be there.

"Look at you," he shouted, "so full of yourself! You think you are so good, don't you? I know what you have done! You don't deserve to be here!"

Suddenly I felt very exposed and vulnerable, like a spotlight had just been illuminated directly on me. I began worrying about what he knew. I knew my life was not perfect; I had done some things I regretted, but how did he know? I felt as if everything I had ever done was suddenly being put on display for the world to see, and I began to feel ashamed. "What's happening here?" I asked with a hint of fear in my voice.

Chuckling, JC replied, "Scared you, didn't I? Do not be afraid; I just had to show you a true picture of yourself to teach you how to forgive and be forgiven."

"Oh, okay," I muttered, still shaking from what happened, "Can we not do that again?"

"Well, that depends on how well you learn what I will teach you, but don't count on it. Nobody gets it right the first time—" there was a slight pause as he looked away briefly "—or the second, or the third, for that matter," he added with a slight chuckle. "Come on. Let's go; we have work to do." With that, he turned again and began walking away.

"Do they ever get it right?" I shouted before slowly following him.

"Not really." I heard him chuckle once more as he continued down the road.

If you have ever been in the military or seen it on TV, you may have experienced a unique training program for recruits known as boot camp. Now, I am not sure if every experience is as bad as it is known for, but there is a purpose behind all the yelling and screaming that most people associate with boot camp.

From the moment the recruits get off the bus they arrive on, they have drill instructors in their faces shouting at them from all angles. There is no welcome bag full of goodies or pamphlets about clubs or events designed to get them acclimated—unless you count the long runs or drills they put them through. There is no super-friendly welcome committee to show them to their room or help them unpack. Instead, they are immediately lined up shoulder to shoulder with intimidating people in their faces, barking orders from all sides, trying to get them to crack.

Many wonder if they made the right choice. "Is this what it's going be like all the time?" they may ask themselves. The good news is that all that yelling and insults eventually stop, but why does it have to be there in the first place? Most people do not like having people in their faces barking orders or shouting insults at them constantly.

In any other situation, many people would be tempted to punch the one yelling in the face. So why is the military different? The difference is that recruits know that all the yelling should not be taken personally. It is simply a tactic to prepare them mentally and get them to perform under stress when it really matters in war.

Boot camp is about tearing you down from your old ways and building you up again with greater mental and physical strength. You will be challenged and pushed beyond what you thought possible. You will no longer be a regular citizen of your country trying to get by on your own merits. Instead, you will become part of a team, transformed into a soldier ready to fight for the freedom of your country and everything it represents.

But how does this relate to our Christian walk?

Why We Must Be Broken

If his children forsake my law and do not walk according to my rules, if they violate my statutes and do not keep my commandments, then I will punish their transgression with the rod and their iniquity with stripes, but I will not remove from him my steadfast love or be false to my faithfulness. *(Psalm 89:30–33 ESV)*.

In the previous chapter I discussed how we must give up our old life to be reborn into a new life with God. Unfortunately, that is easier said than done. We are so used to doing things our way that it is hard to drop everything at the door and start over completely.

Whoever heeds instruction is on the path to life, but he who rejects reproof leads others astray. *(Proverbs 10:17 ESV)*.

Pride is the greatest inhibitor to being broken. No one likes to admit they are weak, especially guys who are expected to be strong and protective. Our culture tends to condition us to fight for ourselves and learn how to survive independently, but this is not how God intended us to live. God disciplines us to conquer pride and be broken to the point of humility. Hebrews 12:5–11 *(NIV)* gives the purpose of God's discipline:

"**My son, do not make light of the Lord's discipline, and do not lose heart when he rebukes you, because the Lord disciplines the one he loves, and he chastens everyone he accepts as his son.**"

**Endure hardship as discipline; God is treating you as his children. For what children are not disciplined by their father? If you are not disciplined—and everyone undergoes discipline—then you are not legitimate, not true sons and daughters at all. Moreover, we have all had human fathers who disciplined us and we respected them for it. How much more should we submit to the Father of spirits and live! They disciplined us for a little while as they thought best; but God disciplines us for our good, in order that we may share in his holiness. No discipline seems pleasant at the time, but painful. Later on, however, it produces a harvest of righteousness and peace for those who have been trained by it.

For most of us it takes time to break down our old ways and to relearn how to be the way God intended us to be. Sometimes, we are broken through our own doing. We are allowed to live our lives as we want until we fail enough that we finally give up and cry out to God for help. God recognizes our nature to want to try things ourselves, so He will sit back and watch as we attempt to handle life's challenges. He knows that what we are doing will likely lead us down the wrong path, but He also knows that trying to convince us of that will only make us turn away from Him more. So instead, He stays a close distance behind, waiting to pick us up and take us back in His arms when we fail and call out to Him.

And you say, "How I hated discipline, and my heart despised reproof! I did not listen to the voice of my teachers or incline my ear to my instructors. I am at the brink of utter ruin in the assembled congregation." *(Proverbs 5:12–14 ESV)*.

The story of the prodigal son found in Luke 15:11–31 is one example of this brokenness. The younger son of the story insisted on receiving his inheritance early so he could run off and live life his way. Unfortunately, after foolishly spending the inheritance his father had given him, a famine entered the country, and he reached a point of need. No longer having the wealth given to him, he became desperate for survival. He had to lower his standard of living and ended up eating with pigs to survive. But after a while, even the pigs seemed to have more than he did.

So what happened next? He did the last thing anyone would want to do: he swallowed his pride and prepared himself to return to his father and ask to be taken back in and given work, essentially admitting he was wrong. His father could have easily denied his greedy son any more help and let him suffer the consequences of his actions, but he did not. Thankfully, his father took him back in with open arms and threw a big party to celebrate his return.

This is an example of what many of us do every day. Many of us demand that God give us opportunities or resources to tackle our goals and then insist on going out and tackling those goals ourselves without God. Often, when we forget God and all He has done for us to get us where we are, we fail. But God waits patiently for us to return. He does not have to say, "I told you so." He opens his arms and pulls us back in, knowing that the lesson has been taught and hopefully understood.

Sometimes it takes more than simply letting you figure things out yourself to break you down enough to come to Christ. Sometimes this is accomplished by taking something away from you that may distract you from God. Other times it takes something drastic to happen. The sad part about this is that many of these "drastic actions" tend to involve you or someone else getting hurt, dying, or losing everything they have. It is unfortunate that you or others must get hurt or suffer before you see that you need to seek God, but remember—God has a perfect plan for everything. Let us explore the result of such an occurrence.

"This illness does not lead to death. It is for the glory of God, so that the Son of God may be glorified through it." *(John 11:4 ESV)*.

No one knows for sure why seemingly innocent people get hurt or die, but in almost all instances one result of that action is that someone will eventually realize their life is short and seek to go after God. Sometimes, the loss of life is truly a means of punishment due to disobedience to God's law. This was the case when He flooded the earth or destroyed cities that chose to turn their backs on God. Other times, the loss may have nothing to do with the direct action of God but is simply a result of our sin as people. God does not wish for those bad things to happen, but

He knows they will, and He can still use those losses to reach out and influence others to turn to Him. Of course, some people may turn away because of those same circumstances, but that is unavoidable. Over time, God may also soften the hearts of those who turned away and bring them back to Him.

No matter how God chooses to break people, His goal is always the same: He wants to build them back up to be followers of His Word. Although it is still a tragedy when someone you love gets hurt or dies, it pales compared to not having God. We must learn how to trust God in all things. This includes the well-being of ourselves, our family, our work, our money, our friends, and everything else in life. Of course, this is hard to do. Therefore, God must often break us down in many ways before we finally learn to trust Him with our entire lives.

"Blessed is the one whom God corrects; so, do not despise the discipline of the Almighty. For He wounds, but He also binds up; He injures, but His hands also heal." *(Job 5:17–18 NIV)*

We Will Be Challenged

As mentioned earlier, part of the purpose of being broken is to eliminate our pride. The other part is to get us all on an equal playing field in our walk with God. As I stated in previous chapters, we all come from different backgrounds and have different expectations in life. Because of this, God must find a way to influence us to change our beliefs to align with His ways.

The act of being broken does not just happen to convert us to Christianity, nor is it only something we experience as new Christians. Brokenness will occur every time we stray from God. Becoming a Christian is not a ticket to an easy life. Many challenges will be designed to teach us new skills as we continue growing in our walk with God.

Unlike a typical boot camp with a set graduation date, the Christian "boot camp" is an ongoing process that usually occurs in stages based on what God knows you can handle. The cool thing about the Christian walk is that you will never stop learning. Every time you believe you have mastered a particular area (which is typically never the case to start with), God will start you into the next stage, suddenly making you feel inadequate all over again. But as in the previous stage, you will eventually learn this stage as well, and the process will continue until you finally stand before God Himself and declare your righteousness through Jesus.

If a day comes when you no longer feel challenged in your walk, and if you are feeling brave, ask God to challenge you. If you have a particular thing in mind that you would like to tackle, pray specifically for that. But be prepared. If you pray for something like more patience, He will answer that prayer far beyond what you expected. He will not just give you easy challenges either so you can easily feel that you accomplished something. He knows exactly what pushes you over the edge in all situations, and He will push that on you as much as possible until you have successfully demonstrated true success in what you were praying for.

The growth that comes from experiences like these is beyond comparison, but they are not without the help of your challenger. If you remember from the previous chapter, a significant part of this new life you have been given is acknowledging that you can do nothing without God. *(John 15:5)* To grow in Christ, you must involve Christ in everything you do. Anything less than that often results in pride, selfish expectations, or even failure.

Count it all joy, my brothers, when you meet trials of various kinds, for you know that the testing of your faith produces steadfastness. And let steadfastness have its full effect, that you may be perfect and complete, lacking in nothing. *(James 1:2–4 ESV)*.

Accepting Forgiveness and Forgiving Others

One of the first challenges many new believers must face is forgiveness. This includes forgiveness for yourself and others.

Many come to God with so much baggage in their lives that they cannot accept forgiveness. They often forget the key point of Christianity—grace. Grace is the act of getting something positive that is not deserved. An acronym you may have heard to describe grace is "God's riches at Christ's expense."

Ephesians 2:8–9 *(ESV)* says, **"For by grace you have been saved through faith. And this is not your own doing; it is the gift of God, not a result of works, so that no one may boast."**

Christ does not wait for us to correct our past actions before accepting us into heaven. Heaven would be empty if that were the case. Romans 5:8 *(ESV)* says, **"God shows his love for us in that while we were still sinners, Christ died for us."**

We must be careful in our walks with God to understand that there is absolutely nothing we can do through our own efforts to make up for the sins we committed. The only way to receive forgiveness for the sins in our past, the sins in our present, and the sins in our future is to acknowledge that our sins have been paid for in full. God patiently waits for us to ask for our free gift and admit our wrongdoing. First John 1:9 *(NIV)* states, **"If we confess our sins, He is faithful and just and will forgive us our sins and purify us from all unrighteousness."**

If we find ourselves repeating what Daniel said in Daniel 9:10 *(NIV)*, **"We have not obeyed the LORD our God or kept the laws he gave us through his servants the prophets,"** look one verse ahead and read, **"The LORD our God is merciful and forgiving, even though we have rebelled against him."** The more we can admit our sinfulness to God, the closer we will be to Him. There is no point in hiding because He already knows what we did, even if we do not.

God's forgiveness is free to everyone who believes, but it also comes with a catch. We must also be willing to forgive if we expect to be forgiven. This is another common roadblock to the growth of a Christian. Many people avoid church or particular people because someone wronged them at some point. They then allow that wrongdoing to dwell in their lives so much that it begins controlling them.

What happens when people end up being controlled by the emotions of an action? It gives the enemy a foothold in their lives. The longer we leave that wound open and unattended, the more we become infected with the filth of war and the weaker we become in the battle for our souls.

So what must we do? As much as it may hurt, we must learn to forgive those who hurt us. It is a lot like pouring alcohol on a wound. It hurts a lot but allows the wound to become clean so proper healing can occur. This does not necessarily mean we have to like them or continue to be friends. We are merely submitting that grievance to the ultimate judge to handle so we can continue on our way. I will talk more about our role as judges in a later chapter, but for now, let us look at why we must learn to forgive.

Matthew 6:14–15 *(NIV)* says, **"For if you forgive men when they sin against you, your heavenly Father will also forgive you. But if you do not forgive men their sins, your Father will not forgive your sins."** This is relatively straightforward. But if we look at the previous chapter in Matthew 5:22–24 *(ESV)*, we will see this:

"But I say to you that everyone who is angry with his brother will be liable to judgment; whoever insults his brother will be liable to the council; and whoever says, 'You fool!' will be liable to the hell of fire. So if you are offering your gift at the altar and there remember that your brother has something against you, leave your gift there before the altar and go. First be reconciled to your brother, and then come and offer your gift."

This implies that we cannot adequately come before God with anger in our hearts. Anger is an emotion stemming from pride.

With this attitude, we are saying that we are better than our offenders and deserve to be treated as such. By saying this, we are opening ourselves to having our wrongdoings judged by someone more significant than all of us combined.

Instead, we are called to follow the instructions in Luke 17:3-4 *(NIV)*: **"If your brother or sister sins against you, rebuke them; and if they repent, forgive them. Even if they sin against you seven times in a day and seven times come back to you saying 'I repent,' you must forgive them."**

If that is not enough, follow what is said in Matthew 18:21–22 *(NIV)*:

"Lord, how many times shall I forgive my brother or sister who sins against me? Up to seven times?"

Jesus answered, "I tell you, not seven times, but seventy-seven times."

The point is people are going to do us wrong. Sometimes they may do so many times. But we are called to forgive every time, regardless of whether they request it. This can be highly challenging, especially if our wrongdoer is a repeat offender or someone who takes something meaningful away from us. Regardless, we must remember our place and purpose. God will judge our wrongdoers accordingly, and the proper action will be made. Our goal is to focus on God's mission for us as individuals and as the church.

Recognize Your Place

Over the next several weeks, I began getting used to this new way of life JC showed me. Every day, I would meet JC early in the morning, and he would teach me something new. The lessons were often hard to deal with as they challenged me beyond anything I could imagine, but they taught me so much about myself that I did not know.

One day while walking around with JC on the base, I noticed some other recruits accomplishing much more challenging tasks.

"JC—that guy needs help!" I exclaimed as I began rushing toward what seemed to be a person struggling in a large fiery furnace.

JC grabbed my shoulder and pulled me back. "Don't worry—he's in advanced training. He is perfectly fine as he is doing things exactly as his leader commanded."

"Oh," I said as I reluctantly turned my attention back to JC. But farther down the road I witnessed another feat that one would consider impossible under normal circumstances.

"Is that guy standing on water?" I asked JC as my attention once again focused on this new distraction. "Oh, I want to do that!"

JC once again chuckled as he often did when teaching me and replied, "One day, but you are not quite ready yet. You still have much to learn."

Disappointed, I once again returned my focus to JC as we went on with the lessons for the day.

Later that night I ran into the guy I saw walking on the water earlier. "Hey—I saw you walking on water earlier. How did you do that?"

"I don't know. My trainer just told me to keep my eyes on him and take a step. It was scary, but he helped me through so much before that I trusted him and took a step. Next thing I know, I was across the pool without getting wet or having to go around."

"That's crazy!" I exclaimed, "You think you can show me how to do that?"

With hesitation, he responded, "Um, I don't know if I can. Why don't you ask your trainer to help you?"

"I did. He said I wasn't ready. I don't get why not; I've done everything else he's told me to do. If you can do it, I should be able to. Maybe I can surprise him and show him I can do more than he thinks."

"Well, I suppose I can try. Do you want to go out to the pool now?"

"Yes, let's do it!"

Since it was late at night, most everyone was in their bunks resting for the night. When my new friend and I got down to the pool, he stood at one end as his trainer did, and I stood at the other, nervous about my ability to do this. I surely did not want to get wet tonight.

"Okay, just keep your eyes on me and step out like you're walking on the ground!" my friend shouted from the other end.

"Is that it—no special way to walk or anything?" I shouted back.

"I don't think so. At least my trainer didn't say so."

"Okay," I said to myself. "Here goes." With that I focused my eyes on my new friend and stepped off the pool's edge—straight down into the water. When I surfaced from the water, I did not see my new friend. Instead, I saw JC with a somewhat angry look on his face.

"What are you guys doing?" he asked sternly.

"I just wanted to show you I can do more challenging things," I said with downcast eyes as if to say, "I'm sorry."

JC responded, "I told you that you were not ready. You must have complete faith in me before you can do something like walking on water or entering a fiery furnace without burning. If you cannot trust what I say now, how will you trust me when it matters? I'm glad you chose to try the water challenge instead of the fire challenge, but still, you made a mistake by doing this without me."

"Lesson learned, right?" I asked while climbing out of the pool.

"I doubt it. You would not be the first to try to do things on your own, and you will not be the last, nor will this be your last attempt—I'm sure. That's why I'm always close by to pull you out of trouble; you recruits tend to get into it way too often. You may not think we are there, but we are. Your life is in our hands."

"We?" I questioned as we headed back toward the barracks.

"You'll see, Allen. You will see."

Ever since the beginning of time, people have tried to venture out on their own and take control of their own lives. Adam and Eve did it when they decided to eat from the tree of the knowledge of good and evil *(Genesis 2:16–17)*, and we do it today when we

Recognize Your Place

constantly think we have our own lives under control and fail to seek God.

Why do we do this? Can't people see that their choices in life rarely, if ever, turn out the long-term results they hoped to achieve? We try to give meaning to our own lives all the time. We seek to achieve many short-term goals to feel important and valuable, yet somehow we miss the long-term success we think we should have.

How often are we rewarded with something only to find ourselves wanting more? We win at something and cheer, and then, of course, we expect to win again. When we don't, suddenly life does not seem so fun anymore. What is the meaning of this?

Life has no meaning if you live according to Solomon in Ecclesiastes. Solomon repeatedly tried to find meaning in everything he did on earth. He tried using his wisdom and found that despite all his knowledge, he still knew nothing compared to the greatness of God. He tried flooding himself with worldly pleasures by building significant wealth, owning everything he could set his eyes on, and essentially trying to fill every man's need through his hard work and wealth. But again, **"everything was meaningless, a chasing after the wind."** *(Ecclesiastes 2:11 NIV)*

In Psalm 127:1 *(NIV)* Solomon writes, **"Unless the Lord builds the house, the builders labor in vain. Unless the Lord watches over the city, the guards stand watch in vain."** Without God as your foundation, everything you are living for is meaningless.

Why toil over making everything perfect, building a great company, or spending countless hours helping your kids figure out their math homework? What is the point? If everything is meaningless, why waste your time doing all of this? Eventually someone will come behind you and undo everything you spent hours, days, or years doing. Someone will take over the company you worked so hard to build from the ground up, and your kids will eventually grow up and start making their own decisions. They will likely never have to figure out those crazy word problems again. So why do it?

Is it to make our time on this earth seem as if it is being used effectively? Is it so our kids can grow older and discover how hard it is to find meaning? Or is it simply to feel good about ourselves, thinking that maybe if we try hard to do something special, we will be remembered forever in the hearts of everyone born after us?

The good feelings we get when we accomplish something big are only temporary. People rarely create such great successes that their names will be in history books forever. Yes, many famous people have done great things in this world, but that number is small compared to the billions of people globally. How many of those people do you think are genuinely happy with their success and fame? They may look happy on the outside, with multi-million dollar homes, millions of fans, and everything they ever wanted. But are they satisfied on the inside? I will take a guess and say that the answer is no for many of these people. They are still searching just as the rest of us do, hoping to find that one thing that fills the emptiness in their heart that they have longed for since childhood.

Let us look at the rich young man who sought to inherit eternal life:

And Jesus, looking at him, loved him, and said to him, "You lack one thing: go, sell all that you have and give to the poor, and you will have treasure in heaven; and come, follow me." Disheartened by the saying, he went away sorrowful, for he had great possessions.

And Jesus looked around and said to his disciples, "How difficult it will be for those who have wealth to enter the kingdom of God!" And the disciples were amazed at his words.

But Jesus said to them again, "Children, how difficult it is to enter the kingdom of God! It is easier for a camel to go through the eye of a needle than for a rich person to enter the kingdom of God."

And they were exceedingly astonished, and said to him, "Then who can be saved?" Jesus looked at them and said, "With man it is impossible, but not with God. For all things are possible with God."

Peter began to say to him, "See, we have left everything and followed you." Jesus said, "Truly, I say to you, there is no one who has left house or brothers or sisters or mother or father or children or lands, for my sake and for the gospel, who will not receive a hundredfold now in this time, houses and brothers and sisters and mothers and children and lands, with persecutions, and in the age to come eternal life. But many who are first will be last, and the last first." *(Mark 10:21-31 ESV)*

Some have found the answer, but so many more are caught up in staying on top of their skill and keeping their fan base or wealth that they never see the true reward of a loving and gracious God. God calls us to live our lives so that even if everything were taken away (which does happen to some people), we would still have Him to bring peace, happiness, and joy into our lives.

You Are Trying Too Hard

So, what if you are trying to live your life for God? You try to do everything the "perfect Christian" should do. You go to church, attend and lead Bible studies, obey all the rules, go on mission trips, and so on. Surely you understand the meaning of life—what it means to be a Christian, right?

To answer this, let us look at the prodigal son parable again. In the previous chapter, I used the parable to illustrate how sometimes we must be broken to see what has been provided for us all along. If you read the whole story, there are two brothers. Let us talk about the older brother now.

You may assume that the older brother was being treated unfairly because he did everything right and did not run away as did the younger brother. The younger brother got what he

The Army of One

deserved. He should not be allowed to waltz back in and receive another part of the remaining inheritance. Right?

Wrong. Let us look at the last five verses of Luke 15. Starting in verse 28 *(NIV)*, Jesus says,

"The older brother became angry and refused to go in. So his father went out and pleaded with him. But he answered his father, 'Look! All these years I've been slaving for you and never disobeyed your orders. Yet you never gave me even a young goat so I could celebrate with my friends. But when this son of yours who has squandered your property with prostitutes comes home, you kill the fattened calf for him!'

"'My son,' the father said, 'you are always with me, and everything I have is yours. But we had to celebrate and be glad, because this brother of yours was dead and is alive again; he was lost and is found.'"

Why did the older brother become so angry? Wasn't he glad to see his brother return home safe? You see, the older brother represents the Pharisees in this story. The Pharisees were people who followed the law to the letter. They even made up their own laws at times to try making themselves look better in the eyes of God. In other words, the Pharisees believed that God enabled them to do good works through their own efforts, thus being able to earn salvation by doing good things.

Unfortunately, all their rules and regulations turned them away from God. In Matthew 15: 1–9 Jesus condemns the Pharisees who previously complained to Him, wondering why He let the disciples eat without washing their hands first. Now, I know that in today's times, this task is practiced because of our advanced knowledge of germs, but back then it was more of a ritual that the Pharisees made to distinguish themselves from ungodly men.

Because the Pharisees assumed that their laws and traditions were just as important or more than what Jesus preached, Jesus confronted them. He stated,

"You nullify the Word of God for the sake of your tradition. You hypocrites! Isaiah was right when he prophesied about you:

"'These people honor me with their lips, but their hearts are far from me. They worship me in vain; their teachings are merely human rules.'" *(Matthew 15:6–9 NIV)*

When the older brother in the prodigal son parable decides to yell at his father and complain about his decision, he puts himself above his father. Like many of us today, he assumed he deserved much more than he was receiving because he did all those "good things" and never disobeyed. He felt cheated when his younger brother got his inheritance early and received part of what was now his.

Being a Christian is not just about following rules or traditions, as many believe. Being a Christian means that you are humbling yourself before the Lord. It also means that you accept the grace God bestows on you. We do not deserve anything that God has given us in life. Everything we have, including our life itself, is a gift from God that can be taken away at any moment.

We will all be given different challenges in life. Some may seem harder than those given to others, but each is a test of faith. When you can overcome the challenges, you must quickly recognize that your success came from God and not your abilities. If you fail to see this, God may intervene and take it all away again.

See which of these two characters you relate to in the following parable in Luke 18:9–14 *(NIV)*:

"Two men went up to the temple to pray, one a Pharisee and the other a tax collector. The Pharisee stood by himself and prayed: 'God, I thank you that I am not like other people—robbers, evildoers, adulterers—or even like this tax collector. I fast twice a week and give a tenth of all I get.'

"But the tax collector stood at a distance. He would not even look up to heaven, but beat his breast and said, 'God, have mercy on me, a sinner.'

"I tell you that this man, rather than the other, went home justified before God. For all those who exalt themselves will be humbled, and those who humble themselves will be exalted."

God would rather you be imperfect, capable of admitting your wrongdoings and crying out to God for help, than to see a self-righteous man or woman before Him who cannot admit to a single mistake.

Are you looking at everything you do right for your salvation, or are you strong enough to admit that you are truly weak? Do you think the traditions created by man will make you a better Christian? Many churches and individuals face this problem: they rely so much on traditions in their services, specific amounts of service to others, or perfect track records that they forget what Jesus says.

Jesus says in John 14:6 *(NIV)*, **"I am the way and the truth and the life. No one comes to the father except through me."** The crucial part of this verse that I have repeated several times in this book is the first two words. There is only one way to God, and that is through Jesus. It is not Jesus plus perfect attendance in all church-related activities. It is not Jesus plus numerous mission trips to foreign countries. It is not Jesus plus a particular way you participate in a church worship service. It is just Jesus.

Traditions and activities within a church may have their place, but the church body must understand that they are used only to get your mind and heart focused on God, not to come to God.

Recognize Your Place

God Is in Control

Have you ever been in a leadership position at work, school, club, or sports team? Leadership is a big responsibility. You not only have to worry about your own successes, but now you must worry about the success of your followers.

There are many great leaders in the world, and some are not so great, but they all have one thing in common: None have complete control over those they lead.

Since this is a military-themed book, let us look at the leadership structure of the army for a moment. In the army there are many ranks. Starting at the basic level of private, you move up in rank to corporal, sergeant, lieutenant, captain, major, colonel, and then general. And between all of those are other ranks, but for the purpose of this book, that gives you the general idea.

The higher you are in an organization, the more people you are responsible for. Does the person at the top, in this case the general, interact with everyone in the organization to give them direction or motivation personally? The answer is often no if the organization is of decent size.

A corporal or sergeant, for instance, would oversee only the people below them in a unit called a squad. These people are usually out on the battlefield and would be doing more of the hands-on work of a mission

Two to four squads put together would form a platoon led by a lieutenant. Between three and five platoons form a company led by a captain or major. And it continues to go up from there. A company becomes a battalion, then a brigade or regiment, then a division, then a corps (such as the Army, Navy, Air Force, Marines, Coast Guard), and finally, the military unit as a whole under the Department of Defense. Different organizational structures may exist for various branches and other organizations, but the concept remains the same.

Each leader in charge of each section has his own responsibilities in leading those below him. Very rarely, if ever, will you see a general out on the field deciding how to carry out a specific mission of a squad. Instead, the general oversees the entire army, deciding whom to attack or how to win a war. Similarly, you will never find a low-level private or sergeant making those advanced decisions.

Regardless of the leadership position within an army, a business, or any other organization, there are always limits to what their leadership covers. Someone else above each leadership level always has the power to override decisions made by lower leadership. Even the general of an army still must answer to the president. The president must still follow our Constitution, Congress, and agreements made with foreign parties. But the ultimate end of the leadership chain ends with the forces of nature and limits imposed by God.

You see, no matter how much we try, we cannot alter the laws of science or the limitations God has given us as humans. Sometimes, we find ways to temporarily get around those laws, such as when we created the airplane to fly, but in the end, our nature is still restricted.

So, what does this have to do with the purpose of this book?

The point of this section is to get you to realize that no matter how much responsibility you may have here on earth, your role in fulfilling the overall will of God is just a bullet point or less in the extent of God's plan. So many people fight in the spiritual war we call life and think they can solve all the world's problems by themselves. They are like a private in an army, thinking he has the perfect plan to win the overall war and then trying to overrule the general's leadership to run the army himself.

It does not matter how smart you are or how much experience you have in each area; if you do not have followers or are not appointed by someone above you, you will not advance in the leadership chain.

Recognize Your Place

The more you trust your true leader, God, the more likely He will use you to do great things in His army. Even the lowly privates can significantly impact the overall war if they follow the instructions of their leaders. It does not matter how old you are or how new a Christian you may be—if you are faithful to God, He will use you.

First Timothy 4:12–16 *(NIV)* states, **"Don't let anyone look down on you because you are young, but set an example for the believers in speech, in conduct, in love, in faith and in purity. Until I come, devote yourself to the public reading of Scripture, to preaching and to teaching. Do not neglect your gift, which was given you through prophecy when the body of elders laid their hands on you.**

"Be diligent in these matters; give yourself wholly to them, so that everyone may see your progress. Watch your life and doctrine closely. Persevere in them, because if you do, you will save both yourself and your hearers."

God will use you, but you must always remember who has ultimate authority. Do not try to take the place of God or attempt more than what God assigned for you. You will only fail and become discouraged if you do.

"Pay careful attention to yourselves and to all the flock, in which the Holy Spirit has made you overseers, to care for the church of God, which he obtained with his own blood." *(Acts 20:28 ESV)*

Discovering Who You Are

After being told once again that I was not ready the other night at the pool, I questioned why I was here. Why was it taking so long for me to accomplish something significant? Seeking an answer, I sought after JC to ask him personally.

I left the barracks and quickly found JC outside as if he were expecting me. He said, "How's it going, Allen? You look troubled."

"Well, I am. I have been here for quite a while now, and I feel like I have contributed nothing. Why am I here?"

JC motioned for me to sit on a nearby bench as he took his place beside me. "Sorry you feel that way, but we had to get your heart right before we could teach you how to be the soldier you were meant to be. Otherwise, you would revert to your old ways, and all the training in the world would accomplish nothing."

"I guess that makes sense—but how much longer do you think it will take before I am ready?" I asked in a disappointed tone and downcast eyes. "I really want to show my worth."

I thought I would be told I had to wait again.

"Well, because you asked me and didn't try to set out on your own path like you did the other day, I'm going to give you a shot. I think we can start early tomorrow."

My eyes lit up as I shook JC's hand with vigor and almost gave him a big hug. "Thank you so much! I won't let you down."

"See you tomorrow, Allen." With that, JC walked away with his usual chuckle, and I returned to the barracks, anticipating what JC had in store for me the next day.

The next day I got up early and rushed out to meet JC before our usual meeting time. I was in such a hurry that I skipped my normal prayer time and other morning routines. I wanted to get there before him to show how eager I was to get started, but as I approached, I found JC on his knees, praying as he always did in the morning.

I approached quietly so as not to disturb him. Realizing that I did not have my own quiet time, I knelt a short distance away and prayed until it was our appointed time to meet. Before I knew it,

JC was tapping me on the shoulder with a friendly grin on his face. "A little eager to get started, I see."

I replied with a slight feeling of embarrassment, "Yeah, I guess so. So, what are we doing today? Combat training? Leadership building? Water walking?" I shot JC a wink and a grin with the last suggestion, knowing he would find it funny.

"Ah, not so fast, Allen," JC said with another chuckle. "Do you trust me?"

"Yes," I responded quickly. I was excited about the possibilities of what I was about to do.

"Good. Today I want you to help serve breakfast, lunch, and dinner for the base."

My heart sank as I responded, "I have to work in the kitchen?"

JC responded sincerely, "You don't have to, but you did say you trusted me. I guess we still have work to do."

"No, I'll trust you. I don't understand it as usual, but I'll trust you."

"Good. You better get going then—lots of hungry people to feed."

One of the most common difficulties both new and old believers face in their Christian walk is determining God's will for their lives. God calls us to give up our old lives and follow Him. The problem is that we often get confused by all the other possible paths that surround us daily. Which one do we choose? How do we know our path is the right one?

Following the right path is a lot like traveling to a popular vacation spot but getting distracted by various roadside attractions along the way. If you do not stay focused on your goal, you will never get to enjoy the greater satisfaction of your true destination.

Many people do not necessarily have the problem of staying focused on a path but simply do not know which one to choose. They know where they want to end up, but they have no clue which road to take to get there. In some cases, they thought they knew, but for some reason, that road was blocked or not currently available, and now they are stuck.

Did you know that a principle behind this could be illustrated by looking at video games? As I am sure you are aware, most games have a goal. If the player is to make it past a few minutes of play, there will also be a set of challenges that must be accomplished before that goal can be obtained. It may be the collection of resources or keys or solving a puzzle. It could also be fighting off enemies or developing strategies to gain the upper hand. Even a classic game like Pac–Man follows this principle. To advance, you must collect all the dots, but you are restricted by walls that limit your way. In addition, you must avoid the ghosts that try to prevent you from winning. So, a simple concept (collect all the dots) still has obstacles that can force you to alter the course you thought you would take in the first place.

So why should life be any different? The creator of the game called life (not the board game) has developed a series of challenges we must complete before our time on earth is done. Again, if the solution were straightforward, we would go through life without satisfaction because it took no effort to get there. Many people wish that God would make life simpler and remove all the hardships we face, but I feel we would be bored if we did not have some of those challenges.

To continue with the video game analogy, let us focus on first-person shooter games. Depending on how modern the game is, most games in this genre have a few things in common. They have a maze-like structure or vast environments with many doors, obstacles, or enemies standing in the way to the finish line.

As you go through the game, you know that you must somehow get from where you are to the next stage of the game to advance. Unfortunately, the logical route that you assume you should take is blocked. So, what do you do? I doubt you give up and say, "I guess this is the end of the game since I can't seem to get through." No, you search for another way through. Sometimes, the alternative route is easy to find, but other times, you must spend a lot of time searching for a not–so–obvious approach or something to unblock the obstacle in front of you, such as a key, a switch, or a hidden entrance.

The Army of One

In life, the road we think God is leading us down will often become blocked with its own challenges forcing us to find an alternative route. God may eventually lead us to that area on the other side of the door, but instead of giving us a straight-through course, He tells us, "Not yet," and that we will have to do something else first. In a video game these alternative paths are built to prevent the game from being too boring and straightforward while building skills or collecting resources for later levels. In real life, they build character and bring us closer to God.

As we go through the game of life we often find ourselves in situations that would cause us to doubt that we are going the right way. We encounter enemies we have difficulty defeating and seemingly impossible circumstances that make us want to quit and give up. However, as in a video game, there is always a way out. God does not give us challenges we would be incapable of handling ourselves or with the help of others. Sometimes we must repeatedly try getting things right, but when we do, we sigh with relief and proceed with more confidence than before, knowing that the finish is near.

To me, one of the most stressful but exciting parts of a game is when you approach a new area and all you hear is the monsters or enemies on the other side. You know that you are about to enter a big mess on the other side, but you also know you must proceed to finish the game. Before entering these battles, what do you do? If you are a daredevil and in full health and ammo, you might rush in and start shooting everything that moves, hoping for the best, but more often than not, you still end up dying. If you are low on health or ammo, you will probably take the time to develop a plan of action to tackle the challenge. Sometimes, you may retrace your steps in the game to ensure that there is no other way around this obstacle. Some people will rush in headfirst to identify what they must deal with, while others will proceed with caution, carefully scoping out all the bad guys. Either way, you will often die the first

Discovering Who You Are

time doing so. The next time you should have a better idea of what you are dealing with so that you can make a plan.

One who is wise is cautious and turns away from evil, but a fool is reckless and careless. *(Proverbs 14:16 ESV)*

In real life, your enemies are people who do not agree with your beliefs or those who want to discourage you or keep you from succeeding. You may face obstacles that prevent you from going in a specific direction or circumstances that make you try harder to win. But in the end, if you have a full bar of spiritual health and God on your side, no matter how many times you may have to repeat a level of your life, God will help you through it. God will never send you into a room full of enemies or obstacles He knows you could never tackle alone.

When faced with a challenge, some of us rush into things without much thought or planning. Occasionally we will make it through all right, but poor planning and forethought often lead to problems. Each new stage of our lives or approach to an unknown should always start with at least a prayer to God for His support and strength to get through whatever we may encounter. Enlisting fellow believers' support is also a good idea if we know we are about to tackle something challenging.

Without counsel plans fail, but with many advisers they succeed. *(Proverbs 15:22 ESV)*

We sometimes face obstacles or circumstances that may make it look as if God has forgotten about us and let us venture down the wrong path, but that is not the case. We wonder how we can get ahead when every step we take seems to be the wrong one.

So, what should you do?

How about turning around? This may mean you must go through some of the same mess you already went through, but if you want to get ahead, you must be going in the right direction. You don't get to the top of the mountain by digging yourself a hole. So why would you expect to get anywhere in life by continuing to do the things that brought you down? God will be with us no matter what direction we end up taking. If we find ourselves going the wrong way, God will be there to get us turned around when we ask for help.

If you find yourself in a challenging situation, God will be there to provide the knowledge of what to do or say. If you feel you are moving toward a dead end, ask God what He is trying to teach you. Maybe you are meant to encounter lost people and bring them back on the right track. Perhaps your journey is intended to develop character so you can be prepared for larger obstacles in the future. Or maybe He wants you to realize that you cannot do things alone and that you need Him there to succeed.

No matter how many doors are blocked or monsters you face, there is always a way out. The game of life may be challenging, but God is always with you to lead you through it. There is one goal but hundreds of ways to get there. Do not worry so much about choosing the right path; be concerned about being well-equipped to handle whatever is on the path you choose. Each challenge you face makes you much stronger and more confident for every following challenge. Do not give up when life seems impossible or when you feel as if all the doors are being shut on you. Keep looking for that way out, and the reward will be worthwhile.

Why Are You Here?

We established that every person has an objective, even if it may not be easy to identify. But why are we here? Are we here to entertain ourselves by accomplishing challenge after challenge for our satisfaction, or does God have a unique goal for every one of us? Is that goal specifically for us? Or is it designed for the greater good of the army we serve? If it is for the greater good of the army, what is our role within that army? These are the questions I will address in this and the following chapter.

If you are like me, you probably ask yourself, "Why am I here?" Perhaps you have an idea of where you see yourself in the future. You may also have no idea and simply live life as it comes. Either way of life is okay, but only if your trust is in God.

I for one have big expectations for my future, a binder full of goals for both business and ministry. But do my expectations match God's expectations for me?

Unfortunately, at the time of this writing, I am struggling. I have a good idea of the end goal I would like to achieve, but I cannot find the door that will get me there. Physically, emotionally, and spiritually, my health bars continue to dip below comfortable levels, but the game must go on.

Knowing that God has a plan for me is the only thing that has kept me going in my personal game of life. There is a solution, but my faith must remain in God. Maybe you are struggling for direction as well. Perhaps you too feel defeated due to the lack of a job or purpose, the loss of a loved one, or poor health. Maybe your life seems to have lost all meaning and worth. If that is true for you, I encourage you to keep going. Your game has not ended, and God still has a plan for you, just as He has one for me.

A famous verse found in Jeremiah 29:11 *(NIV)* related to this topic states, **"For I know the plans I have for you," declares the Lord, "plans to prosper you and not to harm you, plans to give you hope and a future."**

We do not always know why God has put us on the path He has, but if we can follow the direction of Proverbs 3:5–6 *(NIV)*, God will provide:

"Trust in the LORD with all your heart and lean not on your own understanding; in all your ways submit to Him, and He will make your paths straight."

Jeremiah 17:5, 7 *(NIV)* says, **"Cursed is the one who trusts in man, who draws strength from mere flesh and whose heart turns away from the LORD. ... But blessed is the one who trusts in the LORD, whose confidence is in him."**

Now I will admit that these verses are easier said than done. Trusting God when you have been struggling for so long can be difficult. You may feel that He has left you behind or forgotten about you. But we must never give up because we all have a place in this world, and God has a reason for everything. It may take a lot to bring us down to where we have no choice but to depend on God, but when we can do so, we can count on the truth of Philippians 4:19 *(ESV)*, which states, **"My God will supply every need of yours according to his riches in glory in Christ Jesus."**

Consider these verses if you think you may be on the wrong path for your life.

Proverbs 16:9 *(ESV)* states, **"The heart of man plans his way, but the LORD establishes his steps."**

Whatever you do, work at it with all your heart, as working for the Lord, not for human masters, since you know that you will receive an inheritance from the Lord as a reward. It is the Lord Christ you are serving. *(Colossians 3:23–24 NIV)*

You may have a plan, or you may not, but regardless of your path, your work should glorify God. God will work out the other little details if you make that your goal and purpose. You must come to a point at which you can be content with whatever circumstances you find yourself in, knowing that God is with you. You must learn to believe the way Paul believes as stated in Philippians 4:11–13 *(NIV)*:

I have learned to be content whatever the circumstances. I know what it is to be in need, and I know what it is to have plenty. I have learned the secret of being content in any and every situation, whether well fed or hungry, whether living in plenty or in want. I can do all this through him who gives me strength.

What Defines You?

The sad reality of the previous section is that most of us are not content with the circumstances we face. Most of us constantly

Discovering Who You Are

search for something that makes us feel complete. We often forget that God is there to make us whole, so we seek alternative solutions.

Some of us seek significance through what we do. We say, "I am a [doctor, lawyer, teacher, and so on] who happens to be Christian." Our lives revolve around the job we do and what we accomplish. Those in some professions like to have a special title next to their name (doctor, judge, or pastor, for example), but why? Yes, they may have earned a unique degree or have a leadership position, but that is true in many professions.

Do not get me wrong: respecting someone in leadership is important, but respect goes both ways. When you elevate yourself above others by emphasizing your position in your name, you may be going against what it says in Romans 12:3 *(NIV):* **"Do not think of yourself more highly than you ought, but rather think of yourself with sober judgment, in accordance with the measure of faith God has distributed to each of you."**

I do not oppose having a special title designating your position, but that should be its only purpose. If you get upset with people because they call you "Mr." or "Mrs." instead of "Doctor," "Judge," "Pastor," or whatever your title is, then think about what you truly live for. It is easy to enter a state of pride when you forget that God put you in your position. What defines you should be less about your education, work, or social status and more about the values of your heart.

For who makes you different from anyone else? What do you have that you did not receive? And if you did receive it, why do you boast as though you did not? *(1 Corinthians 4:7 NIV)*

Live in harmony with one another. Do not be proud but be willing to associate with people of low position. Do not be conceited. *(Romans 12:16 NIV)*

Be not overly righteous, and do not make yourself too wise. Why should you destroy yourself? *(Ecclesiastes 7:16 ESV)*

You do not necessarily have to have a special title to be caught up in pride. You may derive your significance through how much wealth you have, your beauty, your actions, and the general approval of man. Every one of these things puts the emphasis back on you and not on the glory of God.

Galatians 1:10 *(ESV)* addresses this: **"For am I now seeking the approval of man, or of God? Or am I trying to please man? If I were still trying to please man, I would not be a servant of Christ."**

God has given us all our lives and can easily take them away. He did not give us these lives to elevate ourselves above one another or provide us with a sense of entitlement. Yet in many cases, that is what tends to happen.

"I have the right to do anything," you say—but not everything is beneficial. "I have the right to do anything"—but not everything is constructive. No one should seek their own good, but the good of others. *(1 Corinthians 10:23–24 NIV)*

Jesus gives us these commandments in Matthew 22:37–39 *(NIV):* **'Love the Lord your God with all your heart and with all your soul and with all your mind.' This is the first and greatest commandment. And the second is like it: 'Love your neighbor as yourself.'**

If you follow these laws presented by Jesus, your purpose will be to serve God first and love others second. Nowhere in the Bible does it say to elevate yourself above your peers. All power, wealth, and good have been given to you by God, so we are defined by God, not the other way around.

Do nothing out of selfish ambition or vain conceit. Rather, in humility value others above yourselves, not looking to your own interests but each of you to the interests of the others. *(Philippians 2:3–4 NIV)*

Before going on, we should look at another side that can be equally dangerous to our spiritual health—letting ourselves be defined by the negative labels we or others put on ourselves. Although that will be discussed more in future chapters, it is also important to mention it here.

Discovering Who You Are

Many of us live our lives based on what others think or expect of us. People use others' race, gender, physical attributes, actions, or any number of other traits to assign labels that are often negative or stereotypical to hurt or discriminate against them. Or we end up assigning labels to ourselves based on lies from the enemy, such as "not good enough," "worthless," "stupid," and so on. We may also spend our lives in shame or guilt from past actions.

But, as we will learn more in later chapters, these are all lies. If we let them define who we are instead of listening to how God defines us, we will be ineffective in serving Him.

For you formed my inward parts; you knitted me together in my mother's womb. I praise you, for I am fearfully and wonderfully made. *(Psalm 139:13–14 ESV)*

Of course, the opposite can also be true. Sometimes, we equate traits such as age, appearance, wealth, or success to the value of a person—when inwardly, they could be crooked, greedy, selfish, or other negative things. An example of this is found in 1 Samuel 16 when Samuel was presenting the sons of Jesse to the Lord for Him to indicate which one was to be appointed as king. Jesse brought his seven sons, who displayed "leadership qualities," as he defined them. Perhaps they were tall, charismatic, and strong. Surely the chosen one could be picked from these.

But the LORD said to Samuel, "Do not consider his appearance or his height, for I have rejected him. The LORD does not look at the things people look at. People look at the outward appearance, but the LORD looks at the heart." *(1 Samuel 16:7 NIV)*

Outward appearances do not fool or discourage God. David ended up being chosen for kingship, yet he was not present because Jesse had ruled him out for one reason or another. But God sees what is in our hearts. Even though David made mistakes during his time as king, God still recognized him as a man of God. Could David's brothers have been good leaders? Perhaps, but would their interests have been aligned in service to God or service toward self? Judging by this passage, the answer most likely would have been the latter.

What Is Your Purpose?

A while back I read about the parable of the talents found in Matthew 25:14–30. You might assume I was reading this from the Bible, but I was not. Instead, it came from a business book by Donald Trump and Robert Kiyosaki titled *Why We Want You to Be Rich*.

Robert explained how a youth minister once challenged him and others to explain the meaning behind the parable of the talents. If you are unfamiliar with the parable, a wealthy person gave his servants different amounts of talents (currency) to hold onto while he went on a long trip. Two of his servants invested the money and doubled it while he was gone, while the third servant dug a hole in the ground and hid what had been given to him.

When the master returned, the first two servants returned the money entrusted to them and the additional money they gained. In response to their excellent work, they were entrusted with many things and invited to share in their master's happiness. But when the third servant told the master that he had hidden the money instead of investing it as had the others, the master became angry and replied,

"You wicked, lazy servant! So, you knew that I harvest where I have not sown and gather where I have not scattered seed? Well then, you should have put my money on deposit with the bankers, so that when I returned I would have received it back with interest.

"So take the bag of gold from him and give it to the one who has ten bags. For whoever has will be given more, and they will have an abundance. Whoever does not have, even what they have will be taken from them. And throw that worthless servant

outside, into the darkness, where there will be weeping and gnashing of teeth." *(Matthew 25:26–30 NIV).*

It is worth noting that the talents mentioned in the Bible are no small chunk of change as many likely think. A talent is not simply a coin one may keep in a change purse for everyday expenditures. Instead, one talent is estimated to have been the equivalent of 15–19 years of average wages. (Actual estimates vary between sources due to many means of measurement not being standardized). After a quick Internet search, I discovered that a talent was a unit of weight of approximately 75 lbs., or 33 kg. In monetary terms, this weight measured either gold or silver, silver being the most common, at a value of $846/kg of silver ($27,918/talent) or $56,033/kg of gold ($1,849,089/talent) at the time of writing.

The lord of this story was justifiably angry that the third servant didn't even try to bank the money to collect what would have been a substantial amount of interest. So, what is the purpose of this parable?

With this being a business book, you would assume that Robert was attempting to state that the poor get poorer while the rich get richer or that poor people are lazy and irresponsible. These were the typical answers among his peers, but I do not believe this is all the parable illustrates.

What is it saying, then? I believe the parable can be applied to the modern meaning of the word talent (also known as a skill). When we became Christians, we were all presented with different spiritual gifts. Some were more prevalent than others, but God gave them to us based on what He knew we could do with them.

But how often are we like the third servant? We know we have at least one gift God gave us, as we were each created with a unique purpose. But we often fail to invest time and effort into properly using and growing that gift. Instead, we hide from the world or pretend we do not have any gifts.

The servant in this parable was afraid that the master was unfairly collecting the sowing harvest, in other words collecting the reward without doing the work. However, the servant's purpose in this parable was to take care of the master's money while he was away. If the master simply wanted to keep it safe, he could have hidden it himself. Instead, he trusted his servants, according to their abilities, to go out and invest the money. The third servant's failure to invest or bank the money resulted in his being cast out for being useless for the good of the master.

As with money, if a talent or skill gets set aside untouched, its value is worthless as it produces no gain. It does no good to anyone. Whether we are given money or skill, we really ought to invest in it to create more. If your gift is music, invest the time to practice and play to improve. If you like to program software or cook meals, invest in those things, as they can all be used to glorify God. If you are gifted at making friends, expressing empathy, or even being a good listener, there is always a place for you too.

The more you invest in yourself, the better you will become and the more you can do with that given skill or gift for God's glory. As you continue growing in your faith, those skills might come in handy to support the church or encourage other Christians' growth. You may also become a better person. If you waste your skills and do not invest the time to make them grow, your purpose will be unfulfilled. Even a single talent is worth a lot to the kingdom of God.

The key to all this is that you should at least try. Even if the servant had put the money he had been given into a savings account and collected a minimal amount of interest, that would have been better than simply hiding the money away. If we are given gifts and fail to use them, God has no use for us, which may affect our place in the kingdom of heaven. If we at least attempt to use our gifts for the good of the kingdom, even if they produce little to no reward in our eyes, then God will find favor with us and will not cast us out.

So, what are your gifts? If you have not already done so, there are many spiritual–gift assessments available online that you can take to identify the spiritual gifts you may have. Remember that there is a difference between natural-born talents, skills, and spiritual gifts. All can be used to serve God, but your spiritual gifts are presented only when you accept Christ. You can develop talents and skills through practice and training or just natural–born abilities. Your spiritual gifts are special abilities designed to help the church, and the Christian army grow. Often, your gifts will relate to your talents, but that is not always the case. For example, you may have the talent and ability to study well and learn new concepts quickly. But if you were not given the spiritual gift of teaching, you likely would not be suited for a ministerial position within a church. You may, however, have a place leading a service project or smaller ministries.

First Corinthians 12:4–7 *(ESV)* says, **"Now there are varieties of gifts, but the same Spirit; and there are varieties of service, but the same Lord; and there are varieties of activities, but it is the same God who empowers them all in everyone. To each is given the manifestation of the Spirit for the common good."**

This passage implies that because all gifts are from the Holy Spirit, none should be considered more significant than another. They are all purposed to serve the Lord. Some people may have multiple gifts, and some may have only one prevalent gift, but each person is expected to use whatever they are given for the greater good of the kingdom.

To identify the possible gifts God may have given you, check out the passages in 1 Corinthians 12:8–11 ,28–31 and Romans 12:6–8.

To one there is given through the Spirit a message of wisdom, to another a message of knowledge by means of the same Spirit, to another faith by the same Spirit, to another gifts of healing by that one Spirit, to another miraculous powers, to another prophecy, to another distinguishing between spirits, to

another speaking in different kinds of tongues, and to still another the interpretation of tongues. All these are the work of one and the same Spirit, and he distributes them to each one, just as he determines. *(1 Corinthians 12:8–11 NIV).*

And God has placed in the church first of all apostles, second prophets, third teachers, then miracles, then gifts of healing, of helping, of guidance, and of different kinds of tongues. Are all apostles? Are all prophets? Are all teachers? Do all work miracles? Do all have gifts of healing? Do all speak in tongues? Do all interpret? Now eagerly desire the greater gifts. *(1 Corinthians 12:28–31 NIV).*

We have different gifts, according to the grace given to each of us. If your gift is prophesying, then prophesy in accordance with your faith; if it is serving, then serve; if it is teaching, then teach; if it is to encourage, then give encouragement; if it is giving, then give generously; if it is to lead, do it diligently; if it is to show mercy, do it cheerfully. *(Romans 12: 6–8 NIV).*

God has a plan for everyone. If you are unwilling to do your part to bring people to His kingdom, He may take away the talents He gave you and give them to someone willing to do the job. Do not be a lazy Christian and fail to do your part in supporting God's mission, no matter how small or large your part may be, or you may find yourself kicked to the curb with the unbelievers.

"Each of you should use whatever gift you have received to serve others, as faithful stewards of God's grace in its various forms. If anyone speaks, they should do so as one who speaks the very words of God. If anyone serves, they should do so with the strength God provides, so that in all things God may be praised through Jesus Christ. To him be the glory and the power forever and ever. Amen. *(1 Peter 4:10–11 NIV)*

Becoming United

After meeting with JC, I reluctantly headed to the mess hall to help prepare breakfast for over 10,000 hungry recruits. I was somewhat discouraged once again that JC would give me something beneath what I thought I could do, but I told him I would trust him, so I went. I entered the hall and sought out the kitchen manager to find out what he needed me to do.

"Allen! I was expecting you. So glad you could come. We ended up short-handed today due to schedule confusion and would be in real trouble without you. I know it may seem trivial, but I need you to find, open, and stage all the food packages so the cooks can quickly get to what they need."

"I think I can handle that," I said as I walked toward the kitchen. On the way back, I could not help but think, "Are they incapable of opening their own packaging? Do they really need me here?"

I soon found out how wrong I was. Before I knew it, orders came in from the cafeteria line all the empty or almost empty dishes. All forty cooks were in full gear, cranking out orders to ensure there would be no pause in service.

Every thirty seconds or so I would hear, "Bread! Eggs! Bacon!" or any other menu items we had available. I was rushing back and forth like a madman trying to get their food items prepped and ready to go before they ran out. Lunch and dinner shifts were much the same. I hardly had time to breathe or even think about why I did not want to be there.

At the end of the last shift, I met up with the kitchen manager and JC to have our dinner for the night.

"Hard work, huh?" asked the manager as he patted me on the back while sitting beside me.

"Yes, sir—a lot harder than I thought," I replied.

"Well, I know you didn't want to be here, but you did great! I'm glad you stuck through it and made it your own."

JC added, "Yes, Allen—thank you for trusting me enough to do this. Did you learn anything from it?"

I replied, "Well, I learned that even menial positions have their place on a team. You are right. At first, I did not want to do this. I thought it insulted my abilities and intelligence, but I soon saw what would happen if I were not there. The kitchen would have slowed down a lot if the cooks had to pause and locate or stage their own ingredients."

"I'm glad you could see that, Allen," replied the kitchen manager. "Many people are assigned that position with the same starting viewpoint you had but never see the importance of their role. They move in slow motion, moping around or complaining the whole time. Many never make it back for the lunch or dinner shift."

JC followed that comment by adding, "This is the first task most recruits must complete. If you are unwilling to submit yourself to even the lowest position to serve where you are needed, you are not ready to do the bigger tasks. Not everything you will encounter in battle will be things you enjoy doing or fall within your skill sets. Most things will be dirty work that no one wants to do but must be done for the mission's success and within the team."

"I think I understand," I replied, taking another bite of my food.

"Good," replied JC. "So you want to do it again tomorrow?"

"Well ..." I paused as JC and the kitchen manager stared intently, waiting for my reply, "I'll go wherever you need me, JC."

"Good answer, Allen," JC said as he stood up from the table and patted me on the back as he walked away. "I'll see you tomorrow; I have more things to teach you."

What are the struggles of your life? Maybe you struggle to find your purpose, as noted in the previous chapter. Maybe you struggle with relationships, finances, health, school, or work. Perhaps you struggle with all of these or things much greater.

No matter what you struggle with, how do you handle it? Do you try to go at it alone, afraid to ask for help? Do you seek advice and love from your friends or family? Do you turn to God? If you are like most people, including myself, you probably try to deal with your struggles through your own strength and determination. Sometimes, this is out of pride, for you do not want to appear weak. It may also be because you do not know who to go to or are afraid that you will be further rejected by asking for help or admitting mistakes.

Neither answer is a healthy choice when dealing with struggles, as we cannot tackle every problem ourselves. Even if you succeed in a particular area, this success is usually short-lived without continued motivation or support from those around you.

"Because I have called and you refused to listen, have stretched out my hand and no one has heeded, because you have ignored all my counsel and would have none of my reproof, I also will laugh at your calamity; I will mock when terror strikes you, when terror strikes you like a storm and your calamity comes like a whirlwind, when distress and anguish come upon you. Then they will call upon me, but I will not answer; they will seek me diligently but will not find me. Because they hated knowledge and did not choose the fear of the LORD." *(Proverbs 1:24–29 ESV)*

Being a Christian means you never have to face a struggle alone again. Through God and the community of believers He has placed to live alongside us, we can tackle every battle. Even if you feel alone or lack a church community, God will always be with you if you believe in the truth He offers. You may not always have the physical presence of a body of believers to turn to, but through prayer you can remain connected to the spiritual body of Christ. This is where the "army of one" comes in. As believers, we have become a part of the greatest army known to man. We are called to be united in the Holy Spirit to fight for our Lord, Jesus. He is our commander who loves us and will never let us venture into a situation we cannot escape. We are an army who will fight together and win together. If one part of the army is weak or hurt, the remaining parts are called to come together in the name of Jesus to build that part up again.

Imagine that the body of Christ is like our own human body. Each body comprises different parts, from the brain down to the pinky toe, and is rarely revealed to the public except in warmer climates when everyone is wearing flip-flops or running barefoot. Each part of the body has a specific purpose for the overall working of the human system. Some parts may be more important than others, but no one part can function without a host of other

The Army of One

parts to back it up and support it. Imagine if you break your little toe while running around doing something crazy. Suddenly your whole body responds in pain to the suffering of that toe. Many bodily systems come together to begin healing that toe until it is once again able to function as designed.

That is how we must be as believers. We all suffer from various things, such as relational or health struggles, self-confidence, purity, drugs, and alcohol, or even just being lonely and depressed. Without each other and God, we will never overcome the pain and suffering that result from those struggles.

Let us look at this in another way. Imagine again that you are standing in the middle of a corridor twenty feet wide and you are given the objective of keeping a much stronger and larger person from getting past you. Depending on your strength, you may slow that person down a little, but eventually they will get by because you are not big enough to block the whole passage. Now what happens when that person represents sin? This is how many of us tackle the sin that threatens our lives, and it often proves detrimental to our walk.

But what if we get support from our fellow believers? When our brothers and sisters in Christ stand firm together in the face of sin, that path becomes harder and harder for sin to break through. As many weak individuals come together as one much more robust body of Christ, the enemy becomes the weaker force and cannot pass.

But there is a catch. Each person in your wall of believers must stand firm in their own faith if they are to be as helpful in blocking the sin in your life. If one individual's sin is too great for that person to bear because He has not sought to build up his own defenses, that person will eventually fail against the enemy's unrelenting force. When that person fails, if you depend on them to be a part of your defense, suddenly you will have a significant gap in your wall, and sin will attack you from both sides until you become too weak to defend anymore.

This is the importance of the church body. The Bible says there is strength in numbers. Ecclesiastes 4: 9–10, 12 *(NIV)* puts it this way:

Two are better than one, because they have a good return for their labor: If either of them falls down, one can help the other up. But pity anyone who falls and has no one to help them up. ... Though one may be overpowered, two can defend themselves. A cord of three strands is not quickly broken.

God created us to love and care for the weak. Often, that includes ourselves, but we can't concentrate only on caring for ourselves when there are many others out there with no one to take care of them. When we can put aside our own needs, we can meet someone else's needs. In return, this often makes our personal struggles seem less important or go away completely.

As iron sharpens iron, so one man sharpens another. *(Proverbs 27:17 NIV)*

If your life is not as sharp as it could be, try helping someone else sharpen their own life, and in turn your own life will be sharpened. God tends to meet all your needs and then some when you can unselfishly show His love for others and seek to serve Him in all you do.

He who supplies seed to the sower and bread for food will supply and multiply your seed for sowing and increase the harvest of your righteousness. You will be enriched in every way to be generous in every way, which through us will produce thanksgiving to God. *(2 Corinthians 9:10–11 ESV)*

No Dream Team

If you ask people what their least favorite part of grade school was, many will respond that continually being picked last for sports or other activities was at the top of their list. You may have been either out of shape, uncoordinated, or unpopular. Maybe you did not understand the rules. I fit in most, if not all, of the above categories.

Whatever the case, it often hurts to see person after person picked before you, especially if you know you are just as good as or better than the other person. Some people may not have cared about being picked last because they simply did not care about the game. For many others, though, their self–esteem was often shot down each time they had to go through the team-picking process. They would compare themselves to the other kids in the class or group, wondering why they could not be like them.

As Christians, we sometimes experience similar occurrences. We look around and see people daily who appear to have it all together. They may have many Bible verses memorized, be on the worship team, serve at every event, or be in some form of church leadership. They look like the perfect Christian.

The reality is there is no such thing as the perfect Christian. God does not pick people who have it all together to do His work. He instead takes those who are sinners, like you and me, and teaches them how to play a better game. We learn to live the Christian life from the ground up. When we get too prideful, God may knock us back down again until we realize all our success comes from Him.

As shown in the prodigal son story I shared before, the more someone is caught up in being "the perfect Christian," the less likely they will be helpful to God. This is due to the pride that often comes with self-advancement. God does not need us to fight His battles because He has none. He has already won the war. The only reason we still fight is to show honor to God and to learn how to trust Him.

As mentioned in the previous chapter, everyone has a purpose in the spiritual army of God. No matter how big or small, God can and will use every one of us in unique ways, with and without our potential weaknesses and strengths, but only if we allow Him to.

Because our strength comes from God and not our own, our position in the Christian walk does not matter. We are merely members of a body operated by the head, which is Christ. I've heard many stories of brand-new believers going out and sharing their new faith within hours of becoming a Christian. I also know many who have been Christians for much of their lives yet have never shared the gift God has given them.

Just as each of us has one body with many members, and these members do not all have the same function, so in Christ, we who are many form one body, and each member belongs to all the others. (Romans 12: 4–5 NIV)

Just as a body, though one, has many parts, but all its many parts form one body, so it is with Christ. For we were all baptized by one Spirit so as to form one body—whether Jews or Gentiles, slave or free—and we were all given the one Spirit to drink. Even so the body is not made up of one part but of many.

Now if the foot should say, "Because I am not a hand, I do not belong to the body," it would not for that reason stop being part of the body. And if the ear should say, "Because I am not an eye, I do not belong to the body," it would not for that reason stop being part of the body. If the whole body were an eye, where would the sense of hearing be? If the whole body were an ear, where would the sense of smell be? But in fact God has placed the parts in the body, every one of them, just as he wanted them to be. If they were all one part, where would the body be? As it is, there are many parts, but one body.

The eye cannot say to the hand, "I don't need you!" And the head cannot say to the feet, "I don't need you!" On the contrary, those parts of the body that seem to be weaker are indispensable, and the parts that we think are less honorable we treat with special honor. And the parts that are unpresentable are treated with special modesty, while our presentable parts need no special treatment. But God has put the body together, giving greater honor to the parts that lacked it, so that there should be no division in the body, but that its parts should have equal concern for each other. If one part suffers, every part suffers with it; if one part is honored, every part rejoices with it.

Now you are the body of Christ, and each one of you is a part of it. *(1 Corinthians 12:12–27 NIV)*

God calls us to be united with Him and our brothers and sisters in Christ. Just as in our physical body, the church body does not function at 100 percent when one of its members, or even an entire church or denomination, is not functioning in accordance with God's commands.

Rather, speaking the truth in love, we are to grow up in every way into him who is the head, into Christ, from whom the whole body, joined and held together by every joint with which it is equipped, when each part is working properly, makes the body grow so that it builds itself up in love. *(Ephesians 4:15–16 ESV)*

The church body is not restricted to the people in a particular building. The church body includes every person who believes in Jesus, no matter their level of commitment or knowledge. Because of this, we must be careful not to separate ourselves from that body. There may be times of disagreement within a church, but instead of fighting one another and trying to create our own church, we should look at Ephesians 4:1–6 *(NIV)*:

As a prisoner for the Lord, then, I urge you to live a life worthy of the calling you have received. Be completely humble and gentle; be patient, bearing with one another in love. Make every effort to keep the unity of the Spirit through the bond of peace. There is one body and one Spirit, just as you were called to one hope when you were called; one Lord, one faith, one baptism; one God and Father of all, who is over all and through all and in all.

We should all be on the same team, trying to win others to Christ. The more we separate and argue among ourselves, the weaker we become. As we become weaker and weaker, Satan is given more of a chance to win in our personal battles. It is all right to have different denominations of the Christian faith, but only if their goal remains to bring others to God and is based on what the Bible says and not man. I do not believe any one denomination is better than another, as each presents a different worship style, but there may be cautions to consider when following some denominations.

Some church denominations and individual churches try to change the Bible to work for them instead of trying to change their members to work according to the Bible. Other churches cherry-pick scriptures they want to follow or fail to see the Word's true message. Then they may end up pushing rules or values that are not biblical. These values sometimes come across as hateful to various groups of people outside the church.

Both scenarios are like a squad in an army deciding that they know better than the commander while fighting the war on their own terms. Some might say these teams or individuals are "going rogue." It does not work and only creates more tension within the army you claim to support. Sometimes that rogue squad of people becomes part of the enemy forces themselves. Have you seen any churches that claim to follow the same God as you do, but you would now consider part of the enemy due to their misguided beliefs? We should not let that happen, but it happens all the time because of believers' lack of unity and dependence on God for leadership.

For if we have been united with him in a death like his, we shall certainly be united with him in a resurrection like his. We know that our old self was crucified with him in order that the body of sin might be brought to nothing, so that we would no longer be enslaved to sin. For one who has died has been set free from sin. *(Romans 6:5–7 ESV)*

Many claim to be a part of the body, but they are only dead skin that gets brushed off and turned into dust. Or worse, they become like a disease that decreases the functionality of the real body of Christ. Being part of the body requires constant nourishment and conditioning from God, which comes only if you accept Him as head over your life.

Building Each Other Up in Christ

What do we do when one of our Christian brothers or sisters is in trouble or going down the wrong path? Many modern-day militaries have a "no man left behind" policy, and the Christian army should be the same. Unfortunately, many Christians today adopt the "every man for himself" policy and pay for it through unnecessary suffering.

God calls us to build each other up in Christ, fight for each another, and love. If a body member is hurting emotionally or spiritually, encourage them to keep going and seek God. If a member is stagnant in his growth, help him see what he is missing and point him back toward God. Whatever you do, please do not give up on a fellow believer and count them as lost.

First Thessalonians 5:8–15 and Hebrews 10:24–25 tell us how to do this:

But since we belong to the day, let us be sober, putting on faith and love as a breastplate, and the hope of salvation as a helmet. For God did not appoint us to suffer wrath but to receive salvation through our Lord Jesus Christ. He died for us so that, whether we are awake or asleep, we may live together with him. Therefore encourage one another and build each other up, just as in fact you are doing.

Now we ask you, brothers and sisters, to acknowledge those who work hard among you, who care for you in the Lord and who admonish you. Hold them in the highest regard in love because of their work. Live in peace with each other. And we urge you, brothers and sisters, warn those who are idle and disruptive, encourage the disheartened, help the weak, be patient with everyone. Make sure that nobody pays back wrong

for wrong, but always strive to do what is good for each other and for everyone else. *(1 Thessalonians 5:8–15 NIV)*

And let us consider how we may spur one another on toward love and good deeds, not giving up meeting together, as some are in the habit of doing, but encouraging one another—and all the more as you see the Day approaching. *(Hebrews 10:24–25 NIV)*

Every one of us will face valleys in our walk with God—points in time when we lose hope or are discouraged by our lives. This is normal and part of the growth process God designed for us. Without the support of our godly family, this lack of hope and discouragement can lead to disastrous results. Those on their spiritual peak should help rescue those lost in the spiritual valleys of despair and suffering.

We who are strong ought to bear with the failings of the weak and not to please ourselves. Each of us should please our neighbors for their good, to build them up. For even Christ did not please himself but, as it is written: "The insults of those who insult you have fallen on me." For everything that was written in the past was written to teach us, so that through the endurance taught in the Scriptures and the encouragement they provide we might have hope.

May the God who gives endurance and encouragement give you the same attitude of mind toward each other that Christ Jesus had, so that with one mind and one voice you may glorify the God and Father of our Lord Jesus Christ. *(Romans 15: 1–6 NIV)*

We must not forget that we were not always where we are spiritually. Someone probably helped us get to where we are. Remember: God continually gives us a stream of living water to feed our growth as Christians. It would be wrong for us to try to hold that for ourselves when we see one of our brothers or sisters in desperate need of a source of nourishment.

This is how we know what love is: Jesus Christ laid down his life for us. And we ought to lay down our lives for our brothers and sisters. If anyone has material possessions and sees a

brother or sister in need but has no pity on them, how can the love of God be in that person? Dear children, let us not love with words or speech but with actions and in truth. *(1 John 3:16–18 NIV)*

Learn How to Love

What is love to you? Is love the good feeling you get when you enjoy something? Or is it an action word— something you must work towards and put in some effort? Love has so many definitions and implications that books have been written on it. I will try to summarize it in just a few pages concerning what it means as a believer in Christ.

The love I will describe is not a feeling. It is an action and a representation of who God is. First John 4:7–8 *(ESV)* says, **"Beloved, let us love one another, for love is from God, and whoever loves has been born of God and knows God. Anyone who does not love does not know God, because God is love."**

The Bible clearly defines love in 1 Corinthians 13:4–8 *(NIV)*:

Love is patient, love is kind. It does not envy, it does not boast, it is not proud. It does not dishonor others, it is not self-seeking, it is not easily angered, it keeps no record of wrongs. Love does not delight in evil but rejoices with the truth. It always protects, always trusts, always hopes, always perseveres. Love never fails.

The above passage is self-explanatory. How can you show love to someone if you get impatient or angry with them or treat them wrongly? How do you show love by wishing you had what they have or boasting about what you have and what they do not? Is love shown through dishonesty, selfish gains, or records of wrongdoings? Can you honestly say you love someone if you are unwilling to protect them, trust them, or persevere through hard times?

It seems simple, but many relationships fail even these simple tests. Love fails many people because they never learned to love as God loves. So how do we do this? Second Peter 1:5–7 *(ESV)* gives us a structure to follow in learning how to love like God: **"For this very reason, make every effort to supplement your faith with virtue, and virtue with knowledge, and knowledge with self-control, and self-control with steadfastness, and steadfastness with godliness, and godliness with brotherly affection, and brotherly affection with love."**

To start, one must start with faith. **"Now faith is the assurance of things hoped for, the conviction of things not seen."** *(Hebrews 11:1 ESV)*

It is impossible to love without God's blessing. The only reason non-Christians experience any love is that God extends His love for us while we are here on earth. Without faith, much of the "love" you experience is a false sense of satisfaction that deteriorates over time. This "love" requires a person to continually seek things or experiences to maintain the positive feelings they perceive as love.

Once one has established one's faith, one must add virtue, goodness, or moral living standards to one's faith. In other words, do the right thing. To know what the right thing is, you must add knowledge. Anyone can say what they do is the "right thing," but this passage refers to what is right according to the Bible. The only way to know what is right according to the Bible is to read and study it.

After determining what is right and wrong according to God, you must establish self-control to live it and then the steadfastness (perseverance) to maintain that way of living. It is one thing to know what the Bible says is right and wrong, but if you repeatedly ignore those directions and live life by your own standards, then achieving God's level of love for another is impossible.

Philippians 2:1–4 *(ESV)* states, **"If there is any encouragement in Christ, any comfort from love, any participation in the Spirit, any affection and sympathy, complete my joy by being of the same mind, having the same love, being in full accord and of one mind. Do nothing from selfish ambition** or conceit, but in humility count others more significant than yourselves. Let each of you look not only to his own interests, but also to the interests of others."

According to Peter, as we work our way up the ladder to "true love," the next step is godliness. This results from knowing God's Word and obeying it consistently. As natural-born sinners, we realize that this state of godliness is impossible to achieve without Christ. But Titus 2:11–14 *(NIV)* gives us hope.

For the grace of God has appeared that offers salvation to all people. It teaches us to say "No" to ungodliness and worldly passions, and to live self-controlled, upright and godly lives in this present age, while we wait for the blessed hope—the appearing of the glory of our great God and Savior, Jesus Christ, who gave himself for us to redeem us from all wickedness and to purify for himself a people that are his very own, eager to do what is good.

We will never achieve 100 percent godliness while we have sin in the world, but we have the power to turn from the ungodliness in our lives if we persevere in doing what is right with the faith that God will provide. With even a little godliness in our lives, we can experience the love God wants us to have toward one another. This is about as far as we can share with one another, as the next stage is agape love, which only God can show in its fullest form. Agape love means 100 percent unconditional love toward us. Nothing we can do or fail to do will change God's love for us for better or worse.

But in terms of brotherly love, Colossians 3:12–17 *(NIV)* offers this passage as instruction:

Therefore, as God's chosen people, holy and dearly loved, clothe yourselves with compassion, kindness, humility, gentleness and patience. Bear with each other and forgive one another if any of you has a grievance against someone. Forgive as the Lord forgave you. And over all these virtues put on love, which binds them all together in perfect unity.

Let the peace of Christ rule in your hearts, since as members of one body you were called to peace. And be thankful. Let the message of Christ dwell among you richly as you teach and admonish one another with all wisdom through psalms, hymns, and songs from the Spirit, singing to God with gratitude in your hearts. And whatever you do, whether in word or deed, do it all in the name of the Lord Jesus, giving thanks to God the Father through him.

As you grow in your faith, love for one another will come naturally. God never intended for us to be lost in sin. Thankfully, He has provided a way to experience His love by simply believing in Him and what He did for us through His Son, Jesus. To feel as much of His love as possible while on earth, we must follow Romans 12:9–10 *(NIV)*, which states, **"Love must be sincere. Hate what is evil; cling to what is good. Be devoted to one another in love. Honor one another above yourselves."**

It is also worth noting that you should not pick and choose whom you want to show love to, as God calls us to love our enemies as well.

"But I say to you, Love your enemies and pray for those who persecute you, so that you may be sons of your Father who is in heaven. For he makes his sun rise on the evil and on the good, and sends rain on the just and on the unjust. For if you love those who love you, what reward do you have? Do not even the tax collectors do the same? And if you greet only your brothers, what more are you doing than others? Do not even the Gentiles do the same? You therefore must be perfect, as your heavenly Father is perfect." *(Matthew 5:44–48 ESV)*

If anyone says, "I love God," and hates his brother, he is a liar; for he who does not love his brother whom he has seen cannot love God whom he has not seen. *(1 John 4:20 ESV)*

Although love can be complicated to explain, it is an essential part of Christian living and is the greatest commandment presented by God. The lack of love is the foundation for all sin, while the presence of love is the foundation of righteousness. Love is so essential in our spiritual walk that 1 Corinthians 13:1–3 *(NIV)* states, **"If I speak in the tongues of men or of angels, but do not have love, I am only a resounding gong or a clanging cymbal. If I have the gift of prophecy and can fathom all mysteries and all knowledge, and if I have a faith that can move mountains, but do not have love, I am nothing. If I give all I possess to the poor and give over my body to hardship that I may boast, but do not have love, I gain nothing."**

By diligently seeking how to love as God loves us, we will grow closer to both God and the world of people around us. Our spiritual armies will strengthen, and our unity as believers will be restored.

Graduation Day

After six months of training with JC, my time at training camp was ending. The next day, I would graduate from the safety of camp and enter the battlefield. Was I scared? Yes. I did not know if I was ready to be the soldier JC was training me to be.

It seems as if it was just yesterday when I came into camp and learned how to forgive those who wronged me. Then, I spent more time being put in my place and discovering why I was here in the first place. Just last week, JC had to knock some sense into me again when I tried handling a new recruit's big mistake on my own by lecturing him and trying to set my own punishment for his lack of concern for his peers.

Boy did that backfire on me! Not only did that recruit's trainer not punish him, but I was the one who experienced quite a humbling lecture on my role in the camp when his trainer talked to JC. I soon remembered why judging another recruit's mistakes was not my place. You see, I had an extensive list of marks that could have been held against me if it were not for the camp's grace policy. JC reminded me of every one.

As the day ended, JC and I spent our last hours together in camp, reviewing what I learned and about the future.

"Allen, tomorrow you will graduate from camp and enter the battlefield as a soldier in the army of God. Are you ready?"

"I don't know. I think I am, but what if I'm not? What if I fail?"

"What have I been teaching you all this time, Allen?" JC asked as he placed his hands on my shoulders and looked me straight in the eyes.

"To trust in you, but you aren't going to be out there with me."

"Who said that? I will be with you always. You must remember your basic training. If you can trust me, I will lead you through every difficulty you face, and you will not fail."

"But don't you have to stay here to help other recruits?"

"Every recruit has someone like me who works directly with them, understands their unique personality, and knows exactly what to do to get through to them. There will never be a lack of 'trainers.'"

"So—we're going into battle together?"

"Well, yes and no. I am actually going to battle for you, but I won't be there physically. You will always have constant communication with me as I do the heavy work behind the scenes. Continue to pray endlessly and study the instructions I have given you since day one, and you will overcome every battle you face. If you lose communication and forget what I taught you, you may be on your own for a while until you establish communication again."

I took in what JC said with a slight sense of worry. What if I lost communication? Would I lose my battles and become too weak to fight? I must trust him, I guess. That, after all, is what he has been teaching all along.

This chapter marks the end of section two. This section was about breaking you from your old habits and ways of thinking that might have held you back in your relationship with God. I then showed you how you could be an effective soldier in His army.

In the military, boot camp often serves a similar purpose. You cannot be an effective soldier if you do not learn to get over your ways of thinking and learn how to work as a unit. But just because boot camp is about to end does not mean your training is over. Section three of this book will expand on what you learned in this section and teach you more about who God is and how to fight.

You will frequently have to apply what you learn in this section as you continue growing as a Christian. You will never master any one topic because pride and circumstances always work against you. Still, the more you study and practice the topics outlined by the Bible, the stronger you will be as a Christian.

The path we are on as Christians does not end until the day we die physically. It is a constant race to the finish, requiring ongoing training and motivation to endure. The following passages best describe how we are to persist in our quest as Christians:

I press on to take hold of that for which Christ Jesus took hold of me. Brothers and sisters, I do not consider myself yet to have taken hold of it. But one thing I do: Forgetting what is behind and straining toward what is ahead, I press on toward the goal to win the prize for which God has called me heavenward in Christ Jesus.

All of us, then, who are mature should take such a view of things. And if on some point you think differently, that too God will make clear to you. Only let us live up to what we have already attained. *(Philippians 3:12–16 NIV)*

Therefore, since we are surrounded by so great a cloud of witnesses, let us also lay aside every weight, and sin which clings so closely, and let us run with endurance the race that is set before us, looking to Jesus, the founder and perfecter of our faith, who for the joy that was set before him endured the cross, despising the shame, and is seated at the right hand of the throne of God. *(Hebrews 12:1–2 ESV)*

It takes a lot of self-control and discipline to run the race the way God designed it. Everyone participates in the race, but not everyone knows where they are going or why. Even those who say they believe and know the way may not finish the race. They may teach about the way to the finish, but they never cross that finish line themselves. Some may have heard about the way, but they refuse to believe it is the only way and will seek to direct you down the wrong road. The only way to win your race is to follow God and all that He teaches because He will show you the path you need to take.

Do you not know that in a race all the runners run, but only one gets the prize? Run in such a way as to get the prize. Everyone who competes in the games goes into strict training. They do it to get a crown that will not last, but we do it to get a crown that will last forever. Therefore I do not run like someone running aimlessly; I do not fight like a boxer beating the air. No, I strike a blow to my body and make it my slave so that after I have preached to others, I myself will not be disqualified for the prize. *(1 Corinthians 9:24–27 NIV)*

Your Daily Workout

A common misconception about Christianity is that you do not have to do anything else once you are saved. Although it is true that once you are saved, there is nothing else you need to do to keep your place in heaven, there is still plenty of room for growth.

When you want to grow physically, you need to watch what goes into your body and exercise regularly. When you want to grow spiritually, you must also watch what goes into your body, specifically your mind, and exercise your faith regularly.

The exercises for your faith are often referred to as spiritual disciplines. I will not go into detail about all the spiritual disciplines because much of this book hints at many of these disciplines in one form or another. There is also no defined list of these disciplines in the Bible, so different people will have various thoughts on what should be included. There are, however, a few disciplines that almost everyone who has studied the subject will agree upon.

The most common disciplines that will likely appear on all lists are prayer, worship, fellowship, evangelism, tithing, and serving. The purpose of these, along with any others included in whatever book you read, is to strengthen your relationship with God. Most of these disciplines do not come naturally to us, and we must consciously develop them into working habits. This is why they are referred to as disciplines after all.

God wants us to grow stronger in our relationship with Him and share His name more effectively. How can we be proper disciples if we do not know the truth? How can we be effective soldiers in His army if we are too weak to fight? How can we defeat the enemy if we are unknowledgeable in the methods of spiritual warfare?

Hebrews 5:11–14 *(NIV)* says the following about those who have not exercised these disciplines and have thus failed to grow in their faith:

We have much to say about this, but it is hard to make it clear to you because you no longer try to understand. In fact, though by this time you ought to be teachers, you need someone to teach you the elementary truths of God's word all over again. You need milk, not solid food! Anyone who lives on milk, being still an infant, is not acquainted with the teaching about righteousness. But solid food is for the mature, who by constant use have trained themselves to distinguish good from evil.

Without constant training and trust in the God we serve, many battles and souls who may have had a part in those battles will be lost. Our strength as Christians is not just for our gain but also for the entire body of believers.

If we are not careful, our lackluster attitude to our Christian faith will eventually weaken the body of believers so much that it will seem as if the enemy has won. Although the enemy will never actually win the war, there will be a point in which Christians will be treated as the enemy by much of the population. Unless we train hard and stand firm in our faith as God commands us, the world as we know it will soon be far more overrun with evil. Anyone who still sides with the good will have to go into hiding to escape persecution.

As obedient children, do not conform to the evil desires you had when you lived in ignorance. But just as he who called you is holy, so be holy in all you do. *(1 Peter 1:14–15 NIV)*

Humble Yourself

There is one danger in consistently exercising spiritual disciplines. It is a lot like what you see sometimes in people who exercise regularly and have a perfectly sculpted body. They may look great on the outside and have newfound confidence and look at life, which is good. But, if left unchecked, this confidence often comes packaged with a sense of pride.

According to James 4:6 *(ESV)*, **"God opposes the proud but gives grace to the humble."** To give you an idea of what this means, check out 2 Chronicles 7:14 *(ESV)*:

If my people who are called by my name humble themselves, and pray and seek my face and turn from their wicked ways, then I will hear from heaven and will forgive their sin and heal their land.

Your goal in practicing your spiritual disciplines is not to make yourself look good to others, nor is it a means to achieve a higher standing in heaven. Your spiritual disciplines are meant for you to understand your place in your relationship with God and to come closer to Him. John said in John 3:30 *(ESV)*, **"He must increase, but I must decrease."** When we practice our spiritual disciplines correctly, we should recognize that it was God who allowed us to grow, not our own efforts.

What happens when we think our success in spiritual disciplines, skills, or general life goals comes from anything except God? Often we will brag and try to gain attention to our actions so we can look like a good person to our peers. We put ourselves on a pedestal and say, "Look at me and what I did."

Luke 14:8–11 *(ESV)* gives a good example of what may happen when we decide for ourselves our value to God's mission:

"When you are invited by someone to a wedding feast, do not sit down in a place of honor, lest someone more distinguished than you be invited by him, and he who invited you both will come and say to you, 'Give your place to this person,' and then you will begin with shame to take the lowest place. But when you are invited, go and sit in the lowest place, so that when your host comes he may say to you, 'Friend, move up higher.' Then you will be honored in the presence of all who sit at table with you. For everyone who exalts himself will be humbled, and he who humbles himself will be exalted."

Graduation Day

This means that if you keep showing off and thinking you deserve more, God will do something to let you know your place and who is in charge of your success. When we rely on our power to achieve success, we will eventually reach a failing point. You may have had a lot of fame or recognition before, but suddenly, when something goes wrong and all that fame disappears, you are left with nothing but sorrow and misery.

If you humble yourself, though, God will be the one to show you off. God will be the one saying, "Look what I did," while pointing to you. He does not put self-righteous people on a pedestal. He honors only those who have shown true faith in God by allowing Him to work. If you allow God to build you up, you can rest assured that He will not leave an unfinished or broken piece of art. **"I am sure of this, that he who began a good work in you will bring it to completion at the day of Jesus Christ."** *(Philippians 1:6 ESV)*. He can even use the worst situations to show his power by morphing you into an even greater masterpiece. You will not have to worry about losing your fame or popularity because your worth will be found in Christ.

One's pride will bring him low, but he who is lowly in spirit will obtain honor. *(Proverbs 29:23 ESV)*

When pride comes, then comes disgrace, but with humility comes wisdom. *(Proverbs 11:2 NIV)*

I have often found this principle to be true when playing various games. I have noticed that the people who start making a big deal about being in the lead often lose—while someone else comes from behind and takes the lead. When you are humble about your position in the game, win or lose, you still come out on top because you played for the experience, not the competition. It is always fun to win, but there are two ways you can think about winning in games or life.

If a person's sole purpose is to win, they may sometimes go to extreme lengths to do so. Sometimes, they may try to cheat or manipulate the game to work in their favor. If they win, these

The Army of One

people often rub it in the other players' faces and make a huge deal about it. Sometimes the "losing party" is left feeling horrible because of the winner's words. The game is no longer fun.

Thankfully, there is a thing called "healthy competition." If you go into a game playing for fun, yes, there will still be a winner and a loser, but in the end, both parties still have fun. The game is played fairly within the rules, so no cheating occurs. The game's purpose is less about winning and more about the experience with the person you are playing with. The result may include one person celebrating victory, but the losing parties still had fun and can often celebrate with the winner.

The point is this—when you go through life, you can play to win through your own efforts, or you can play to please God and enjoy the experience He has planned for you. You must realize that the perfect plan with a perfect outcome has already been laid out for you, but you must choose to follow it. There is a reason the path to salvation is so narrow, according to Matthew 7:13–14. The reason is that so many people try to win the game of life through their own abilities and ultimately lose altogether.

In Luke 13:30 *(NIV)* Jesus says, **"There are those who are last who will be first, and first who will be last."** This is referring to the very principle I have been discussing. It makes no difference how close to the finish you think you are—unless God has a part in your finish, you will not be allowed to enter the kingdom of heaven.

Brothers and sisters, think of what you were when you were called. Not many of you were wise by human standards; not many were influential; not many were of noble birth. But God chose the foolish things of the world to shame the wise; God chose the weak things of the world to shame the strong. God chose the lowly things of this world and the despised things— and the things that are not—to nullify the things that are, so that no one may boast before him. It is because of him that you are in Christ Jesus, who has become for us wisdom from God—that

is, our righteousness, holiness and redemption. Therefore, as it is written: "Let the one who boasts boast in the Lord." *(1 Corinthians 1:26–31 NIV)*

No Place to Judge

There is one more danger that comes from practicing your spiritual disciplines. Often as people learn a particular skill or set of rules, including those found in the Bible, they suddenly feel the need to teach others. The problem with this is that it usually goes beyond teaching and turns into personal judgments when someone else does something wrong.

How often have you witnessed someone who does not dress by your standards? Maybe they are covered in tattoos or piercings, and your standard is long skirts and turtlenecks with plain colors. Or perhaps you witnessed someone out at a restaurant having a glass of wine or a few beers, and your standard is not to drink alcohol at all. What was your first reaction to those cases? If you are judgmental, often the reaction is "Oh, they must not be Christian because they aren't following my standards."

The problem with this reaction is that you do not have the power to judge someone's heart by just looking at them. There are many people covered in tattoos who are strong Christians, just as there are many people who may dress very modestly who are not. When I have been out evangelizing, I have sometimes avoided people based on how they look. Some people look scary, intimidating, or mad at the world, so I think they would not be interested in hearing what I say. Those very same people, however, need Jesus just as much as you or I do. If I assume someone will never become Christian because they look or act a certain way, then I am not doing my job and may be subject to the same judgment that I have placed on them. Having said that, however, I would not advise going up to people who seem aggressive or hostile, especially not alone. This is not a matter of judging their salvation but rather a matter of your safety. Do what you can, but do not put yourself in danger. It's not your job to save everyone.

"Do not judge by appearances, but judge with right judgment." *(John 7:24 ESV)*

So not judging people based on appearance is easy to understand, but what about judging people's actions? If you see a lawbreaker, they should pay the price, right? Well, yes and no. If they have sinned, then they do deserve the same punishment that every one of us deserves. In God's eyes, this means we will end up in hell. But everyone who sins also has the opportunity to receive the same forgiveness that we do for our sins, and only God can extend that grace completely.

Did you ever realize that the sins you judge the most in others often tend to be ones you struggle with or have struggled with in the past? I believe this is because we want to hide our actions by focusing on someone else. Or we may think, "That person is doing it too," or "To a greater extent than me, so I must be okay."

Jesus addresses this in John 8:7 *(ESV):* **"Let him who is without sin among you be the first to throw a stone at her."**

You see, it is very easy to turn the focus off ourselves by seeking to find someone else doing the same sin or something worse. But God says all sin is punishable by death without having the grace of God. Just because we have gone through the training and shown signs of improvement in our lives does not mean we have reached perfection. Until that day comes, which it won't, we have no right to judge others for their sins when we have so many of our own that must be addressed.

"Judge not, that you be not judged. For with the judgment you pronounce you will be judged, and with the measure you use it will be measured to you. Why do you see the speck that is in your brother's eye, but do not notice the log that is in your own eye? Or how can you say to your brother, 'Let me take the speck out of your eye,' when there is the log in your own eye? You hypocrite, first take the log out of your own eye, and then you

will see clearly to take the speck out of your brother's eye." *(Matthew 7:1–5 ESV)*

Therefore you have no excuse, O man, every one of you who judges. For in passing judgment on another you condemn yourself, because you, the judge, practice the very same things. We know that the judgment of God rightly falls on those who practice such things. Do you suppose, O man—you who judge those who practice such things and yet do them yourself—that you will escape the judgment of God? *(Romans 2:1–3 ESV)*

Many churches and individuals insist that specific actions or people groups will go to hell because they do not match their beliefs. Sometimes, they are right in that a particular action is a sin and is punishable by spiritual death, while other times, the offender's "sins" are just a violation of a rule made by man. Whatever the case, these churches or individuals fail to understand the basic gospel, which states that Jesus died for all sins—past, present, and future—and for all people who accept His name and His sacrifice in taking the punishment for us.

We cannot decide the state of someone's heart, nor do we know if God may change that person's heart in the future. Yes, that person may have to suffer various consequences here on earth for their actions, but when it comes to going to heaven or hell, we have no right or ability to judge that person. When we insist on doing so, we are setting our own standard of salvation, and that standard may be used against you when you are standing before the real Judge in heaven.

What if we see a brother or sister in Christ doing something wrong? Should we turn our backs and pretend it did not happen? This is where the answer can be a little tricky to understand, and it often depends on your relationship with the person. There is a difference between going up to a person and saying, "You sinned. You are going to hell if you don't change," or saying, "You sinned, but because I love you and don't want to see you fall away from God, I want to help you."

To give you an example, let us say you have a friend who you know cheated on a significant test. You know it was wrong, and he could be expelled for doing so. Do you turn him in? Do you pretend it did not happen and hope he does not do it again? Or do you confront him, letting him know his actions were wrong, and try to help him learn the material so he does not have to cheat again?

Let us examine the consequences of each action. Some examples purposefully exaggerate the worst possible scenario to illustrate the point.

You turn him in.

In this case, you will most likely lose a friend as he will be expelled and never trust you again. Because he has been expelled, he may have a hard time reaching his educational goals, and the rest of his life may be affected negatively because of that one bad report on his student record. He may have trouble getting a respectable job and, in turn, may have difficulty finding a good spouse because he is not making much money working at the local fast-food joint. That one action set a course of failure in his life.

Pretend it did not happen.

In this case, your friend may have gotten away with cheating. But now, because he successfully cheated on one test without being caught, he thinks, "Why bother studying?" for the next test. Your friend soon develops a habit of cheating and getting away with it. He goes through school without being caught and ends up with a great job because of his seemingly impressive grades. The only problem is that your friend still has the cheater mindset and falsifies an important financial report. This time, he gets caught and gets sent to prison, spending a large portion of his life behind bars.

Confront him.

Depending on your relationship with this person and the situation, your friend will likely be defensive initially, probably denying cheating at all. But after explaining to your friend that you only want to help so he does not end up in trouble, he explains that he resorted to cheating because something terrible happened in his life and he did not have time to study but needed a good grade. You tell him you understand and recommend that he confess to his teacher and explain the situation. Your friend reluctantly agrees and talks to his teacher. The teacher admires your friend's honesty and decides not to report the instance to the school but does have to fail your friend on that test. In this case, the teacher does not offer a make-up test, but there are still several other tests in the semester in which you offer to help your friend study. Your friend then completes the remaining tests under the teacher's watchful eye and barely passes the class. Ultimately, your friend leaves with a clean conscience and a closer relationship with you.

There are two additional points I would like to make about the example I just gave. The first is that you rarely know why people do what they do. A lot of sinful behavior stems from desperation. In this case the friend needed a good grade but did not have time to study because something happened in his life. (Family troubles are a big cause.) In other situations, people give in to sin so they are not lonely anymore or to fill some void in their lives. All they want to do is fit in, even if it is with the wrong crowd. Most people do not start their lives with bad intentions, but because of various circumstances, one thing led to another, and they let themselves get locked up in the bondage of sin.

The second point is this: when you confront someone, it must be out of love for that person. When a brother or sister becomes too weak to tackle a sin on their own, we need to lift them up and fight the battle with them. Remember: we are supposed to be one body under Christ. When one member is weak, it weakens the whole body.

Look at the following verses for instructions on interacting with fellow believers who have fallen into sin:

"If your brother sins against you, go and tell him his fault, between you and him alone. If he listens to you, you have gained your brother. But if he does not listen, take one or two others along with you, that every charge may be established by the evidence of two or three witnesses. If he refuses to listen to them, tell it to the church. And if he refuses to listen even to the church, let him be to you as a Gentile and a tax collector." *(Matthew 18:15–17 ESV)*

If you see any brother or sister commit a sin that does not lead to death, you should pray and God will give them life. I refer to those whose sin does not lead to death. There is a sin that leads to death. I am not saying that you should pray about that. *(1 John 5:16 NIV)*

Accept the one whose faith is weak, without quarreling over disputable matters. ... Who are you to judge someone else's servant? To their own master, servants stand or fall. And they will stand, for the Lord is able to make them stand. ... Therefore, let us stop passing judgment on one another. Instead, make up your mind not to put any stumbling block or obstacle in the way of a brother or sister. *(Romans 14:1, 4, 13 NIV)*

Do not speak evil against one another, brothers. The one who speaks against a brother or judges his brother, speaks evil against the law and judges the law. But if you judge the law, you are not a doer of the law but a judge. There is only one lawgiver and judge, he who is able to save and to destroy. But who are you to judge your neighbor? *(James 4:11–12 ESV)*

PART 3
PREPARING FOR BATTLE

10

Knowing Your Leader

Dear Journal,
This is it! This is the moment I have been training for. Today I will enter the battlefield. Am I ready? I don't think so. Do I need to be? JC says I am ready, so I will trust him.

Today I meet my leader, the one who is strict yet full of grace when I mess up, the one who has never lost a war and never will, the one whose sole existence is worth fighting for with all my might.

I cannot help but wonder if he will like me. JC told me not to worry about that, but I still have a lot to learn. I mean, just yesterday I made a big mistake and was lectured once again. What If I make a mistake on the battlefield, where it matters? Will he kick me out of his army? Will he get tired of picking me up when I repeatedly fail?

Here he comes! I have to go. I'll report back when I'm able.

I AM, King of Kings, Lord of Lords, Father of heaven and earth, Alpha and Omega, Everlasting Father, Creator, Comforter, Righteous Judge, or Almighty God.

No matter what you call our God, the message is clear: God is in control. God was here before all and will remain here after all. Through Him alone, we have life, purpose, and freedom.

Everything that was, everything that is, and everything that will be comes from God *(Psalm 89:11)*. His very existence far exceeds our imagination. He is all-knowing, all-present, and all-powerful. You cannot hide from God, you cannot keep a secret from Him, and you cannot defeat Him.

He holds not only our lives but also the world in His hands—and not only the world but also the universe and all of creation. He knows the name of every star in the sky *(Isaiah 40:26)* and has records of every hair on your head *(Matthew 10:30)*. He controls all nature *(Jonah 1:4; Jeremiah 10:13)* and provides for every creature's needs *(Psalm 104)*.

God's attributes surpass our deepest understandings. His timing is perfect, and His choices are just. He has wisdom and love that cannot be beaten. His love for you is unconditional, unchanging, unrelenting, and undeserved.

God is all you need.

***

In the beginning was the Word, and the Word was with God, and the Word was God. He was in the beginning with God. All things were made through him, and without him was not any thing made that was made. In him was life, and the life was the light of men. The light shines in the darkness, and the darkness has not overcome it.

The true light, which gives light to everyone, was coming into the world. He was in the world, and the world was made through him, yet the world did not know him. He came to his own, and his own people did not receive him. But to all who did receive him, who believed in his name, he gave the right to become children of God, who were born, not of blood nor of the will of the flesh nor of the will of man, but of God.

And the Word became flesh and dwelt among us, and we have seen his glory, glory as of the only Son from the Father, full of grace and truth. *(John 1:1–5, 9–14 ESV)*

If you are a Christian, your purpose in life is to serve God. But how many of you can say you truly know the God you serve? Even the most versed Christians have a limited understanding of God. Our human brains cannot comprehend the full magnitude of who God is. There are no words that will do Him justice nor comparisons that will adequately represent His full power in our lives and the world in which we live. Yet we must have some frame of reference to guide our understanding of the God we serve.

The purpose of this chapter is to do just that. In this chapter, I will illustrate one of the most misunderstood aspects of

Christianity, the Trinity. Remember—my explanations are just a tiny part of who God is. Because the concept of the Trinity is not a natural occurrence within our laws of nature, the illustrations I provide may not adequately explain the extent of the relationship.

Before the beginning of time there was one God. Within that one God are three persons: the Father, the Son, and the Holy Spirit. The Father is not the Son or the Holy Spirit. Likewise, neither of the others is equal to the remaining two, yet all there are equally God. Each has a unique function and purpose distinct from the others, but they are all the same deity with equal power in our lives.

The best illustration I have heard to help explain the Trinity relates to candles. If you lean three lit candles together with their wicks touching, there will be one flame, yet if you separate the three candles, each will have a flame identical to the first and of the other. The separation of the candles does not diminish the flame of any of the candles, nor does returning the candles to a central flame create a stronger flame.

Although the term Trinity is not found in the Bible, the first indication of a multi-person God can be found in Genesis 1:26 *(ESV)*, when God said, **"Let us make man in our image, after our likeness."** There are also references to a plural God in Genesis 3:22; 11:7; and Isaiah 6:8.

Until the New Testament, only two parts of the Trinity were identified. The Lord made Himself known to a select few to give them direction, and then the Holy Spirit surrounded the individuals to carry out the task they commissioned. The Holy Spirit was never a permanent and personal part of the individual until the introduction and death of the third part of the Trinity, Jesus.

Even though only two parts of the Trinity were recognized in the Old Testament days, there has always been the third, but He did not yet have the physical form that He did in the gospels. Numerous prophecies throughout the Old Testament alluded to the coming of this third part, but He was not revealed until several thousand years of human history had elapsed. It is through the introduction of the final member of the Trinity that salvation became possible. Without any one part of the Trinity, salvation is not possible.

It is worth noting that Jesus may have appeared as the "Angel of the Lord" a few times[1] throughout the Old Testament. This is believed to be the case because in these instances the angel accepted worship from those he visited and claimed the ground as "holy ground." Other angels would reject any attempts at worship, as in Revelation 22:9

Although I cannot explain why God exists in a Trinity, I can do my best to describe each part of the Trinity's purpose in our lives according to the Bible. To do this I will relate their roles to roles you may see on a battlefield. That is the theme of the book, after all.

The Father

The first part of the Trinity I will discuss is the Father. This is not because He is more important than the others but because you must start somewhere, and this is the order in which they are usually mentioned. It is also the Father whom we are first introduced to in the Bible.

"Truly, truly, I say to you, the Son can do nothing of his own accord, but only what he sees the Father doing. For whatever the Father does, that the Son does likewise. For the Father loves the Son and shows him all that he himself is doing." *(John 5:19–20 ESV)*

The Father's role is to plan, direct, and send. His role most relates to a general in an army as He is the "brains" of the operations. He is the one who coordinates all the routes we are to take and makes sure they line up at the exact right moment to accomplish our mission. He also knows the results of every other

---

[1] Genesis 16:7–14; Exodus 3:2-4; and Joshua 5:15 are a few examples thought to be an angelic form of Jesus.

course we can take and has created each with a way out when we start to wander down the wrong path.

Trust in the LORD with all your heart and lean not on your own understanding; in all your ways submit to Him, and He will make your paths straight. *(Proverbs 3:5–6 NIV)*

Because He knows what we will do before we do it, His will for our lives will be carried out perfectly. He may even use our disobedience for His glory (though we may have to suffer more by not listening the first time). Romans 11:1–12 shows that even when an entire people group disobeys God's Word, good can still come from it. The disobedient Jews were cast out, and the Gentiles were accepted as part of God's family.

The Father is also the one who establishes the rules of life, both our own and everything around us. Being the rule-maker, He is also the ultimate judge of our lives. Only He can establish the means to salvation, which is absolute perfection. Anything less than perfection would disrupt the unity between Himself, the Son, and the Holy Spirit. To account for this, He had to send His Son, who is also perfect, to come down and purify our hearts with a personal sacrifice that only the Son could perform.

The Father is strict but gracious to those who follow His direction. He knows we will mess up many times in our lives, but He will never give up on us when we do. Numbers 14:18 and 1 John 1:9 best express this fact.

The LORD is slow to anger, abounding in love and forgiving sin and rebellion. Yet he does not leave the guilty unpunished. *(Numbers 14:18 NIV)*

If we confess our sins, he is faithful and just to forgive us our sins and to cleanse us from all unrighteousness. *(1 John 1:9 ESV)*

This does not mean that we all have a get-out-of-jail-free card and can do whatever we please. God still expects us to at least try following His rules and striving for perfection to the best of our abilities. He established two essential rules that, if followed perfectly, would also eliminate all sin in our lives.

These can be found in Matthew 22:37–39 *(NIV)*:

'Love the Lord your God with all your heart and with all your soul and with all your mind.' This is the first and greatest commandment. And the second is like it: 'Love your neighbor as yourself.'

Any deviation from those rules, no matter how small, results in a departure from the course God designed for us, so we get lost. This is where the second two persons of the Trinity come in.

The Son

He is the image of the invisible God, the firstborn of all creation. For by him all things were created, in heaven and on earth, visible and invisible, whether thrones or dominions or rulers or authorities—all things were created through him and for him. And he is before all things, and in him all things hold together. And he is the head of the body, the church. He is the beginning, the firstborn from the dead, that in everything he might be preeminent. For in him all the fullness of God was pleased to dwell, and through him to reconcile to himself all things, whether on earth or in heaven, making peace by the blood of his cross. *(Colossians 1:15–20 ESV)*

The role of the Son, first and foremost, is to carry out the will of the Father. This is stated in John 6:38 *(ESV)* when Jesus says, **"For I have come down from heaven, not to do my own will but the will of him who sent me."** The Son is the human form of God. He experienced the same pain and suffering that we do and was equally tempted, if not more so, than any of us *(See Matthew 4:1–11)*. The difference between the Son in His human form and us is that He did not give in to any of those temptations. Because of this, He is the only one capable of being with the Father without any special provision.

In our lives, the Son is like the guide in the Trinity. In a military sense, the Son, Jesus, might be like a colonel out on the field carrying out the instructions of the general. In his angelic appearance in the Old Testament *(Joshua 5:15)*, He is referenced as "the commander of the Lord's army." If we follow His instructions, He will get us through any obstacles that come our way.

In the Bible, this idea is carried out by referring to Jesus as the shepherd of our lives *(John 10:1–21)*. A shepherd's whole purpose is to safely lead his sheep to green pastures and care for the sick. His flock trusts only him and will follow him wherever he takes them.

Jesus says, "I am the good shepherd; I know my sheep and my sheep know me— just as the Father knows me and I know the Father—and I lay down my life for the sheep. I have other sheep that are not of this sheep pen. I must bring them also. They too will listen to my voice, and there shall be one flock and one shepherd. The reason my Father loves me is that I lay down my life—only to take it up again. No one takes it from me, but I lay it down of my own accord. I have authority to lay it down and authority to take it up again. This command I received from my Father." *(John 10:14–18 NIV)*.

Although we are referred to as the sheep in the Bible, we often do not give Jesus our complete trust and attention. Instead, we choose to find our own "green pastures." Many of us "follow Jesus" by taking the lead, only looking back occasionally to ensure He is still behind us.

Have you ever done this? While following someone to a destination, instead of following behind the person who truly knows the way, you get excited thinking you know the destination, so you go ahead only to look back and realize the person you were supposed to be following is not there with you. Sometimes parents with kids may hide around a corner while keeping a close eye on their children and watch as their children suddenly realize that their parents are no longer behind them. Temporary fear enters children's lives as they look for the person who is supposed to protect them. Parents do this to teach their kids that they should stay with them to avoid getting lost, and Jesus often does the same thing to us.

Even as adults we often think we know the direction we need to take in life. We try to find our own way while sometimes leaving Jesus in the dust. We must then cry out to Jesus, just as a child would cry out to his parents, to get us out of the mess we got ourselves in as we become lost.

Although Jesus is referred to as the Son in the Trinity, He is very much like a father figure in our lives. He will allow us to make mistakes to strengthen us. He will not micromanage our lives or demand perfection because He knows perfection is impossible. Instead, He watches and waits patiently as we try hard to succeed, only to fail and call out to Him. Only then will He pick us up and encourage us to go on.

Sometimes, this will happen repeatedly, with not even a minute between failures. But Jesus does not get mad at our failures. He likely chuckles to Himself, wondering when we will learn to give Him control.

In John 15:5 *(NIV)*, Jesus says, **"Apart from me, you can do nothing."** This does not mean we need Jesus to do our everyday tasks, such as eating or caring for ourselves, though God also plays a big part in those things. But we need Jesus for any chance of spiritual advancement, from our initial salvation to our continual growth in Christ.

Without Jesus, our failures would have much more significant consequences. Our act of disobedience to God the Father is punishable by death. When we try going our own way, someone still has to be punished for not following the Father's orders. Jesus was the one to take that punishment.

He loves us so much that instead of letting us receive the full wrath of the Father, He submitted Himself to God's punishment by being painfully beaten and hung up on a cross to die in one of the most painful deaths possible. Jesus paid for every act of disobedience we performed because He loved us.

For there is one God and one mediator between God and mankind, the man Christ Jesus, who gave himself as a ransom for all people. *(1 Timothy 2:5–6 NIV)*

Think about that for a moment. Jesus became a living sacrifice to pay for our sins. Every time we sin or try following our own path, it is almost like spitting in the face of the one who saved us. But instead of getting mad and condemning us to where we belong, He stays with us, hoping that one day we will truly recognize what He did for us and decide to turn around and let Him lead us down the right path of sanctification and righteousness.

The heart of man plans his way, but the LORD establishes his steps. *(Proverbs 16:9 ESV)*

Jesus's life on this earth as a man was short-lived. In His ministry of only a few short years, Jesus taught us everything we need to know to have a chance of salvation. It is so simple that many people refuse to believe it and still attempt to achieve salvation by their own means. Believing in what Jesus did for you on the cross and choosing to follow Him will grant you a place in heaven. Even without the physical presence of Jesus in today's time, you can still "follow Jesus" through the final piece of the Trinity, the Holy Spirit.

"But the Advocate, the Holy Spirit, whom the Father will send in my name, will teach you all things and will remind you of everything I have said to you. Peace I leave with you; my peace I give to you. Not as the world gives do I give to you. Let not your hearts be troubled, neither let them be afraid." *(John 14:26-27 NIV)*

The Holy Spirit

If the Father is the general and the planner of our lives and Jesus is our leader and guide, who is the Holy Spirit? To me, the Holy Spirit is like our GPS. I once saw a church sign that referred to this not as a global positioning system but as a "God-positioning system." I don't think that's far off.

Think about it: when Jesus returned to be with the Father, we still needed a guide to get us through our tough times. In Jesus's human form, He couldn't be a physical guide for all believers. There was just not enough of Him to go around. As God, He could have multiplied himself so there would be one of Him for every person, as I alluded to in my mini-story throughout this book, but He had a better solution. Jesus had to go so we could receive the greatest benefit to us all: the inclusion of the Holy Spirit. Read this in John 16:7–11 *(ESV)*:

"Nevertheless, I tell you the truth: it is to your advantage that I go away, for if I do not go away, the Helper will not come to you. But if I go, I will send him to you. And when he comes, he will convict the world concerning sin and righteousness and judgment: concerning sin, because they do not believe in me; concerning righteousness, because I go to the Father, and you will see me no longer; concerning judgment, because the ruler of this world is judged."

So as new believers, we will all be equipped with this individualized guide who dwells in us. This guide will do much the same as Jesus did in leading us down the right path, but still, we must listen. Just as with a GPS in a car with that annoying voice telling you which way to go, we can also ignore the direction of the Holy Spirit. Of course, when we ignore the GPS or the Holy Spirit, the same outcome often occurs—we get lost.

The Holy Spirit is often represented on TV by those little conscience angels that argue back and forth on your shoulders when you have a difficult decision to make between right and wrong. Of course, the Holy Spirit would be the angelic-looking one, representing good. Although no little angels appear on your shoulders in real life, this is a decent representation of what goes on.

There is a constant battle between good and evil that the Holy Spirit helps you fight daily if you let Him. Since the Holy Spirit is a part of the Trinity as well, and therefore God, He knows what is coming ahead in your life and is working to properly prepare you for it or lead you out of harm's way if you listen. But all too often we still have the enemy voice in us, placed by Satan, who is just as determined to throw us off course. Sometimes, we do not even need the demon voice to lead us off the path. He has conditioned us so much to ignore the Holy Spirit that we often do it ourselves without prompting.

Romans 8:4–5 *(ESV)* explains why we need the Holy Spirit:

In order that the righteous requirement of the law might be fulfilled in us, who walk not according to the flesh but according to the Spirit. For those who live according to the flesh set their minds on the things of the flesh, but those who live according to the Spirit set their minds on the things of the Spirit.

Recognizing and being filled by the Spirit is an ongoing task that takes a lot of work. Jesus says in John 14:16–17 *(NIV)* that the Holy Spirit will be with us forever when we become Christians:

"And I will ask the Father, and he will give you another advocate to help you and be with you forever— the Spirit of truth. The world cannot accept him, because it neither sees him nor knows him. But you know him, for he lives with you and will be in you."

The purpose of the Holy Spirit is to intercede for us when we are too weak to accomplish an obstacle ourselves: **"The Spirit helps us in our weakness. For we do not know what to pray for as we ought, but the Spirit himself intercedes for us with groanings too deep for words"** *(Romans 8:26 ESV)*.

The Army of One

The Holy Spirit also gives us the words we should say when sharing God's truth: **"For it will not be you speaking, but the Spirit of your Father speaking through you."** *(Matthew 10:20 NIV).*

The need for the Holy Spirit is a great one: **"For all who are led by the Spirit of God are sons of God. For you did not receive the spirit of slavery to fall back into fear, but you have received the Spirit of adoption as sons, by whom we cry, 'Abba! Father!' The Spirit himself bears witness with our spirit that we are children of God."** *(Romans 8:14–16 ESV).*

Without this part of the Trinity, we would be so lost that we would never find our path to salvation. God did a great thing by making Himself a part of every one of us who accepts His name.

And it is God who establishes us with you in Christ, and has anointed us, and who has also put his seal on us and given us his Spirit in our hearts as a guarantee. *(2 Corinthians 1:21–22 ESV; see also: Ephesians 1:13–14).*

As soon as we accept Christ as our Savior, the Holy Spirit enters our hearts. But the process does not stop there. The indwelling of the Holy Spirit is one you must continually keep track of. The Holy Spirit will intercede for you, but often you must ask Him.

There is a great analogy for this that compares your life to a house. Each room of the house represents different parts of your life where you may occasionally need help. One room could represent your love life or your relationships with others. Another room could be your finances, your education, or your job. Taking it further, different rooms could represent your tendency for specific sins (pride, lust, greed, and such). This can be taken as deeply or as shallowly as you wish.

Now if you were honest with yourself, most, if not all, of the rooms of your "house" are a total mess compared to what they should be. Perhaps the room representing your family life is in total shambles. Not one thing is in order. It is such a mess that you try to hide it. You put it in the back of your mind, shut the door, and pretend it is not there. Or perhaps you keep adding to the mess like a hoarder until it gets so deep that it is practically impossible to use it.

As you know, God is the creator of your life, so in this analogy He is the architect of your house. He knows the way it is supposed to look better than you do. When you accept the knock at the door to your heart *(Revelation 3:20)*, you allow God into your house through the Holy Spirit. The mere presence of the Holy Spirit in your home is enough to get you into heaven, even if He stays in the foyer. But if we want Him to intercede, we need to give Him the tour.

We often show God only the parts of our house that are reasonably in order, even if not perfect. We want our new guests to think that we are doing well in our lives. But remember—God is the architect. He knows when there are rooms you are not showing Him. Sometimes He may ask about them while at other times He will wait patiently for you to invite Him into those spaces.

This is the hard part. The Holy Spirit will not enter a room of your life until you invite Him. All those rooms you are ashamed of, God knows they are there, and He knows how much of a mess they are. Through the Holy Spirit, God would love to help us get our rooms back to looking the way He designed them. He is a perfectionist, after all. Some rooms may take a short time to get in order, while others could take years. But every day we must ask God to continue working on every room we want to return to the way it was meant to be.

Notice I said every day. This is not a one-time contract deal where we set the terms and expect God to show up every day to clean. We must call upon Him every single day and work alongside Him to get our rooms cleaned up. When we start throwing more trash in on top of God as He works, He will walk out until we are ready to take the cleaning process seriously.

For the desires of the flesh are against the Spirit, and the desires of the Spirit are against the flesh, for these are opposed to each other, to keep you from doing the things you want to do.
(Galatians 5:17 ESV)

The Army of One

The final question you must ask yourself daily is "Am I ready to let the Holy Spirit change my life?" It is usually easy to invite God into your house, but it is often challenging to humble yourself so much to give God the full tour of the house, to show Him how much of a mess you have made of His one-of-a-kind creation, to admit how much you have been buried in sin and pain and then have attempted to dig your way out of it is probably the hardest thing you will ever do—but it is what God calls us to do.

God wants to help us. That is why He sent the Holy Spirit to live with us for the rest of our lives. He knows how much we have buried ourselves in trash and filth. He knows the skeletons we have hiding in our closets. He knows what we try to hide and do not want Him to see. But He does not care about those things. All He wants is to get His house back to how He designed it, regardless of how long it takes. So open your house to God and watch Him work. It may be painful at points—but the end is always worth the means when God is involved.

11

The Armor of God

"Suit up! It is time to go to war! Meet me in the briefing room in ten minutes."

"War? I'm not ready for war."

"Yes, you are, soldier! Put on your armor and follow me."

"This equipment looks a little primitive, doesn't it? How is this going to protect me from bullets?"

"You still haven't learned to trust us much, have you? This equipment is all you need to protect you from the enemies you will fight. Do as I say when I say it, and the battle will be won. Remember to be in constant communication. Do not go off the planned course, and you will be fine. If you do, rely on your GPS to get you back on course as soon as you realize you are off track."

"Okay, General. I trust you. I'm just scared."

"I know you are, soldier, but I've never lost a war and don't plan on starting now. All you have to do is believe that I will get you through wherever I send you and be ready to go when I say go. I will do the rest. Are you ready?"

"Well, General, I don't know how this will turn out, but let's go to war."

War has changed a lot over the years— from the weapons we use to the fighting style we endure. Our enemies have changed, and our freedoms have been tested. However, within every war common factors help determine the winner and the loser. Those factors are how well the sides can defend themselves and how well they are prepared to fight back.

This chapter explains how God has equipped us to fight the battles each of us encounters. The spiritual warfare against Satan is real, and we must all properly prepare ourselves to fight—or we will lose.

The Army of One

God has outlined exactly what our spiritual armor is. This chapter aims to expand on that to tell you what it is, how to use it, and what it is not.

The armor of God is found in Ephesians 6:10–18. Verses 11–12 *(NIV)* tells us why we need to have God's armor: **"Put on the full armor of God, so you can take your stand against the devil's schemes. For our struggle is not against flesh and blood, but against the rulers, against the authorities, against the powers of this dark world and against the spiritual forces of evil in the heavenly realms."**

Notice how this passage states that our struggle is not against flesh and blood but against spiritually evil forces. These forces are not forces that any earthly armor can handle. Instead, these forces attack your conscience, and you need the spiritual armor provided by God to protect you fully.

In the following verse the passage says we need our armor **"so that when the day of evil comes, you may be able to stand your ground."** This is a crucial point to understand. God tells us to **"Be on your guard; stand firm in the faith; be courageous; be strong. Do everything in love."** *(1 Corinthians 16:13–14 NIV)*.

In fact, the Bible tells us to stand firm or uses related terminology at least twenty-seven times[1] in the Bible. Our responsibility is not to seek evil and try to defeat it without help. We would never be able to. Instead, we are called to stand our ground when evil comes knocking at our door and let God fight for us.

However, there are times when our mission may seem more offensive. These are times when God directs us to go out and evangelize or rebuke a brother who has fallen. But those efforts should be based on God's Word and done only with his backing and direction. God tells us where and when to go, and we are to

---

[1] Exodus 18:23; Deuteronomy 10:20; Joshua 23:6; Psalm 40:2; Isaiah 26:4; Matthew 10:22; 24:13; Acts 11:23; 1 Corinthians 15:58; 16:13; 2 Corinthians 1:24; Galatians 5:1; Ephesians 6:11, 13; Philippians 1:27; 4:1; Colossians 1:23; 4:12; 1 Thessalonians 3:8; 5:21; 2 Thessalonians 2:15; Hebrews 3:6, 14; 4:14; 10:23; 1 Peter 5:9; 2 Peter 3:17

follow His command. We are called to stand up for our beliefs and fight against sin, not seek it out.

Every one of the pieces of armor I am about to describe is meant for defense against evil forces, including the sword. If we properly maintain and wear the armor of God, then evil forces will never be able to get past us.

The rest of the passage lists the armor we are to wear.

Stand firm then, with the belt of truth buckled around your waist, with the breastplate of righteousness in place, and with your feet fitted with the readiness that comes from the gospel of peace. In addition to all this, take up the shield of faith, with which you can extinguish all the flaming arrows of the evil one. Take the helmet of salvation and the sword of the Spirit, which is the word of God.

And pray in the Spirit on all occasions with all kinds of prayers and requests. With this in mind, be alert and always keep on praying for all the Lord's people. *(Ephesians 6:14–18 NIV)*

Belt of Truth

The very first piece of armor the Bible mentions is probably one of the last things anyone would put on when getting dressed in today's time—the belt. Why is this?

The belt, or more specifically the belt of truth, is the first item mentioned because knowing the actual truth is the core of Christian beliefs. Truth is represented as a belt because it was used for more than holding up a soldier's pants in the period this was written. The belt was designed with a thick material to help protect the vital organs in the body's midsection or core. A gut wound to a soldier was often fatal, just as how not knowing the truth of God can be fatal in our spiritual battles against Satan.

Many people, especially non-Christians, like to think that truth is relative. In other words, it's the belief that what may be true for one person may or may not be true for another. Although I agree that sometimes the truth may have different applications that vary from person to person, the underlying truth cannot be relative. There will always be one truth and many non-truths in the form of lies, misinterpretations, or false teachings. Unbelievers often argue this statement of relative truth, so let me explain my reasoning.

Let us say you have a bucket on a table before you and ask four people what it is. The first person comes along, flips it over, and starts beating on it. To him, that bucket is a drum.

The next person is a little short, so she takes the bucket, puts it on the floor, and uses it as a step stool to obtain something out of reach.

A third person comes up and decides the bucket would make a lovely flowerpot for her plants.

And finally, the last person comes along on the way to a costume party dressed as a knight who lost his helmet. So what does he do? He cuts a couple of eye holes in the bucket and runs off with the bucket on his head, ready for battle.

Four different people came along and found four separate applications for that bucket. But the truth is that the bucket was designed as a container to hold or carry various contents.

People try doing this all the time with the Bible. They claim that because everyone can pull different applications from Scripture, the message's truth does not apply to them if they choose not to believe it. Unfortunately, it does not work that way.

As with the bucket, the problem with the truth is that people always try to manipulate it to make it work for them. They then call that the truth instead of acknowledging the absolute truth. They do not care what its designer says it is. Instead, they try to convert it to what best suits their interests. Some people even try to take stuff out of the truth to fit their needs, like the guy who cut a couple of holes in the bucket.

The truth becomes less effective when people alter it from its original purpose. You see, the truth, like this bucket, can be only one thing. Sometimes, it may have several applications, but its overall purpose remains the same. When God gave us the truth through His Word, He never intended for us to pick and choose what we want to believe, as some religions and people do.

I warn everyone who hears the words of the prophecy of this book: if anyone adds to them, God will add to him the plagues described in this book, and if anyone takes away from the words of the book of this prophecy, God will take away his share in the tree of life and in the holy city, which are described in this book. *(Revelation 22:18-19 ESV) (See also Deuteronomy 4:2; 12:32)*

We are left with an imperfect system when we remove parts of God's truth from our lives. It may suit your needs for a little while, but eventually you will be left with a mess left behind by the holes in the system, just as if you tried pouring water into a bucket full of holes. The more you attempt to remove or alter pieces of the truth, the less effective it becomes. It is often too late when you realize that the "truth" you are living is a total disaster. You will have to spend a lot of time patching the holes and cleaning up the messes you made to return to the original truth.

Two technical terms are used when dealing with the handling of the truth in the Bible. The first is exegesis, and the second is eisegesis.

Exegesis is "a critical explanation or interpretation of a text or portion of a text, especially of the Bible." This is done by studying the original manuscripts, the culture, writing styles, and more to uncover a text's true meaning.

Eisegesis, on the other hand, "is an interpretation, especially of Scripture, that expresses the interpreter's ideas, bias, or the like, rather than the meaning of the text."

Discovering the truth through proper exegesis should be our goal as Christians. Far too many people attempt to make the Bible fit their worldview instead of trying to adapt their actions to fit the lessons of the Bible. It is worth noting that sometimes our attempts to find the truth can be misguided if the material we study from is already tainted. We can only do our best with the resources we have available to us, but we must be careful not to put blind trust into every new frame of thought that might be presented. Test everything against the scripture to see if it aligns.

The truth will always win out, no matter how much someone may argue otherwise. Regarding religion, there are a few "truths" that people pass around. Christians say that there is one God. Atheists say there is no god. Some religions state that there are multiple gods or that you even have the potential to become a god. One of these groups must be right. You cannot simultaneously have no god and a single God just because one person chooses not to believe, and the other does. One will be correct, and the other must live with the consequences.

John 14:17 *(ESV)* tells us that truth comes from the Spirit, **"whom the world cannot receive, because it neither sees him nor knows him. You know him, for he dwells with you and will be in you."**

Everything in the Bible is considered trustworthy because it is God's Word. It is meant to be read as a whole to get the full effect of its message. When we cherry-pick what we want to believe, the Bible loses its effectiveness in our lives. Just because part of the Bible is hard to understand or written in a style that doesn't make sense to you doesn't make it any less accurate. It only means you have more studying to do to get the whole meaning. The more you study it, the clearer your understanding of the actual truth of the Bible will be.

However, we must also understand that we operate on a very limited knowledge of the authors' original influence and God's overall will and knowledge. The combined knowledge of everything on earth from the past to the present is likely less than a percent of the total knowledge available to obtain. This means we need to be careful when we learn something new or think we have come up with some revolutionary insight so that we don't claim it to be some sort of proof to end all arguments. People have been debating aspects of the Bible since the day it was written. It's good to study and try to gain new insights into biblical meanings, but we must be careful not to claim that our conclusions are the only right conclusions unless there is no other way to view the subject or God explicitly states something as fact.

Breastplate of Righteousness

The second item in the armor of God is the breastplate of righteousness. Since the belt was designed to protect the lower organs, the breastplate was designed to protect the upper organs, specifically the heart.

The heart is the central organ responsible for circulating oxygen to the rest of the body through our blood. Unfortunately, it also circulates any impurities that may be present in our blood. Similarly, the heart is often referenced as the home of our conscience, emotions, and self-worth. In other words, what we believe is influenced by where our heart is.

Therefore, we have the instructions in Matthew 6:20–21 *(NIV)* to **"store up for yourselves treasures in heaven, where moths and vermin do not destroy, and where thieves do not break in and steal. For where your treasure is, there your heart will be also."**

When we become Christians, we are instructed to guard our hearts, as Proverbs 4:23 *(NIV)* states: **"Above all else, guard your heart, for everything you do flows from it."**

The breastplate of righteousness does just that. Righteousness is the state of moral perfection required by God to enter heaven. As defined by the Greek word dikaios, righteousness means observing divine laws or being upright, faultless, innocent, and guiltless. Unfortunately, due to our sinful nature, **"There is no one righteous, not even one"** *(Romans 3:10 NIV)*. Jesus freed us from sin when His righteous blood covered our own to purify our imperfections.

When we fight our spiritual battles, we must have the full cover of Jesus's righteous protection over our hearts. If unconfessed sins or other impurities exist in our lives, our most vital organ is left exposed to the enemy. By remembering that we have been set free, we are more likely to recognize the things that tempt us before they have a chance to affect our hearts.

To prevent sin from wreaking havoc on our lives, we must put on our breastplate of righteousness daily. It will take time to heal sins that have already affected us due to weak armor, but it can happen through the grace of God.

Test me, LORD, and try me, examine my heart and my mind; for I have always been mindful of your unfailing love and have lived in reliance on your faithfulness. *(Psalm 26:2–3 NIV)*

We must constantly remind ourselves of God's saving grace and do as it says in 2 Timothy 2:22 *(ESV)* to achieve the complete righteousness that God desires: **"Flee youthful passions and pursue righteousness, faith, love, and peace, along with those who call on the Lord from a pure heart."**

Therefore, as God's chosen people, holy and dearly loved, clothe yourselves with compassion, kindness, humility, gentleness and patience. Bear with each other and forgive one another if any of you has a grievance against someone. Forgive as the Lord forgave you. And over all these virtues put on love, which binds them all together in perfect unity. *(Colossians 3:12–14 NIV)*

Footgear of Readiness

The third piece of the armor of God is shoes. It may not seem that they should be that important to mention, but they are. Can you walk over some of the rougher terrains you have encountered if you did not have shoes? Our shoes protect our feet so that we can go places we would not otherwise be able to go without experiencing severe pain or discomfort.

The Armor Of God

If you have ever shopped in a shoe store, you may have noticed that there are often hundreds, if not thousands, of shoes to choose from. Some vary just by the look on the outside, but most are designed with a particular purpose. There are shoes designed to help with athletic activities and others to protect your feet in dangerous environments. There are also shoes designed to look good on a special occasion or to create a few laughs when walking around.

You would not find someone wearing fluffy bunny slippers on a construction site or someone wearing combat boots trying to do ballet. When God instructs us to put on shoes of readiness from the gospel of peace, He teaches us that we need a particular shoe type.

We must be ready to move when God instructs us to do so. When we move, we might be called to share the gospel or use it to defend ourselves against attacks.

When we are called to share with someone, we must be ready. First Peter 3:15 *(NIV)* instructs us, **"Always be prepared to give an answer to everyone who asks you to give the reason for the hope that you have."** Failing to be prepared with a message of hope is a missed opportunity to reach the lost.

Alternatively, when Satan attacks, if we do not know the promises of the gospel, we can quickly lose our footing and be knocked off track. By wearing the shoes of readiness of the gospel, we can rest assured that our feet can handle any obstacles on the course that God has set for us.

My steps have held fast to your paths; my feet have not slipped. *(Psalm 17:5 ESV)*

This piece of armor can relate to my first analogy of this book, which compares our Christian walk to being in an expansive jungle with no apparent way out. We know many things would harm our feet in a jungle if unprotected. Similarly, many things can immobilize us in our walk with God if we are unprepared with the gospel.

The Army of One

If you have ever seen a war movie in which a soldier loses the use of one or both of his legs during an intense fight, he is often given a gun and left to defend himself as his fellow soldiers try to prevent enemy advances. If the battle goes on long enough, often, the other soldiers die, and it is just the wounded soldier versus the enemy. Because he has lost his legs, he cannot get up and hide or charge the enemy. Any movement he could pull off would likely be a slow crawl or scooting across the ground. In most situations like this, that soldier also ends up dying as well because he cannot get away when the enemy approaches.

If you are not prepared with the truth of the gospel to move you out of danger, you are like the soldier left to defend himself with the bit of ammunition he has left. Do not lose your ability to walk the spiritual life by not being ready with the gospel to move you when the enemy forces are too strong.

Therefore, if anyone cleanses himself from what is dishonorable, he will be a vessel for honorable use, set apart as holy, useful to the master of the house, ready for every good work. *(2 Timothy 2:21 ESV)*

Shield of Faith

This God—his way is perfect; the Word of the LORD proves true; he is a shield for all those who take refuge in Him. *(Psalm 18:30 ESV)*

Faith is one of the greatest weapons of war and one easily confused with worldly thoughts. But what is faith? In the Bible, faith is described as having absolute trust in God as our creator and leader. Hebrews 11:1 *(ESV)* defines faith as **"the assurance of things hoped for, the conviction of things not seen."**

It means that even when things are not going our way, we trust God will pull us through. Faith is also a gift from God so that we may be saved. Ephesians 2:8–9 *(ESV)* says, **"For by grace you have**

The Armor Of God

been saved through faith. And this is not your own doing; it is the gift of God, not a result of works, so that no one may boast."
My shield is with God, who saves the upright in heart. *(Psalm 7:10 ESV)*

The shield of faith is the first line of defense against Satan's attacks. In verse 16 the shield is the only armor that includes instructions on what to do with it. That is, the shield is the piece of armor **"with which you can extinguish all the flaming arrows of the evil one."** *(Ephesians 6:16 NIV)*.

Before we discuss how to use the shield, we should discuss what these flaming arrows represent. Flaming arrows were often used in combat many years ago because they did more damage on impact. Not only would they cause a puncture wound, but they would also spread and burn the body and anything else in the vicinity. The arrows from Satan are lies that penetrate our bodies and can cause significant damage if not quickly extinguished.

So why is faith so hard a spiritual weapon to master? The answer is that we think we can recognize and defeat the lies Satan throws at us without help. Many people claim to have the faith to get them through the trouble they face. They then go on with their lives without any real biblical backing to their claim and no works to prove it. They think that because God rescued them from a lie of the enemy before, they are immune to future deceit. Or they see how another Christian was delivered from sin and just assumed God would deliver them the same way without taking any tangible steps of their own.

Let me give you a modern example of how this could play out. Imagine that there was a guy out there who always played one of the popular football video games. He became good at the game and was known by some of his friends as the best at it; he always made the right plays and would win almost every game he played. This person recognized his skills and one day decided to try out for his college football team. Quickly, he discovered how unprepared he was. Sure, he knew the rules, strategies, and maybe some of the plays needed to win, but he was not prepared physically. He knew what to do, but because he had never actually trained for it or exercised to improve his skills and strength, his knowledge of the game was not enough when it came down to facing the larger challenges before him—actual players.

It is easy to claim you have the faith needed to perform when the need arises, but unless you regularly practice that faith in the real world or take steps to act on that faith, you will be in for a shock the moment opposition hits. When tough times hit us and we are isolated, scared, and no longer know what to do, will our faith still protect us from the evil that may come our way? That question must be addressed to fully master the shield of faith that God has provided to defend his honor.

In Matthew 17:20 *(NIV)* Jesus says to His disciples, **"Truly I tell you, if you have faith as small as a mustard seed, you can say to this mountain, 'Move from here to there,' and it will move. Nothing will be impossible for you."**

If this is true, why aren't we seeing many mountains getting up and moving? A mustard seed is relatively small, so wouldn't at least a few people have enough faith to move those mountains? I am sure quite a few people might have the faith to accomplish this task, but it just does not happen for two reasons.

First, there is rarely a reason for a mountain to move, so that thought does not go through people's minds. But if it did, because of the simple fact that most people have no legitimate reason other than to test God, the mountain will never move.

Now I know that when God refers to mountains, He refers to any significant life obstacle, such as sin or our struggles, that may get in our way and disrupt our path to freedom, but the same test applies. When we ask God for protection or say that we believe He will guide us through, are we asking or saying this with 100 percent faith that He will provide, or are we saying the words hoping what He did for someone else He will do for us? Will we be able to accept an answer that we may not want with the full belief that God knows exactly what He is doing and will not abandon us? Will we be willing to move when God tells us to, knowing that the enemy cannot defeat us?

I talk to people often who claim to believe in Jesus 100 percent but at the same time question if they are doing enough. Or they struggle with some sin, so there is some doubt. If this describes you, then you don't believe in Jesus 100 percent. You are still relying on yourself or some external factor to secure your place in heaven.

Having faith in things we have seen work many times before is easy. But when someday one of those things does not work as it used to, it also becomes quite easy for us to turn our backs on God and question why He did not do as He did all the other times. The key to mastering the shield of faith is knowing that you cannot be defeated no matter what you do if you are moving under God's protection and guidance.

Therefore, among God's churches we boast about your perseverance and faith in all the persecutions and trials you are enduring. *(2 Thessalonians 1:4 NIV)*

Although this section has dealt more with the defensive side of faith, it is essential to know that it also takes a great deal of faith to perform God's offensive missions.

The Bible says in James 2:14–17, 26 *(ESV)*, **"What good is it, my brothers, if someone says he has faith but does not have works? Can that faith save him? If a brother or sister is poorly clothed and lacking in daily food, and one of you says to them, "Go in peace, be warmed and filled," without giving them the things needed for the body, what good is that? So also faith by itself, if it does not have works, is dead.**

For as the body apart from the spirit is dead, so also faith apart from works is dead."

One point to note about the previous verses is that this is the equivalent of what many modern-day Christians do. They may see someone in need, and instead of helping according to their abilities, often their response is "I'll pray for you." Whether or not they pray is a different matter altogether, but assuming they do, is it enough? I realize that not everyone is equipped to handle everyone's problems, but sometimes God has put us in people's paths to be the solution, and we use that Christian phrase as an excuse not to do what God has directed us to do. It's a perfect example of saying you have faith with your mouth but not showing it with your actions.

God has promised us many great things if we believe in Him. But many of us fail to receive these things because we forget God called us to act. We are to be good and faithful servants. Servants serve others out of the same love God has for us. We cannot simply sit back and wait for God's gifts to be dropped into our laps or rely on an overused phrase, hoping someone else can bless that person in need. We must act—following through with what God calls us to do. Many of us fear the outcomes of such missions, but that is where the shield comes into play. A shield has no purpose, though, if all we do is hide in fear. The greatest demonstration of faith starts with our making that first step into the unknown, trusting in the words of God to get us through.

Without faith, it is impossible to please him, for whoever would draw near to God must believe that he exists and that he rewards those who seek him. *(Hebrews 11:6 ESV)*

Helmet of Salvation

The next piece of armor in the passage covers the body's last vital organ, the brain. The helmet's role is to protect people from injuries to the head that might create lifelong damage or death. The helmet of salvation is no different. The helmet of salvation is your protection against self-doubt and discouragement that can greatly hinder your walk with God and cause spiritual death.

When Satan attacks, he likes to plant lies in our heads meant to distract us from God. It is easy to believe those lies and get disoriented in battle when the enemy delivers a knock-out blow to the head. If we do not take the precautions to protect ourselves from those attacks, those blows will often push us away from the faith and truth that every other piece of armor strives to protect.

Salvation, in the biblical sense, means we have been set free from sin and delivered into God's protection. We are granted salvation when we believe and accept that Jesus died for our sins so we may be with God.

While we are still here on this earth, however, we must be prepared to fight the evil that is still present in our lives. Unfortunately, many of us as Christians fail to recognize the importance of the salvation we receive, or we act as if it is hindering our thoughts and desires, so we place our helmets on a shelf somewhere.

Let us look at another scene sometimes found in war movies. What happens when someone removes their helmet because it gets in the way during a battle? Often the next scene is of the soldier receiving a fatal shot or blow to the head, all because their helmet was not securely fastened in place to prevent it from blocking their view or from otherwise being a distraction.

Resist him, standing firm in the faith, because you know that the family of believers throughout the world is undergoing the same kind of suffering. *(1 Peter 5:9 NIV)*

We must recognize the enemy's presence and treat our helmet of salvation carefully. Every day we wake up, we must remind ourselves that God has set us free while putting on our helmets. As we go through our days, the enemy will throw everything he has at us to try to get us to lose focus or deny our salvation. But if we wear our helmets securely on our heads, then we will get through those battles. Lies will reflect off, and the deadly blows will not penetrate our heads. No matter how rattled we may get, we will rest assured knowing that God still has His protection over us.

Many believe you can lose your salvation either through continual sin or by simply walking away. But without going too deeply into this debate, as it can be a book in itself, I would like to offer two points. One, when God sets you free from something, you are free. If you continue holding on to past mistakes or sinful ways, you will be limited in your service to God, but you are no longer chained to that lifestyle.

And two, once you have experienced freedom, no one can enslave you to sin again. Yes, our flesh will want to return, but our spiritual bodies will be cleansed and covered by the blood of Jesus. There is no undoing that. The more we can embrace the power of our spiritual selves, the less we will return to our flesh.

Let us then with confidence draw near to the throne of grace, that we may receive mercy and find grace to help in time of need. *(Hebrews 4:16 ESV)*

May you be **"strengthened with all power, according to his glorious might, for all endurance and patience with joy; giving thanks to the Father, who has qualified you to share in the inheritance of the saints in light. He has delivered us from the domain of darkness and transferred us to the kingdom of his beloved Son, in whom we have redemption, the forgiveness of sins."** *(Colossians 1:11–14 ESV).*

Sword of the Spirit

If we were to ask the average person, they might assume that the sword is the offensive weapon in this list of armor, while everything else is geared toward defense. I agree and disagree with this conclusion.

We are told to stand firm in our faith to defeat the sin that tries to defeat us. But God does not just expect us to stand there and take a beating with nothing to fight with. Instead, He has provided a strong weapon specifically designed to defeat sin.

The Armor Of God

God will never send us into the world seeking out sin to battle because that is not our fight, but He sends us out on rescue missions to find the lost and lead them back to God. Along the way, we will likely meet a lot of resistance that we must be prepared to fight to succeed. So, in this way, we can say that the sword could be considered an offensive tool. But, if you look at it, we are to fight only when directly attacked.

Second Corinthians 10:3-5 *(NIV)* says, **"For though we live in the world, we do not wage war as the world does. The weapons we fight with are not the weapons of the world. On the contrary, they have divine power to demolish strongholds. We demolish arguments and every pretension that sets itself up against the knowledge of God, and we take captive every thought to make it obedient to Christ."**

When God sends us on a mission, or even if we struggle to grow in our understanding of God, we must be prepared with a sword to fight the evil that comes our way. But what exactly is this sword? If you have been involved with the church long enough, you would likely have heard that the sword is your Bible, or more specifically, as described in the passage, the Word of God.

Are you just supposed to smack people upside the head with your Bible if they sin against you? With some of the large study Bibles on the market, this could work, but that is not what the passage means when referring to using the Word of God as a weapon.

The best example of the Word of God being used as a defensive tool is by Jesus in Matthew 4:1-11, when He was tempted by Satan himself after fasting in the wilderness for forty days and nights. When He was weak and hungry at His most vulnerable time, Satan offered Jesus several "easy way outs" to get Him to go against God's will and thus make Him a sinner like the rest of us.

For each of the temptations, Jesus did not reply with physical threats, violence, or petitions, as so many people resort to today.

Nor did He contemplate back and forth with Himself, trying to justify why God would not mind if He gave in.

Instead, He responded with the recorded scripture of His time, now known as the Old Testament. According to 2 Timothy 3:16–17 *(NIV)*, **"All Scripture is God-breathed and is useful for teaching, rebuking, correcting and training in righteousness, so that the servant of God may be thoroughly equipped for every good work."**

When you find yourself in conflict, no matter how big or small, and before you let it pound away at your faith, you should be well-equipped with scripture to stop the attack before it penetrates your armor. **"For the word of God is living and active, sharper than any two-edged sword, piercing to the division of soul and of spirit, of joints and of marrow, and discerning the thoughts and intentions of the heart."** *(Hebrews 4:12 ESV)*.

Knowing the truth found in the Bible will help you defeat anything that Satan tries to throw at you, but it also comes with a warning. As with any other weapon, the Sword of the Spirit requires a lot of skill and training to use correctly. You should be careful using it unless you know what you are doing, or you can cause more harm than good to yourself and others.

You may wonder how simple words from the Bible could hurt you, but it is a common occurrence. It happens every time that scripture is taken out of context. For example, using the same passage of Matthew 4:1:11, someone may quote part of verses 8–9 to try convincing you that God will give you all the kingdoms by bowing down and worshiping Him:

[He] showed him all the kingdoms of the world and their glory. And he said to him, "All these I will give you, if you will fall down and worship me." *(Matthew 4:8–9 ESV)*

But if you read the full context, you will see that it is the devil making this claim to tempt Jesus, not a promise from God. So the interpretation is false and potentially dangerous if a new believer or uninformed Christian uses this to frame their faith.

The Armor Of God

You see, God intended the passages of the Bible to be read as a whole. Even though there are many different stories and styles of writing in the Bible, and many different people wrote the various books over many years, they all still serve one purpose—to tell others about God's power.

When we pull scripture out of context to fulfill our agenda, we manipulate the truth and do not hear the whole story. You do not usually need to quote an entire passage when referencing verses, but you should ensure that the verse you are quoting represents the truth you are trying to proclaim. Taking someone's word on what a passage means is also not enough. To master your skill, you must study the scripture to make your own conclusions about the meaning. A complete understanding of the Bible depends on carefully analyzing how everything relates. You can get a basic understanding of different topics by reading various verses in the passage's context, but your learning does not stop there.

Each passage of scripture can be studied on a multitude of levels, with each level revealing more and more about who God is. The deepest levels of study involve years of learning beyond the simple words you see on paper. To understand the entire message God is trying to teach, you must not only read the words but also know the culture, history, and other things about the passages in question.

Often, you will find that various passages finally make sense when you realize that the people in biblical times had a much different culture than we do. In doing a word study, you will see that a word like love in the Bible may have different Greek or Hebrew words to describe various meanings of that word. Love, for instance, has four different Greek words used in the Bible and two to three others that are not used. Confuse them, and your understanding of a passage could change.

You should also read the text as closely as possible to the original text to ensure that meaning has not been lost in translation if you are trying to get the deepest possible understanding. There are often debates about which translation is the best or closest to the original text, and I won't get into that here. But if you compare various translations to see if they agree in meaning, you can get a good idea of what the original passage likely intended. If there are big differences in translation or interpretation, it would be wise to study that passage to see why and to make your own educated decision. But usually, the popular translations will all lead you right when you focus on what's important and God's Word as a whole. The Holy Spirit will ensure that you hear the truth if you put your faith in Him.

As you can see, the Bible offers a lifetime of study and instruction. It is not a "read once and you are done" type of book. People have spent days, months, or even years diving into single verses, passages, or books to get a very deep understanding of the message.

Regardless of the level of mastery you choose to pursue, the sword will always be enormously powerful when used correctly. The more you know about the Word of God, the greater the chance you will avoid temptation when the enemy strikes.

I want to caution some who may be guilty of over-studying certain words or passages. Of course, they will say there is no such thing as over-studying, but if you start reading into things that aren't there because you found some obscure connection to this or that, you risk altering the message of the gospel. Some things really are as simple as they appear on paper. You don't need to start manipulating scripture to find secret codes or whatever else you think is there. Maybe it is there, maybe it isn't. I don't know. But your focus should remain on the saving grace of Jesus and trying to reach lost souls, not dissecting every word or letter, hoping to find some secret message that thousands of years of human history have never uncovered.

Power of Prayer

The last item I will discuss is not officially part of the armor of God, but it is mentioned and is an important part of your battle preparation. In modern-day gear, this would be your source of communication with your commander—your radio. This piece of gear is the power of prayer. **"Do not be anxious about anything, but in every situation, by prayer and petition, with thanksgiving, present your requests to God. And the peace of God, which transcends all understanding, will guard your hearts and your minds in Christ Jesus."** *(Philippians 4:6–7 NIV).*

Prayer is your direct line of communication with God. When God sends you on a mission, He does not expect you to go in blind to defeat the enemy yourself. The only way the battles of the Bible were won for the good side was when the people listened and talked to God through prayer or a direct word from Him.

Prayer can be hard sometimes because background noise (distractions) makes it hard to hear the response God is giving you. But as in a real battle, you must do your absolute best to find a place where a signal is clear, as a wrong move could mean someone's life or a failed mission.

You should never make any strategic move, either offensive or defensive, when it comes to spiritual warfare or your worldly battles without first receiving instructions from God. When He tells you to move, you better do so because the enemy could be coming in full force to bring you down. When He tells you to stand and fight, follow His instructions and you will not be defeated. Because God knows all and can see all, He can steer us straight through any obstacles that may otherwise get in our way.

Without prayer, we often try to fight our battles ourselves, and we usually lose. We may get it right occasionally, but we are battling blindly without communication and our field guide, the Bible. As in other parts of our battle gear, our communication gear can also be misused if we are not careful. There is an effective way to pray and a less effective way. Let us look at some examples.

Telling your commander how to direct you in battle does no good when in a war. All too often this is exactly what we as Christians do when fighting our battles. For example, there is a difference between praying, "God, please give me the strength to give up this sin," and "God, you are my strength; please take this sin from me and direct me to freedom."

The difference may seem insignificant and subtle to most of us. I often pray the first way myself and often get no results. I still find myself struggling with the same sins over and over. If you think about it, the first thought process often stems from our desire to fight the battles ourselves. We see the problem and acknowledge it, but we still want to oversee removing it from our lives.

The second way of praying is acknowledging a problem and giving it to God to take care of while waiting for His instructions on how to proceed. Waiting is always the most challenging part, but if we listen to God's voice and do not try to solve our problems with our own strength, I do not believe we will have to wait long. Just don't forget that we should also act when He instructs us to do so.

Jeremiah 17:5–9 *(ESV)* addresses this: **"Thus says the Lord: 'Cursed is the man who trusts in man and makes flesh His strength, whose heart turns away from the Lord. He is like a shrub in the desert, and shall not see any good come. He shall dwell in the parched places of the wilderness, in an uninhabited salt land. Blessed is the man who trusts in the Lord, whose trust is the Lord. He is like a tree planted by water, that sends out its roots by the stream, and does not fear when heat comes, for its leaves remain green, and is not anxious in the year of drought, for it does not cease to bear fruit.' The heart is deceitful above all things, and desperately sick; who can understand it?"**

God takes care of those who believe in His command. When you ask for direction through prayer, take the time to make sure you understand what He is trying to tell you. Do not let your thoughts interrupt His communication with you, or you may find yourself heading into circumstances you were not meant to enter. No matter where you end up, proper communication with your commander can get you back on course so your mission can be completed.

God gave us a spirit not of fear but of power and love and self-control. *(2 Timothy 1:7 ESV)*

Rejoice always, pray without ceasing, give thanks in all circumstances; for this is the will of God in Christ Jesus for you. Do not quench the Spirit. *(1 Thessalonians 5:16–19 ESV)*

12

Knowing Your Enemy

Attention, soldiers! As you know, you all have been a part of a huge war threatening how we live, think, and interact with one another. Our freedom is being compromised every day the enemy is allowed to roam. Today, I will be introducing you to this enemy. His name is Lucifer. He is also known as "Satan," "the devil," "the father of lies," "the beast," "the god of this age," and "the deceiver," among others.

As I am sure you heard, Satan is an immensely powerful enemy capable of infiltrating our defenses in the subtlest of ways. His army is massive, with his followers and demons found in nearly every area of our lives. Undoubtedly, his influence is in this very room as his army's tactics tend to go unnoticed, even by the most well-trained soldiers.

Satan is known for his power of deception. Be aware. Wear your armor everywhere and continue studying and practicing your field manual. He will strike at the slightest hint of weakness, so you must always be on guard.

There is no way to defeat Satan on your own accord, so please do not try, as it will put you right where he wants you. He is not invincible, however. To win, we must work together and follow the general's commands as closely as possible. We leave no man behind. The fight will be difficult but not impossible. Follow our instructions carefully and work as a unit, and you will get through this war.

Okay, soldiers—get out there and let's win this war!

What is a book about spiritual warfare without talking a little about the enemy we are fighting? Many of the results of the enemy's work have been discussed in the earlier chapters, but this chapter and the next are dedicated to who our enemy is and how he attacks.

By now you know that our enemy is Satan, an angel created by God, just as you and I were created by Him. Like you and me,

The Army of One

this angel became infiltrated with a sin called pride and was cast out of heaven. He did not go alone, though. He took an entire third of the angel population with him as he was cast into the lake of fire.

Although Ezekiel 28:12–19 is directly talking about the prince of Tyre, it is believed that this passage also alludes to the fall of Satan:

'You were the seal of perfection, full of wisdom and perfect in beauty. You were in Eden, the garden of God; every precious stone adorned you: carnelian, chrysolite and emerald, topaz, onyx and jasper, lapis lazuli, turquoise and beryl. Your settings and mountings were made of gold; on the day you were created they were prepared.

You were anointed as a guardian cherub, for so I ordained you. You were on the holy mount of God; you walked among the fiery stones. You were blameless in your ways from the day you were created till wickedness was found in you.

Through your widespread trade you were filled with violence, and you sinned. So I drove you in disgrace from the mount of God, and I expelled you, guardian cherub, from among the fiery stones.

Your heart became proud on account of your beauty, and you corrupted your wisdom because of your splendor. So I threw you to the earth; I made a spectacle of you before kings. By your many sins and dishonest trade you have desecrated your sanctuaries.

So I made a fire come out from you, and it consumed you, and I reduced you to ashes on the ground in the sight of all who were watching. All the nations who knew you are appalled at you; you have come to a horrible end and will be no more.' *(Ezekiel 28:12–19 NIV)*

So, what does this have to do with us? You see, at one point Lucifer (Satan) was one of God's most beautiful and powerful angels. Lucifer held a high rank in the spiritual army and was thought to be God's second in command. As with many in the world today, Lucifer was not happy with being only second best. Because of his beauty and power, he rebelled against God to obtain the worship meant for God. God, in return, banished Lucifer down to earth, where he became ruler of the earth and the influencer of most of our struggles today.

Let no one say when he is tempted, "I am being tempted by God," for God cannot be tempted with evil, and he himself tempts no one. But each person is tempted when he is lured and enticed by his own desire. Then desire when it has conceived gives birth to sin, and sin when it is fully grown brings forth death. *(James 1:13–15 ESV)*

Like it or not, the moment we are born, Satan's power takes hold of us, and we become slaves to the evil ways of the world. The battles we fight every day are due to conflicts between the flesh (under Satan's control) and the Spirit of God. Although it is true that Satan is not the direct cause of all our struggles and pain regarding temptations of the flesh, he does have a strong influence over how we choose to react when trials come our way.

Our battles can either be won for Christ or be won for Satan. Before anyone becomes a Christian, their battles are counted only as wins for the enemy side. After accepting Christ as our Lord and Savior, it becomes possible to change the outcome of each battle to a win for God.

Satan's entire purpose of existence is to prevent us from joining or fighting in God's army. He fully understands how powerful we can be as Christians if we learn how to use God's power properly. The more we seek God and seek to become like God, the more Satan will throw at us to try to catch us in a stage of weakness. Satan wants to see us fall so that he can get a foothold in the church, but to do that, he must trick us. How he tricks us depends on the individual, but there is one thing Satan is good at—knowing exactly what it takes to distract us from God.

Contrary to popular belief, Satan does not have a single ounce of direct control over our lives. God must approve everything he does. Why God approves of Satan's attacks is hard to understand, but a glimpse of the reason is found in the Book of Job. We will look at that a little later.

If Satan has no control, how is it that we struggle so much in sin and find it nearly impossible to avoid? The answer lies in the intelligence that Satan gathers about us all. Satan and his army of demons have studied every one of us so intensely that they know every little thing that sets us off, everything that tempts us, everything that will boost our ego and everything that makes us question ourselves and our abilities.

Satan does not make us sin, but he provides the best opportunities for us to do so. Only through God's power can we recognize these traps and avoid or overcome them. Unfortunately, most of us are nowhere near skilled enough in God's ways to see everything that has the potential to harm us. Satan's traps are so heavily disguised that we often overlook them or think they have come from God Himself.

So, what can we do?

The best method of avoiding Satan's traps and attacks is to be properly prepared. His attacks are inevitable and unrelenting. He will find the slightest hint of weakness in your defenses and bombard you in every conceivable direction until you break. The chapters before this discussed the importance of wearing your armor and being united with your brothers and sisters in Christ to form a solid wall of defense around the church body.

Unfortunately, far too many Christians fail to put their armor on daily, or they try to fight without help, so the wall of defense is easily broken as Satan moves in undetected and unchallenged. By the time we realize we are under attack, Satan has wreaked havoc on the church and individual lives.

The Roaming Lion

Be alert and of sober mind. Your enemy, the devil, prowls around like a roaring lion looking for someone to devour.
(1 Peter 5:8 NIV)

One of the most popular questions among Christians and non-believers is why God allows Satan to roam the earth in the first place. If he has no control and must ask God's permission to make his attacks, why does God allow it? The answer to these questions is difficult to understand from a merely human perspective, but through the book of Job, I hope to offer a hint of a reason.

If you are unfamiliar with the story, you know Job was a wealthy man with a large family. He is also regarded as being blameless in that he always strived to do what was right in the eyes of God. This is not to say he was sinless, but he was a godly man, and God recognized him as such.

One day when God was meeting with His angels, Satan was in attendance. After inquiring where Satan had been, God mentioned Job, stating, "There is no one on earth like him; he is blameless and upright, a man who fears God and shuns evil."
(Job 1:8 NIV. See also Job 2:3).

True to his nature, Satan questioned the legitimacy of God's claim. Surely Job's "faith" is nothing more than the result of a seemingly good life, he claimed. Satan was sure that if everything Job had were taken away, Job would surely curse God. God knew His faithful servant, however, and allowed Satan to put Job to the test. In just a short time, Job lost almost everything that meant anything to him. All his livestock and even his children were now gone in a series of misfortunes that would cripple any man.

Through all of this, Job did not curse God. So Satan once again approached God, who then allowed him one more shot to test Job. This time, Satan was permitted to go after Job's health. As a result, Job was inflicted with loathsome sores from head to foot. At this point, Job was understandably upset. Not only did he lose

The Army of One

everything he had, but now he was in extreme physical pain. Once again, despite the recommendation from his wife, he refused to curse God.

The rest of the book consists of a poetic dialog between Job and three of his friends, which ends with God himself confronting Job. This series of dialogs can teach a few lessons.

You Can't Always Count On Friends

First, you cannot always count on your friends or even family members to support you when you go through struggles. This is the sad reality many of us live in and one I alluded to in an earlier chapter. All of us will go through trials at some point in our lives. Many of these trials will test the faith of even the most dedicated Christian. When these trials happen, it is common for friends and family to step in and offer unsolicited advice to the struggling party. Depending on their own faith in God, this advice may go against everything you know to be true about yourself or everything you believe about your God.

Job's friends insisted that Job must have sinned greatly to deserve such punishment, but Job, and more importantly God, knew that he had done nothing of the sort. Because of his friends' increased focus on this suspected wrongdoing, Job lost focus on living for God and turned toward trying to prove his innocence to his friends and God. If that pattern were repeated in our lives, our faith would also be challenged. We may turn toward cursing God for our sufferings when we do not receive the answers or the life we think we should have. Therefore, it is essential to surround yourself with people who have equal or greater faith than yourself. When you suffer, you need equal-minded people who will help encourage you, fight for you, and get you back on track to where you need to go.

Although Job's friends messed up with their false interpretation of the situation and added insult to injury, they did not do everything wrong. Job's friends did the right thing when they simply sat and grieved with Job for seven days as he processed what was happening. They spoke only when Job indicated he was ready to talk by speaking himself.

You never know what someone may be going through internally when they face a struggle. Being too quick to speak to help someone may only amplify the pain they are experiencing. That pain can become resentment against you if you fail to understand the situation. This, in turn, could lead to the person feeling isolated or angry, assuming that no one understands what they are going through.

If you feel isolated from the world, Hebrews 4:15–16 *(NIV)* lets us know that we are not alone in our struggle:

For we do not have a high priest who is unable to empathize with our weaknesses, but we have one who has been tempted in every way, just as we are—yet he did not sin. Let us then approach God's throne of grace with confidence, so that we may receive mercy and find grace to help us in our time of need.

Quick to Listen, Slow to Speak

When someone is hurting, do not be too quick to speak or try to fix things yourself. James 1:19 *(NIV)* says, **"Everyone should be quick to listen, slow to speak and slow to become angry."**

It is far too easy to jump to conclusions about a situation when we first hear of a conflict with someone we know and even easier when it is about someone we do not know. We live in a culture in which news travels extremely fast and misinformation can spread rapidly, causing people to form opinions without learning all the facts. Casting judgment or offering advice without knowing the full details of a situation can further victimize a truly innocent person or lead them down a path they need not be on.

Every distraction caused by unnecessary judgment or inaccurate advice can be counted as a win for Satan. Each distraction pulls our attention away from the race we are called to run. It is hard enough to get through our struggles on our own, but with God's help, we find that He can use those trials as growth opportunities if we can keep our faith in check.

James 1:2–12 *(NIV)* addresses this when it is written, **"Consider it pure joy, my brothers and sisters, whenever you face trials of many kinds, because you know that the testing of your faith produces perseverance. Let perseverance finish its work so that you may be mature and complete, not lacking anything. If any of you lacks wisdom, you should ask God, who gives generously to all without finding fault, and it will be given to you. But when you ask, you must believe and not doubt, because the one who doubts is like a wave of the sea, blown and tossed by the wind. That person should not expect to receive anything from the Lord. Such a person is double-minded and unstable in all they do.**

"Believers in humble circumstances ought to take pride in their high position. But the rich should take pride in their humiliation—since they will pass away like a wild flower. For the sun rises with scorching heat and withers the plant; its blossom falls and its beauty is destroyed. In the same way, the rich will fade away even while they go about their business.

"Blessed is the one who perseveres under trial because, having stood the test, that person will receive the crown of life that the Lord has promised to those who love him."

A Testing of Faith

The next lesson is that trials can happen to anyone, good or bad. There is no rule in place that states that everything must go right when people spend their lives trying to do good. Bad things do happen to good people, just as good things happen to bad people. It is impossible to have complete control over everything life brings us. In an instant, everything you have and know could be altered, and your life will never be the same again. Sometimes these life alterations can be for the good, but the ones we hear about are often for the worst.

It is never easy to accept why God would take away someone you love or something you have worked hard for, but there is always a reason. Even smaller trials, like getting stuck in traffic, may have a reason. Often we do not learn the reasons for our trials until much later in our lives, if at all, but if you trust in God, you can be sure that He has a plan. For many, this fact alone does not make the trial any easier to get through. Even the most dedicated Christian will go through periods of questioning after a tragedy or hard times. Many will question if God cares or why their loved ones were taken and not themselves. They may question why they were even brought into existence in the first place. Many might contemplate suicide, believing that without their loved ones or the things they worked so hard for, there is no further point in continuing the life they lived.

Despite what we may think, God does care—more than we know—and there is always a purpose, whether we see it or not. Our trials are a test of our faith, a faith of greater worth than gold. But why test it? As seen in the passage above from James, testing our faith produces perseverance. God needs to know you are with Him when things get tough. It is easy to say you believe in God when everything is going well, but when things get tough, will you still follow behind your leader, or will you be running in the opposite direction, giving up on the very thing that gave you a new life?

Examine yourselves, to see whether you are in the faith. Test yourselves. Or do you not realize this about yourselves, that Jesus Christ is in you?—unless indeed you fail to meet the test! I hope you will find out that we have not failed the test. But we pray to God that you may not do wrong—not that we may appear to have met the test, but that you may do what is right, though we may seem to have failed. For we cannot do anything against the truth, but only for the truth. For we are glad when we are weak and

you are strong. Your restoration is what we pray for. *(2 Corinthians 13:5–9 ESV)*

First Peter 1:6–9 *(ESV)* gives insight into how our trials are designed to test our faith:

In this you rejoice, though now for a little while, if necessary, you have been grieved by various trials, so that the tested genuineness of your faith—more precious than gold that perishes though it is tested by fire—may be found to result in praise and glory and honor at the revelation of Jesus Christ. Though you have not seen him, you love him. Though you do not now see him, you believe in him and rejoice with joy that is inexpressible and filled with glory, obtaining the outcome of your faith, the salvation of your souls.

God allowed Job to be tested to see if he was the soldier of God he claimed to be. Again, we see similar examples to this sometimes in movies or books. A new soldier is kidnapped by people pretending to be the enemy and then tortured greatly to see if he would give up his nation's secrets if he were to be captured for real. Of course, the staged kidnapping and torture seemed real to the soldier. If the soldier passed, he could join the fight. If he gave in to the pain of the torture and shared critical information that could compromise the war, he would not be allowed on the battlefield. We do not want people fighting for us who are too easy to break if captured. There is no critical information in God's army that we might give up, but there are critical people. God wants Christians who believe in the mission and are willing to follow Him at all costs.

Our mission is to proclaim the faith of the gospel so that others may be saved. You give the enemy a great advantage if you turn your back at the slightest hint of a struggle. He now knows he does not have to worry about you fighting against him, and he may come after you and feed you lie after lie until you end up fighting for him. It is natural to waver in your faith during times of trials. The outcome of such wavering largely depends on the foundation of learning and support you built up before going into battle. Lay a solid foundation, and you will stand to defeat anything that comes your way. Fail to lay that foundation, and you will fall at the first disruptive force that comes your way.

Do not be afraid of sudden terror or of the ruin of the wicked, when it comes, for the LORD will be your confidence and will keep your foot from being caught. *(Proverbs 3:25–26 ESV)*

No Power Is Greater Than God's

The final lesson from the Book of Job is that God has complete control. At the beginning of the book God wanted to show Job off. He knew that Job loved God more than anything he owned and more than his family and health. God wanted to let everyone in heaven know, including Satan himself, that Job was indeed a man after God's heart. So why did Job have to suffer for months to prove this point?

Job was a righteous man, but he was by no means perfect, and God knew this. Despite his strong focus on God, Job's life still had impurities that needed to be addressed. One of these impurities was pride. During the conversation between Job and his friends, Job repeatedly attempted to defend his righteousness, even going as far as to demand a presence with God to prove his case. To most of us, this seems like the expected thing to do. If you know you are not guilty, defend yourself. But in God's eyes, this was a sign of pride lingering deep within Job.

God desires 100-percent perfection in our lives. None of us will ever achieve it, but God is continually refining us to get us as close to it as possible to achieve our highest reward in heaven. In this instance, Job had to suffer so that pride could be revealed and handled before it hindered Job's walk with the Lord.

The author of Psalm 66:10–12 *(NIV)* expresses the thoughts of many who have experienced the refining fires of God:

The Army of One

> **For you, God, tested us; you refined us like silver. You brought us into prison and laid burdens on our backs. You let people ride over our heads; we went through fire and water, but you brought us to a place of abundance.**

At the end of the Book of Job, God came down and talked to Job directly and made it clear who had control of all things. God laid the foundation of the earth, not Job. He created the heavens and the seas, He commanded time as well as the weather, and He has been not only to the extents of the earth, farther than anyone else has ever been or ever will be, but also throughout the universe above. Every living and nonliving thing is under the control of the almighty one. Nothing we say or do will ever compare to the power of our living God.

There are some brilliant people in the world—no doubt about it. You would assume that many of them must have spent their childhood memorizing a set of encyclopedias. They are so full of knowledge that it is exceedingly difficult to debate with them if you ever choose to do so, and they are also capable of some interesting conversations. But even these people, who know so much, know only a fraction of the world's knowledge.

The point is that we are so limited in our knowledge of the world that trying to understand God's reasoning with our limited knowledge is about as helpful as trying to empty the Pacific Ocean with a teaspoon. We see only what is around us. We cannot see how our actions today could affect us tomorrow or far into the future. We do not know how our decisions today could impact many others who cross our path directly or indirectly. And we do not see when those little hardships we may face in our day-to-day lives are there to protect, grow, or strengthen ourselves or those around us.

We have no business instructing God about how to run the world, yet so many of us try. Thankfully, God brushes most of these statements and requests due to our simple ignorance of His reality. But occasionally he humbles us as He did Job. When God revealed himself to Job, Job was quickly put in his place and replied to the Lord, **"Surely I spoke of things I did not understand, things too wonderful for me to know."** *(Job 42:3 NIV)*.

Faith requires believing in things we do not understand or see. Satan's goal is to distract us from that faith by any means possible. If you keep your eyes on Jesus as He guides you through your struggles, you will come out on top every time and be rewarded with God's eternal glory.

For our light and momentary troubles are achieving for us an eternal glory that far outweighs them all. So we fix our eyes not on what is seen, but on what is unseen, since what is seen is temporary, but what is unseen is eternal. *(2 Corinthians 4:17–18 NIV)*

13

Types of War

"Captain—we are under attack!"

"Stand your ground, soldier! Where are the attacks coming from?"

"We are being hit from all sides, sir! We have been infiltrated!"

"There must be a hole in our defense. Regroup everyone together and continue holding your ground! Make sure your shields are in place and armor on. We cannot have any more casualties. Allen, get on the radio with JC! Wait for the general to provide instructions on when and how to make our move! Till then, do not let the enemy get in your head. Remember what you were taught, and we will win this!"

"Sir, yes sir!"

In the previous chapters we learned why Satan attacks. In this chapter we will learn about how he attacks and how we can prepare for and defend against those attacks. By now you should know about the armor of God, but if you do not know how to use it, it will take you only so far. Knowing how the enemy attacks so you can have a plan to defeat him is another critical tactic in the fight against evil. If you are not prepared with a strategy to get you out of different kinds of attacks, you risk becoming a sitting duck as the enemy catches you off guard and continues pounding away at your weaknesses until you become too crippled to fight.

You can think of this chapter as a playbook for various scenarios you may face. Of course, every situation may require tweaking these plays to handle the unique circumstances of your battle. Still, with these strategies and your trust in God for instruction, you should be adequately prepared to fight just about any attack that comes your way.

For this chapter, I will be comparing Satan's attacks with a few different types of warfare that exist in today's time, as well as from the past. Satan and his demons have several different methods of breaking our focus from God. Some attacks are obvious, while others are more subtle and often go unnoticed until it is too late. All can have disastrous results on you and the church body if left unchecked.

Biological Warfare

The first type of warfare that I will compare is biological. Biological warfare is the use of biological toxins or infectious agents such as bacteria, toxins, viruses, or fungi with the intent to kill or incapacitate humans, animals, or plants as an act of war.

The most obvious comparison to this is the sin in our lives. Since the fall of Adam and Eve in the Bible, sin has spread like a virus throughout all humanity. It has wreaked havoc on the human population and all living organisms, including animals and plants, both directly and indirectly. From the day we were born, the virus of sin has already been in our DNA. Even the sweet, innocent babies who know no better are infected from birth through no fault of their own.

Like a virus, sin is impossible to stop with our own power. Both sins and viruses ingrain themselves so deeply in our inner workings that the most we can do is try to control the symptoms as much as possible to make them more comfortable to live with. Sometimes, we can control both sin and viruses to a point at which we do not always see them, but they always linger, waiting for the right conditions to surface again.

Satan knew the power of biological warfare before biological warfare was a thing. By the tempting of just one person in the garden and that person giving in, the future of humanity was then doomed to a certain death apart from God. Read Genesis 3 for the results of this initial sin.

Types Of War

Although there is nothing we can do to remove the sin virus from our lives, we can do things to prevent further exposure to the different levels or strains of sin that can enter our lives. Like a virus, multiple variations of sin exist, and they constantly manipulate themselves for each unique host. By taking steps to prevent further infection, you can more comfortably live your life with the knowledge that there is a light at the end of your tunnel.

One of these steps relates to the clean rooms you may have seen or heard of in labs, hospitals, or sensitive technology manufacturing facilities. You might know that they often require people who enter such rooms to wear special clean suits and undergo a cleansing process before and after entering the rooms. These suits serve one of two purposes or both, depending on the kind of lab.

The first purpose is to keep outside contaminants out of the clean room. In this case, the slightest speck of dust or outside influence of any sort could destroy or alter the results of whatever the scientists are working on.

The second purpose of such a suit is to keep potential contaminants from getting to you. This case is typically found when working with dangerous chemicals or other substances that could be extremely harmful to you, or potentially humanity if even the slightest bit of the substance were exposed to the outside environment.

Both types of clean rooms and the requirements of God have a few things in common. If you have followed along with me in this book, you will know that God requires 100 percent perfection for us to be with Him. You will also know that achieving 100 percent perfection on your own is impossible. So, God gave us a solution—a hazmat suit, so to speak.

In him we have redemption through his blood, the forgiveness of our trespasses, according to the riches of his grace. *(Ephesians 1:7 ESV)*

God provided our hazmat suit—the covering by the blood of Jesus—when He allowed His Son to die on the cross for our sins. **"Indeed, under the law almost everything is purified with blood, and without the shedding of blood there is no forgiveness of sins."** *(Hebrews 9:22 ESV).*

How much more will the blood of Christ, who through the eternal Spirit offered himself without blemish to God, purify our conscience from dead works to serve the living God? *(Hebrews 9:14 ESV)*

Jesus's blood is so pure that any impurities we may have inside us are eliminated when we reach heaven, and as such, we can be with God. But still, there is more. On earth we still live with sin in our hearts. Jesus's blood may have freed us from the hold sin has on us, but we are often unable to release the hold we have on sin. In this case, we need to perform our cleansing process known as spiritual breathing.

As with the decontamination process you may see in a clean room, spiritual breathing is a daily cleansing process meant to clear our conscience of the sins we accumulate every hour of every day. Before God even hears our prayers, he expects us to recognize our sins so we can come to Him with a clean heart.

John 9:31 *(ESV)* says, **"We know that God does not listen to sinners, but if anyone is a worshiper of God and does his will, God listens to him."**

The author of Psalm 32:3 *(ESV)* also states, **"For when I kept silent, my bones wasted away through my groaning all day long."**

Like a virus, unconfessed sin will linger in our bodies and make us feel sick. Through an act of spiritual breathing, we can be made clean in the eyes of God, and He will hear the desires of our hearts.

The first step of spiritual breathing is exhaling the bad, that is, confessing the sins you know you have committed. By confessing, you agree with God that you are guilty and want a change in attitude and action regarding that sin. It is often not enough to make a blanket statement such as "Forgive me of my sins." God has already forgiven all sins of those who believe in Him. Why ask for something that was already promised to us when we accepted Christ? Instead, we must be willing to admit our guilt for specific sins. What good is forgiveness if you do not know what you are being forgiven for?

If you do not know your long list of sins, God can reveal them to you. Pray like David in Psalm 139:23–24 *(ESV)*: **"Search me, O God, and know my heart! Try me and know my thoughts! And see if there be any grievous way in me, and lead me in the way everlasting!"**

You will never be able to list every sin you have ever committed due to lack of time and knowledge of the sins as God sees them, but the more you are willing and able to humble yourself before God, the more God will reward you with His blessing. This leads us to the second step—inhaling.

Inhaling the good means surrendering control of your life to God. **"You were taught, with regard to your former way of life, to put off your old self, which is being corrupted by its deceitful desires; to be made new in the attitude of your minds; and to put on the new self, created to be like God in true righteousness and holiness."** *(Ephesians 4:22–24 NIV)*

This simple process of exhaling the bad and inhaling the good allows us to have the greatest connection to God.

First John 1:6–10 *(ESV)* says, **"If we say we have fellowship with him while we walk in darkness, we lie and do not practice the truth. But if we walk in the light, as he is in the light, we have fellowship with one another, and the blood of Jesus his Son cleanses us from all sin.**

"If we say we have no sin, we deceive ourselves, and the truth is not in us. If we confess our sins, he is faithful and just to forgive us our sins and to cleanse us from all unrighteousness. If we say we have not sinned, we make him a liar, and his word is not in us."

Finally, the last thing to help prevent further attacks of this biological warfare is to make deliberate efforts not to go places where you may be further affected. Sounds simple enough, but so many people fail at this, myself included, that it must be mentioned. If you struggle with certain sins, do not put yourself in situations where you know you will act out those sins or relapse if you have been trying to cleanse yourself of those particular sins.

Simple examples of this would be avoiding bars if you struggle with drunkenness, avoiding certain websites or locations if you struggle with lust or impurity, or avoiding the modern-day equivalent to the water cooler if you struggle with gossip (for many, this involves social media).

The Bible gives some extreme instructions in Matthew 18:8–9 *(ESV)*: **"If your hand or your foot causes you to sin, cut it off and throw it away. It is better for you to enter life crippled or lame than with two hands or two feet to be thrown into the eternal fire. And if your eye causes you to sin, tear it out and throw it away. It is better for you to enter life with one eye than with two eyes to be thrown into the hell of fire."**

The point of this passage is that we may have to make extreme changes to live the holy life that God desires for us. We often do not like those changes, and some changes may hurt because they are so engraved in our nature. If we desire true righteousness, though, those changes must be made.

Much of the pain we suffer due to sin is caused by continually putting ourselves in situations in which we know we will likely fail. Every time we do that, we give the sin virus more fuel to grow in our bodies. The more we allow it to grow, the further separated from God we become due to our impurities.

CYBER WARFARE

The next type of warfare is cyber warfare, which is one of the newest types of warfare to make its acquaintance. With the advent of computers and technologies that a large portion of the world relies upon for their day-to-day activities, cyber warfare is a genuine threat to our daily lives. Its attacks can disable websites and networks, disrupt or disable essential services, or steal or alter all kinds of data—all without ever seeing the victim.

In this comparison, instead of computers, the mind is attacked. Like hackers, Satan is very skilled at manipulating the programming of our minds. Although our minds are capable of many incredible things, they are also very vulnerable to attack. Through careful manipulation over a long time, our minds have a high potential to gradually become reprogrammed with lies meant to distract us from our service to God.

These lies may include feelings of inadequacy, superiority, innocence, or extreme guilt. These are not the only lies that Satan may be feeding you, but they are likely the biggest.

Many of us have stories that lead to at least one of the lies above. People who struggle with inadequacy likely grew up with people constantly telling them they were not good enough. Perhaps they were teased continuously, ridiculed by peers or parents, or abandoned or rejected by someone they thought loved them. Throughout their lives, these statements by others accumulated so much that when these people finally got out on their own, the thoughts remained. This conditioning made it difficult for them to believe in themselves, and as a result, many let life slip by without achieving anything of significance. Scared of rejection, some people found building relationships or finding meaningful jobs hard. Within the church, most of these people also avoided volunteering to serve because they felt they did not have what it takes to be used by God.

On the other hand, some people were reprogrammed to feel superior to their peers. These people may have come from privileged backgrounds in which everything was provided for them. Perhaps they were born with highly desired traits such as natural athleticism, high intelligence, or beauty. There was little they could not get or do while growing up. As a result, the need to spend much effort on something was a foreign concept to them. However, some worked their way up from unprivileged backgrounds or undeveloped abilities. Then, somewhere along the way, they forgot how it felt to be at the bottom and began treating those below them with little respect as they plowed over anyone who stood in the way of their perceived success.

The lie of perceived innocence often relates to the superior-minded, while the extreme guilt often relates to the insecure. Whether the person believes, "I never did anything wrong," or "I can't do anything right," both are lies that Satan wants them to believe, so their focus is not on God's truth but instead on their self-worth or lack thereof.

The focus or effectiveness of our minds can often be influenced by our worldly passions as well. In the computer world, this could be described as a denial of service (DoS) attack. In this book, this is simply being too busy to be of any use to God. DoS attacks work by overloading a server or computer with so many requests that it can no longer perform the duties it was meant to do. Hackers use these attacks to bring down entire networks and thus bring productivity to a screeching halt. Satan uses our work, passions, and other distractions so we become so focused on the meaningless aspects of the world around us that we forget our true purpose of serving God. Even taking on too many roles at church can be a distraction if you are not careful. You may think you are doing well by serving God in so many areas, but the busyness that comes from excess service tends to distract you from what God wants to teach you. It is like a parent who works long hours at a job to provide for his family—but, while doing so, fails to build an actual relationship with the very family he is trying to provide for.

Satan not only attacks our minds with lies or excessive distractions. Sometimes he manipulates our thinking with partial truths as well. In the computer hacker world, this is known as phishing. Phishing makes a site look legitimate to gain the end user's trust, so they give up sensitive information. Satan's plan, however, was not so much for information as it was for power. In Matthew 4:1–11 He attempted to trick Jesus by tempting Him to sin after a long forty-day fast. Satan manipulated scripture to get Jesus to rely on His own strength instead of relying on the Father's strength to get Him through His moment of weakness. If Jesus gave in to even one of the three temptations that Satan proposed, none of us would ever have a chance in heaven because Jesus's blood would no longer be pure.

As you can see, the lies and distractions of the devil can have significant consequences on the lives we live. If we do not take steps to stop these attacks, we will be useless soldiers in God's army. If you go into battle thinking you will lose, you are pretty much guaranteed to lose. If you go into battle thinking you have a better way, you might as well be fighting for the other side. And if you go into battle with your cell phone in your hand, music in your ears, and your favorite sitcom playing on the TV while you attempt to carry on a conversation with several friends and finish that project that's due in two days, I think you can guess what would happen.

So, how do we protect ourselves?

When a new computer is purchased, the end-user has two choices. They can take steps to protect it right away with antivirus software and a decent backup solution, or they can wait until they get infected and then spend countless hours trying to undo the damage done by the infection. Sometimes the damage is so great that the user has no choice but to wipe everything and start over, potentially losing years of work, important data, and cherished memories. To counteract and prevent cyber warfare against our minds, Christians have the same choices and similar consequences.

The first steps in preventing future cyber attacks on your mind are recognizing your weaknesses and taking precautions to prevent access to those weaknesses by the enemy. God has a use for those who can admit they are weak and struggling, whether through insecurities, pride, constant distractions, or any other lies Satan may throw at you. Paul wrote in 2 Corinthians 12:10 *(NIV)*, **"That is why, for Christ's sake, I delight in weaknesses, in insults, in hardships, in persecutions, in difficulties. For when I am weak, then I am strong."**

When we can admit our weaknesses and come to God, He becomes the protector of our minds, and we can be confident in knowing that we will not go down because of these attacks. But **"if anyone thinks he is something, when he is nothing, he deceives himself. [Let] each one test his own work, and then his reason to boast will be in himself alone and not in his neighbor."** *(Galatians 6:3–4 ESV)*.

As with a computer, our minds need antivirus protection and a solid backup system for when things go wrong. **"My flesh and my heart may fail, but God is the strength of my heart and my portion forever."** *(Psalm 73:26 ESV)*.

No matter where you may be in life, God's backup plan can restore you to a working operating condition if you call on His name. **"Such is the confidence that we have through Christ toward God. Not that we are sufficient in ourselves to claim anything as coming from us, but our sufficiency is from God."** *(2 Corinthians 3:4–5 ESV)*.

Many companies protect their systems against exploitation by completely reloading programs and servers from scratch on a random schedule. This ensures that no malicious code is hidden away in a file that could potentially destroy their system or compromise data, and it also prevents hackers from knowing when to stage their attacks for optimal destruction.

Similar preventative maintenance should be performed regularly to avoid a total reboot of your human operating system. This is accomplished by constantly reloading the truth regarding areas of your life that may have been infected with lies. Diving into God's Word regularly will help keep your system running smoothly, as the lies and distractions will have no place to hide.

Depending on how bad your system is to begin with, this reloading might take some time. As with computer viruses, lies find ways to reintroduce themselves despite your best efforts to remove or control them. Through the constant reliance on your antivirus program (God) and the constant effort to reload your brain with truth by the daily reading of the Word, even the most troublesome attacks can be reversed or stopped.

Trench Warfare

The final comparison is trench warfare, a type of combat in which opposing troops fight from trenches facing each other. Trench warfare historically happened when two opposing sides had a lot of firepower and desired to win but nowhere to move. So, they dug in and fought for years with little progress from either side until advances in technology came in and changed the game.

The goal of trench warfare was attrition: progressively grinding down the opposition's resources until they could no longer wage war. As a result, many thousands of lives were lost during WWI and WWII. Any advance from either side into "no man's land" (the area between the two battle lines) was guaranteed to lose many lives.

So again, what does this have to do with Christianity? In the spiritual sense, trench warfare is the fighting between groups both inside and outside the church that often serves no purpose in winning the war that God has us fighting. As a church, many lives are lost or wounded spiritually every week as differences of opinion cause unnecessary conflict among community members. Similar arguments are repeated with no one ever agreeing. Below are just a few of the battles that take place daily between different members of the communities in which we live.

Church vs. Science

If you have ever been out evangelizing or talking to a group of non-believers about spiritual topics, you may have noticed that some specific issues come up repeatedly. Evolution, creation, and miracles are the big three in this category.

For whatever reason, a large population refuses to believe that a god had any part in how our world came to be. They instead claim that we appeared simply due to various scientific events.

Without going too deeply into defending one way or another, I want to point something out. Science and the church's beliefs can coexist and often support each other. Many people, however, ridicule the concept of faith because they believe in science. They fail to realize that most science comprises ordinary men's theories and thus requires just as much faith in an ordinary man's word as in God's.

Why can't science and faith work together? I am not personally fond of studying scientific topics intensely, but I enjoy watching documentaries about our world and universe on TV. Why? Because they show that God is in control of everything. Ultimately, it does not matter if we evolved from monkeys, appeared out of the explosion of a star, or just materialized from nothingness. I do not think we will ever find the true answer to any of those questions, but there is one thing we can know for sure. That is, God would have had to be involved regardless. Every single theory that scientists present would have had to have a creator of some sort, making it all work together the way it does at its exact moments.

Think about all the conditions that would have to be made perfect for every living thing on this earth to survive in its respective environment. Even in the harshest climates where food and water are scarce, God has provided a way for the few plants and animals that inhabit those lands to survive.

"Look at the birds of the air: they neither sow nor reap nor gather into barns, and yet your heavenly Father feeds them. Are you not of more value than they?" *(Matthew 6:26 ESV)*

The point is that no matter how we may have come to be, there had to be a creator to make it happen. Although figuring out how things work together is fun, the results of these discoveries should not make you doubt that a creator is behind them all. Instead, you should be in awe of the complexities involved and realize they could not have happened by chance.

Whether you understand everything that goes into making something work or not should not influence your decision about how it came to be. I do not see many people out there questioning the existence of the people who designed the airplane, the phone, the space shuttle, or the superconductor in Switzerland because they understand something had to make it happen. Will we ever know how these inventors figured it out? The answer is no for most of us. But will the lack of understanding in the process make you question the result? Likely not—so why do we question God's creations?

Church vs. Itself

I appeal to you, brothers, to watch out for those who cause divisions and create obstacles contrary to the doctrine that you have been taught; avoid them. For such persons do not serve our Lord Christ, but their own appetites, and by smooth talk and flattery they deceive the hearts of the naive. *(Romans 16:17–18 ESV)*

Another big example of trench warfare happens within the church itself. As seen in an earlier chapter of this book, the Christian body is supposed to be united under one head, Christ. Unfortunately, this is often not the reality if you look at it. Far too often, various church groups divide themselves and have harsh arguments among their supposed brothers and sisters in Christ. These arguments distract from the purpose that the church is supposed to serve and create great opportunities for the enemy to attack.

But avoid foolish controversies, genealogies, dissensions, and quarrels about the law, for they are unprofitable and worthless. *(Titus 3:9 ESV)*

How can a church, whose entire purpose should be to love God and love one another, effectively do God's work if most of its time is spent arguing among itself? It cannot. By taking part in such arguments, the opposing trenches in the war do not even have to put much effort into the fight or expend their own troops because they can sit back and wait for the church to destroy itself.

In the first place, I hear that when you come together as a church, there are divisions among you, and to some extent I believe it. No doubt there have to be differences among you to show which of you have God's approval. *(1 Corinthians 11:18–19 NIV)*

What are these arguments that turn the church against itself? Sometimes they are trivial things, such as what color the sanctuary carpet should be, types of furniture or decorations to use, or usage of building space and land. Other issues may include alternate viewpoints on scripture or perceived biblical truths.

I want to focus on the latter set of arguments. Several big debates between Christian bodies have been big enough to form entire denominations around opposing viewpoints.

Romans 14:13–23 shows an example of whether certain foods should be eaten. Some abiding by the old covenant may say some foods are unclean. In contrast, those accepting the new may say otherwise. Different passages in the Bible may convict people in various ways. But if they are not essential to salvation, we must learn to respect each other's differences of conviction and focus on what God is doing in our own lives. If we are convicted one way based on our faith, God will honor that faith. If we violate our convictions, it may become a sin, even if God made provisions for the action or belief itself. If you make a rule for yourself and fail to keep it, God may hold that against you. I'm sure it would be forgivable, as with every other sin, but there might still be consequences.

Unfortunately, many viewpoints that divide God's people have nothing to do with salvation. We get so focused on things, such as whether the earth was created in a literal seven days or figuratively, that we miss the bigger picture—God created the earth! It does not matter how He did it or how long it took.

By the word of the LORD the heavens were made, and by the breath of his mouth all their host. ... For he spoke, and it came to be; he commanded, and it stood firm. *(Psalm 33:6, 9 ESV)*

All things were made through him, and without him was not any thing made that was made. *(John 1:3 ESV)*

If God wanted us to know the details of a particular event, it would have been said in a way that created no room for argument. Regarding events such as the creation, He would have given us more than a couple of pages to explain if it was vital for us to understand all the details. You must remember that many things in the Bible are things only God can achieve and are beyond comprehension with our human minds. What we see written is there to describe the event in a way we can understand. The reality of the event will likely never be something we can explain away with science or any other means besides faith in God.

In the creation example, God exists outside of time, so the times provided are just a means to explain the creation in a way humans can relate to based on Earth's days. Different planets have different days, and confining God to Earth's time creates unneeded confusion. There may or may not be an actual order of events, considering no one was there to witness it. The reality is that all God would have to do is speak, and any level of detail He desired in creation would be performed instantly. God does not need a waiting period for things to develop, as we do. We will never understand the timeless existence in which God resides, so generalizations had to be made.

Did you ever notice that there are more passages with detailed genealogies of people we never heard of or care much about than there are about the creation of the earth? Yet many of us skip over those passages as they can be tedious to read and instead try to figure out details of subjects God did not provide. I believe there is a reason we as humans were the last to be created—so we would not have to worry about it.

The church should focus on the issues that bring life and salvation or have a definitive answer, not things that do not make much of a difference in the grand scheme of things. Yes, it would be cool to know for sure, but since we do not, we will have to wait to read the FAQ list when we get to heaven if we want to know. But I feel we will be too preoccupied with worship, and many of our pressing questions will no longer be important to us.

Church vs. Alternative Lifestyles/Beliefs

The final type of trench warfare is the daily battles between beliefs from people outside the church. These are the people in the trenches on the other side of the battlefield. Some of these groups are directly opposed to Christian views and are doing everything they can to stop the movement's advances. Others may have similar goals but perhaps different teachings leading to alternative truths. Both can be dangerous in battle if not handled effectively.

The latter groups are often not a direct threat to Christianity. Instead, they dig their trenches away from the battlefield and usually stick within their community. The problem comes when members of our side wander and stumble into one of these other groups. At first glance, everything may seem peaceful and possibly even calmer than the battles within the Christian home team due to the previously mentioned issues. However, the problem lies in the fact that the god they worship is often not the God of the Bible. And despite what others may think, there is only one God and one way to heaven. Remember, just because someone thinks their way is true does not make it so. Only one of us can be right.

It is the first group of people that I want to focus on now: people who have made it their mission to destroy or prevent Christianity. This is often the atheists of the world but may include other religions as well.

Before I continue, I do want to point out that there are a few types of atheists. Many choose not to believe in any God and go on about their lives without bugging anyone. These are the people who will likely bring up scientific arguments or otherwise want some proof of God's existence when questioned. They often are not necessarily against Christianity or any other religion but have not given them much thought. These people may also be referred to as agnostics.

Other atheists, however, make it their mission to prove there is no God. They love to debate and throw out many arguments to competing Christians that may stump believers who are not prepared to handle such questions.

I do not understand why atheists fight so hard against something they claim does not exist or why they are worried about Christians whose message should be about spreading love. But for some reason, they despise that message and would rather live by their own hateful or selfish ways than principles meant to bring life to people. I suspect that many had a bad experience with someone claiming to be Christian and, in turn, decided to make the entire Christian community their enemy. This is why Christians should strive to live up to God's standards. We may be forgiven for our sins, but living a sinful lifestyle may turn others away from the faith.

Many of us will get caught in one of these battles at various points in our lives. We will try our best to give that life-changing point that saves humanity or at least the person in front of us, but unfortunately, these debates rarely produce a victor.

It can be discouraging to stand up for your beliefs only to be outplayed, bullied, or even persecuted for them. However, the mission God has given us has never been to win every argument or go on an offensive to fight against every person who tries to remove Christianity from our culture. So, should we have these debates? Yes and no.

Sometimes, it can be fun to get into healthy discussions about beliefs. It can test your knowledge and faith in what you claim to believe. Sometimes, your discussions can also plant the seed in the other person to get them to think more about God in ways they may never have heard before. Whether or not they switch sides then and there is not up to you. That is up to God. You will have more nos than yeses when you tell others about God, but that does not mean your efforts were without gain. Years later, after a continued search from that person, they may eventually find their way to Christ and become your brother or sister in the spiritual family of God, all because you planted or watered the seed for spiritual growth.

However, there is a warning. You must be careful with what you say. The wrong words could easily deter someone from Christianity. If you sound judgmental or hostile or share wrong teachings, your words or actions could destroy any previous attempts at growth for anyone listening or observing what you say or do. If you do not know something, it is better to say so or arrange to have someone more knowledgeable talk to the other person than to defend yourself with potentially false teachings.

Some atheists are against the church because they were wronged in some way in their past. They may be fighting based on emotional pain instead of recognizing the truth and facts presented to them. If logic and facts do not get a person to respond, try to figure out why they feel the way they do. If you cannot get that information or they refuse any logical argument, it is often best to end the conversation and give it to God. Pray for them as soon as you can after the conversation ends and as often as it comes to your mind. It is not your responsibility to convert them. Show them love to the best of your ability if circumstances allow, and let God do the rest.

The last thing you want to do is fuel their fire or fall into the traps they throw at you, trying to get you to falter. Everything you do should be with love toward that person. Do not call them names, ridicule them, or pass judgment—it is not your place. It is always better to show love to someone, even if you disagree than to turn them away with hostile arguments or accusations.

Ephesians 4:18 *(ESV)* says these people **"are darkened in their understanding, alienated from the life of God because of the ignorance that is in them, due to their hardness of heart."**

First Peter 2:15–17 *(ESV)* says, **"For this is the will of God, that by doing good you should put to silence the ignorance of foolish people. Live as people who are free, not using your freedom as a cover-up for evil, but living as servants of God. Honor everyone. Love the brotherhood. Fear God. Honor the emperor."**

Battles of the trenches should be avoided as much as possible; do not seek them out. But when they come to you, be ready to fight. And be willing to back off when you are in over your head. Let God do the fighting. If your words are not from God, you should not be speaking them when put in these situations. Anything less than God's Word will result in the enemy gaining ground and putting the Christian body at unnecessary risk.

See to it that no one takes you captive by philosophy and empty deceit, according to human tradition, according to the elemental spirits of the world, and not according to Christ. *(Colossians 2:8 ESV)*

PART 4
THE HOLY WAR

14

Battle Wounds

"Captain—we are under attack!" I shouted into the radio as bullets rang out behind me.
"Where is it coming from, soldier?"
"Inside the north gate, sir. We have been infiltrated."
"What? How did that happen? Who was on guard?"
"I was, sir. They had fake credentials and paperwork. They tricked me into letting them in."
"If anyone gets hurt out there, it's on you, soldier! Lock down the base and pray no one gets hurt."
It was all my fault. I had let my guard down by not verifying the identity of the people coming through the gate. People were getting hurt because of me.

Throughout this book I have discussed various struggles people face and presented truths based on the Bible to help overcome those struggles. But the reality is that many of us have been in the fight so long that instead of being in the proper condition to fight, we are left wounded and hurt. We have lost our hope and will to fight, and we are left wondering if this pain is worth it.

I am lumping myself in with those statements because even after writing this and the many chapters with the Bible's answers, I am also struggling with those very things. This chapter has been the hardest to write in the entire book. It was at least two years between this and the previous chapters because I did not know what to write. Even when I finally wrote something, I sat on it for another few years and rewrote it a few times. I did not feel that I could present a book with what I was proclaiming to be the answers when I had struggled so much in believing in my heart that what I said was true for others was also true for me.

The Army of One

Ever since I was young, I have felt the enemy has been attacking me hard, trying to distract me from the mission laid out for me. I believe that God has a plan for my life beyond anything I could come up with myself. I also believe the enemy is aware of that plan and has been doing everything in his power to stop me. As a result, trying to follow that plan and understand it has been quite challenging.

There have been many times I have wanted to give up on this project. I often think I am not good enough or worthy to teach when there were times I could not even accept it for myself. And there have been times when I thought my sins would disqualify me from being of service to God. But then I reread what I wrote many years before and reminded myself that God can and will use anyone who trusts Him. This is not about me. This is about sharing what God has put on my heart to share over the last ten-plus years as I have written these chapters piece by piece. Much of what has been written is God's words to me as much as His words to you, perhaps more so. I cannot give up because I have been wounded in my walk. I cannot give up because I struggle to see the finish line, and I cannot give up because past struggles have knocked me down. I must get up, brush myself off, and keep moving, as my purpose may be just around the corner.

I cannot let Satan win. Regardless of my current obstacles or past actions, God's truth will never change. I will not let Satan stop me from completing my mission, no matter how much pain he has brought to my life. This is God's battle now, as it should have been from the start. As with many of God's recruits, I tried going my own way, fighting my own battles, and losing. I forgot or ignored many of the truths I have proclaimed in this book.

The content of this book was never written to elevate myself above my fellow believers. Everything written has been lessons God has been trying to teach me, and I hope these lessons will also inspire you in your personal battles.

Rest and Healing

As we have seen, the wounds we get while fighting our battles are due to fighting without God's help. But God's plan for us does not change just because we face hardships. He has accounted for our getting lost and wounded but continues to call for us. Every step of ours has been accounted for, even those that lead us off course.

The steps of a man are established by the LORD when he delights in his way; though he fall, he shall not be cast headlong, for the LORD upholds his hand. *(Psalm 37:23–24 ESV)*

There comes a time for many of us when we wonder why we are fighting these battles. As we have learned from previous chapters, the enemy is always on the prowl, searching for ways to knock us off course. It can be increasingly difficult to continue getting up when you feel that everything that could go wrong is going wrong.

Perhaps your circumstances have left you with little hope for a positive future. No matter what you do, you feel as if you will never overcome the obstacles in your path. You have been knocked down so often that you became too weak to get up on your own accord.

Perhaps your wounds have led to some addiction by which to hide from your pains. Perhaps that addiction has caused even deeper wounds as it led to you doing something you would not have normally done in the right state of mind. If left untreated, addictions could result in the loss of family or friends, your job, freedom, or even your life, causing further wounds not just to you but also to those close to you. Even if you think no one else is getting hurt by your addictions, that is rarely ever the case, and it is not what God wants from you.

Regardless of your circumstances, if you feel attacked from all sides, it is vital that you take time to heal. Our God is not only our leader as we go into battles but also our healer when we are wounded. If we go the wrong way and don't follow the directions He set out for us, He will still come to our aid when we call out to Him.

When the righteous cry for help, the Lord hears and delivers them out of all their troubles. The Lord is near to the brokenhearted and saves the crushed in spirit. Many are the afflictions of the righteous, but the Lord delivers him out of them all. He keeps all his bones; not one of them is broken. *(Psalm 34:17–20 ESV)*

It is so easy to get knocked off track that sometimes you can see it happening right before your eyes. I experienced this once when I observed two teenage girls talking with each other in my church. It was a simple interaction, but it has stuck with me for some time because it reminded me of some pains in my own life. It all started with one girl asking another why she always has such cute outfits—and following up with "I don't have anything like that." But it was the look of disappointment and obvious jealousy that followed that convinced me that the enemy had just attacked her self-worth.

I did not know the girl, but hopefully she was strong enough in her faith not to let that fester. She is probably just like the rest of us, constantly striving for more. We continually compare ourselves to others and wonder, "Why not me?" or "Why can't I have that?" We place our worth on what we have, what we do, what we look like, or who we know instead of letting our worth come from the God who created us. There is a reason that God included warnings in His Word against envy. He knew how much it could destroy us if we let it distract us from the mission He set out for us.

I have another friend at church who told my study group about a conversation he had with his daughter in the aftermath of the racial tensions in America in 2020. His daughter asked him, "Why would a God who loves me let me be born Black in times like this?"

As you can expect, this threw my friend off guard as he did not know how to answer. However, through his faith in God, he provided an answer that I believe will greatly motivate his daughter to do great things in the world as she gets older.

He said, "You were not born Black as a punishment in a time like this, but you were born Black for a time like this because you are meant to be a solution, not the problem."

You see, the world, as with the enemy, is quick to throw labels at us that make us think we are worth less than we are. When we let race, gender, age, looks, social status, or past actions define who we are, we lose track of the fact that we are called God's children—created in His image, complete with a plan and a purpose for our lives. Nothing—I repeat, nothing—can change that fact.

It is easy to lose hope when you forget or are unaware of the promises God made for you. Even the author of Psalm 42:11 *(ESV)* experienced this when he wrote, **"Why are you cast down, O my soul, and why are you in turmoil within me? Hope in God; for I shall again praise him, my salvation and my God."**

Not everything we desire will go the way we expect. The closer you are to God, the more likely this may happen, but more often or not, God has different plans or detours He needs you to take before you advance in your mission. Therefore, it is essential to **"Rejoice in hope, be patient in tribulation, be constant in prayer"** *(Romans 12:12 ESV)* and remember **"that all things work together for good for those who love him, who have been called according to his purpose."** *(Romans 8:28 NIV)*.

"For I will restore health to you, and your wounds I will heal, declares the LORD." *(Jeremiah 30:17 ESV)*

When we find ourselves worrying about how others think of us or how a particular problem will be handled, it distracts us from the end goal. Jesus said in Matthew 6:33–34 *(NIV)*, **"But seek first his kingdom and his righteousness, and all these things will be given to you as well. Therefore, do not worry about tomorrow,** for tomorrow will worry about itself. Each day has enough trouble of its own."

Remember that lowly shepherd I mentioned in chapter one—you know, the one who was to become King David? God promised him a kingship and descendants who would one day lead to the birth of Jesus and the world's salvation. It would have been easy for him to give up at many points in his mission set by God. If you think you have enemies, try having an entire army looking to kill you.

Not only did his whole family look down on him due to his size and profession, but when he did finally come to power, he abused it. He slept with a married woman and then had her husband killed in battle to cover it up.

But he did not give up. He wrote in Psalm 71:20 *(NIV)*, **"Though you have made me see troubles, many and bitter, you will restore my life again; from the depths of the earth you will again bring me up."**

Even with his struggles and mistakes, God still described him as "a man after my heart," as described in Acts 13:22 *(ESV)*: **"And when he had removed [Saul], he raised up David to be their king, of whom he testified and said, 'I have found in David the son of Jesse a man after my heart, who will do all my will.'"**

When our hearts are set on God, our mistakes can be erased from God's judgment by calling out to Him again. **"Then the Lord knows how to rescue the godly from trials, and to keep the unrighteous under punishment until the day of judgment."** *(2 Peter 2:9 ESV).*

Our stubbornness to give God control, or our inability to forgive ourselves or others, accounts for many of the wounds in our lives. But God never stops loving us. Here are some of the promises and instructions from God:

You will again have compassion on us; you will tread our sins underfoot and hurl all our iniquities into the depths of the sea. *(Micah 7:19 NIV)*

"Forget the former things; do not dwell on the past." *(Isaiah 43:18 NIV)*

"So do not fear, for I am with you; do not be dismayed, for I am your God. I will strengthen you, I will help you; I will uphold you with my righteous hand." *(Isaiah 41:10 NIV)*

God is our refuge and strength, an ever-present help in trouble. *(Psalm 46:1 NIV)*

Instead of your shame you will receive a double portion, and instead of disgrace, you will rejoice in our inheritance. And so you will inherit a double portion in your land, and everlasting joy will be yours. *(Isaiah 61:7 NIV)*

"Very truly I tell you, whoever hears my word and believes him who sent me has eternal life and will not be judged but has crossed over from death to life." *(John 5:24 NIV)*

Addressing the Wounds

We are afflicted in every way, but not crushed; perplexed, but not driven to despair; persecuted, but not forsaken, struck down, but not destroyed; always carrying in the body the death of Jesus, so that the life of Jesus may also be manifested in our bodies. *(2 Corinthians 4: 8–10 ESV)*

With every war, people's lives are forever changed. Whether physically, mentally, or emotionally—war always leaves people wounded in one way or another. Spiritual war is no different. Satan knows how powerful people can be if allowed to challenge him. So, he will stop at nothing to get Christians to lose focus on their objective.

For me, this manifested as the lie that I was not good enough and my worrying about things I could not control. I have battled with depression, anxiety, and other health and personal challenges that severely impacted my ability to pursue my mission effectively. Instead of reaching out to my Christian family for help, I mostly

The Army of One

isolated myself and tried fighting my battles alone due to a long life of rejection and disappointment from others.

Like many, I was teased or rejected during my childhood and struggled to fit in. This affected me even in college and beyond, as I had trouble building meaningful friendships. I feared being hurt again. Although I have had many goals and ambitions and the ability to achieve them, I often failed to do so because I believed the lies that I was not good enough to have success. The enemy buried me under so much pain, false beliefs, and seemingly impossible obstacles that I have been struggling for years, trying to unburden myself and pursue what God has called me to do.

At several points in my life, I have wanted to give up and put an end to the pain that never seemed to go away. Every time I took a step forward, something else would come along and knock me two steps back. The only reason I kept getting up and pressing forward was knowing that God had a plan for my life.

Most of us know Jeremiah 29:11 *(NIV)*, which states, **"For I know the plans I have for you," declares the Lord, "plans to prosper you and not to harm you, plans to give you hope and a future."** Many people stop there when offering comfort to those who are struggling. But if we continue to verses 12–13, we see, **"Then you will call on me and come and pray to me, and I will listen to you. You will seek me and find me when you seek me with all your heart."**

Call on God and pray. I have done that many times, but did I do it wholeheartedly? Perhaps not. How could I when I felt God had rejected me due to my suffering or life mistakes? How could I when I had held onto sin and lies for so long?

God calls us to turn from such things, but Jesus died on the cross to cover those transgressions. So where was I going wrong? Why couldn't I escape the grasp of sin that kept me from truly connecting with God? Why, throughout my entire life, did it seem as if the world was against me? Why was it that no matter what I did, I struggled to find peace?

Romans 7:14–18 *(ESV)* addresses these questions: **"For we know that the law is spiritual, but I am of the flesh, sold under sin. For I do not understand my own actions. For I do not do what I want, but I do the very thing I hate. Now if I do what I do not want, I agree with the law, that it is good. So now it is no longer I who do it, but sin that dwells within me. For I know that nothing good dwells in me, that is, in my flesh. For I have the desire to do what is right, but not the ability to carry it out."**

What does this mean? One of the hardest parts about Christianity is that although our sins have been forgiven and we have been set free, the enemy is still there, firing away, trying to prevent us from escaping his grasp. Romans 7:21–23 and 8:1–2 *(ESV)* tell us, **"So I find it to be a law that when I want to do right, evil lies close at hand. For I delight in the law of God, in my inner being, but I see in my members another law waging war against the law of my mind and making me captive to the law of sin that dwells in my members.**

"There is therefore now no condemnation for those who are in Christ Jesus. For the law of the Spirit of life has set you free in Christ Jesus from the law of sin and death."

Until we can learn to give God everything, the sin we are born with will continue fighting against us and often win. This is where I went wrong. Even though I knew the truth of God—the spiritual law—and wanted to obey it, I failed to practice it. I was so wounded that I did not know how I was ever going to escape. How could I possibly be a soldier in God's army if I could not even handle my own battles? If I were not good enough for the world, how could I ever be good enough to serve in Christ's army? These are all the lies the enemy wants us to believe, and unfortunately, in me he succeeded.

Second Corinthians 12:9–10 *(ESV)* has an alternate view: **"But he said to me, 'My grace is sufficient for you, for my power is made perfect in weakness.' Therefore, I will boast all the more gladly of my weaknesses, so that the power of Christ may rest** upon me. For the sake of Christ, then, I am content with weaknesses, insults, hardships, persecutions, and calamities. For when I am weak, then I am strong."

Titus 3:3–7 *(ESV)* also states, "For we ourselves were once foolish, disobedient, led astray, slaves to various passions and pleasures, passing our days in malice and envy, hated by others and hating one another. But when the goodness and loving kindness of God our Savior appeared, he saved us, not because of works done by us in righteousness, but according to his own mercy, by the washing of regeneration and renewal of the Holy Spirit, whom he poured out on us richly through Jesus Christ our Savior, so that being justified by his grace we might become heirs according to the hope of eternal life."

The grace of God is all we need. Remember: we were never meant to fight our battles alone. Doing so only causes pain and anguish as we repeatedly try to overcome the trials of the world, only for them to continue piling on until they overcome us. By turning over our battles to God, we go from being a weak force against the enemy to having the full backing of the most powerful force in the universe fighting to protect us—God Himself.

The Lord is faithful. He will establish you and guard you against the evil one. *(2 Thessalonians 3:3 ESV)*

When we can find our strength in God, we can rest assured that we **"will not need to fight in this battle,"** but we should **"stand firm, hold [our] position, and see the salvation of the Lord on [our] behalf. Do not be afraid and do not be dismayed. The Lord will be with [us]."** *(2 Chronicles 20:17 NIV, bracket items added)*. God wants to fight for us. We go through our suffering so God can receive glory as we learn to depend on Him for our lives.

"Come to me, all you who are weary and burdened, and I will give you rest. Take my yoke upon you and learn from me, for I am gentle and humble in heart, and you will find rest for your souls. For my yoke is easy and my burden is light." *(Matthew 11:28–30 NIV)*

Finding Victory

As hard as it is to go through these trials, the enemy will never have victory over us if we strive to follow Jesus completely. **"Submit yourselves therefore to God. Resist the devil, and he will flee from you."** *(James 4:7 NIV).*

God calls us to **"Share in suffering as a good soldier of Christ Jesus. No soldier gets entangled in civilian pursuits, since his aim is to please the one who enlisted him."** *(2 Timothy 2:3–4 ESV).*

Imagine if our nation's soldiers were distracted by every personal problem they faced. Their focus would not be on the battle they were called to fight. This lack of focus could result in fellow soldiers getting hurt or missions being rendered incomplete due to failure. God also has missions for us; we cannot let our struggles distract us from our call to serve.

I thank Christ Jesus our Lord, who has given me strength, that he considered me trustworthy, appointing me to his service. *(1 Timothy 1:12 NIV)*

So why must we share in sufferings if God wants us to be focused on the missions He has set for us? Wouldn't it be easier for everyone involved if God relieved us of our suffering to begin with? Surely God knows that some people's pain will be too much for them and will make them run from God instead of running toward Him. This is precisely the point. What army wants soldiers who run away when facing obstacles? God needs soldiers committed to His cause and committed to following Him regardless of obstacles encountered.

Second Corinthians 10:3–6 *(ESV)* gives this word: **"For though we walk in the flesh, we are not waging war according to the flesh. For the weapons of our warfare are not of the flesh but have divine power to destroy strongholds. We destroy arguments and every lofty opinion raised against the knowledge of God, and take every thought captive to obey Christ, being ready to punish every disobedience, when your obedience is complete."**

The Army of One

To become strong soldiers for God, we must learn to **"count it all joy, my brothers when you meet trials of various kinds, for you know that the testing of your faith produces steadfastness. And let steadfastness have its full effect, that you may be perfect and complete, lacking in nothing."** *(James 1:2–4 ESV)*.

Trials do not just go away because we joined God's army. First Peter 4:12–13 *(ESV)* tells us to expect them: **"Beloved, do not be surprised at the fiery trial when it comes upon you to test you, as though something strange were happening to you. But rejoice insofar as you share Christ's sufferings, that you may also rejoice and be glad when his glory is revealed."**

So not only are we supposed to share in Christ's suffering, but we are also called to rejoice in that suffering. It seems counterintuitive, doesn't it? It is not normal human behavior. Am I expected to have joy that I was teased as a child? Am I supposed to have joy when I struggle to build meaningful relationships? How about my poor health or the constant barrage of challenges? According to God's Word, the answer is yes.

It does not matter if we feel we have let people down or have been let down by others. It does not matter how much we have lost or how little we have gained. And it does not matter if every one of our plans for our lives has been disrupted. We are still expected to find joy. But why?

Romans 5:1–5 *(ESV)* has an answer: **"Since we have been justified by faith, we have peace with God through our Lord Jesus Christ. Through him we have also obtained access by faith into this grace in which we stand, and we rejoice in hope of the glory of God. Not only that, but we rejoice in our sufferings, knowing that suffering produces endurance, and endurance produces character, and character produces hope, and hope does not put us to shame, because God's love has been poured into our hearts through the Holy Spirit who has been given to us."**

To explain this passage, let us look at one of the largest causes of trials in our lives—sin. When we allow sin to run rampant in our lives, it can be like letting a rhino into a china shop; surely things will be broken. But when we have the faith to follow Christ, our sins will be justified. This means we have been made righteous or found not guilty when we face the ultimate judge. It means that the rhino in the china shop has been restrained and carefully led out of harm's way. The problem may be that we allow it back in to wreak havoc once again. If we can fully accept what Christ did for us, we will have peace knowing that God has us in His hands. Even if a few things get broken along the way, our faith in God's promises will give us peace in knowing that we will soon receive the crown of life *(James 1:12)*.

The crown of life sounds great, but it still does not explain our suffering. The remaining half of the Romans 5 passage explains the reasoning. Suffering produces endurance. When athletes prepare for their events, they push themselves regularly to a failing point. That is the point at which their muscles cannot handle much more without first resting so the muscles can be rebuilt stronger. The more often you push your muscles like this, the stronger they get and the longer they endure each subsequent trial before breaking again. Each time we experience a life struggle, we also go through a period of being broken and rebuilt by God. Remember boot camp? Each time we are knocked down, we are expected to get back up, lasting a little longer each time before we crash and burn all over again.

As we establish endurance, we also produce character. It takes a certain level of discipline and courage to willingly allow yourself to go through the pain that comes from trials. Waking up every day knowing that you are likely to be put through yet another test can be very difficult when you don't have an end goal in mind. But as Christians and athletes both know, our pains are being endured for a purpose, so we do everything it takes to win the prize waiting for us.

This leads us to the next part: hope. What is the point in building endurance and developing a good character of discipline if you have nothing to fight for? No goal, no purpose. Our hope is our reason for doing what we do, knowing we will be rewarded through our hard work and struggles. Romans 4:20–22 *(ESV)* says, **"No unbelief made him waver concerning the promise of God, but he grew strong in his faith as he gave glory to God, fully convinced that God was able to do what he had promised. That is why his faith was 'counted to him as righteousness.'"**

Just as the athlete trains to compete for the prize, we compete knowing that we have a prize of eternal life in Jesus. Paul also exclaims this commitment in Philippians 3:13–14 *(ESV)*. He writes, **"Brothers, I do not consider that I have made it my own. But one thing I do: forgetting what lies behind and straining forward to what lies ahead, I press on toward the goal for the prize of the upward call of God in Christ Jesus."**

Colossians 3:23–24 *(ESV)* also tells us, **"Whatever you do, work heartily, as for the Lord and not for men, knowing that from the Lord you will receive the inheritance as your reward. You are serving the Lord Christ."**

Our goal is to serve God. The hope we get through our trials is that God will deliver us and allow us to serve in the battle for the lost, and there is no shame in that. Every trial we face is meant to strengthen us, teach us, or get us to turn our eyes back to God. Some trials are designed so you may be a witness of God's power to others who are hurting.

Why was I teased as a child? So I could develop a heart for the oppressed and ostracized today. Why do I struggle to build relationships? Perhaps so that my relationships will become stronger or that I will love more as God loves. Why do I observe so many relationships fail, including my own? Perhaps so I can learn what not to do when my time comes. Why do I continue to get knocked down despite my best efforts to move forward? Perhaps because I was so stubborn in giving my all to God, He needs to teach me some things that I am just not learning with all the world's distractions.

Battle Wounds

Is it painful? Yes. Do I believe this will be a long-term hindrance to my life? No. Only time will tell how God plans to use these trials to build me up in His image.

When going through a trial, especially a long-term one, it can be challenging to see the light at the end of the tunnel, but there is always an end, and God will see us through from start to finish if we trust in Him.

You see, the truth is that I am good enough to be used by God, and He still has a plan for me despite a life of pain, mistakes, and self–doubt. He gave me a set of talents that I doubt He will allow me to waste due to insecurities and challenges.

I do not know how His plan will manifest or how soon, but all I can do is follow what James 1:5–8 *(ESV)* says: **"If any of you lacks wisdom, let him ask God, who gives generously to all without reproach, and it will be given him. But let him ask in faith, with no doubting, for the one who doubts is like a wave of the sea that is driven and tossed by the wind. For that person must not suppose that he will receive anything from the Lord; he is a double-minded man, unstable in all his ways."**

Even though it can be helpful to seek help from other believers when dealing with troubles, it is essential that **"Your faith might not rest in the wisdom of men but in the power of God."** *(1 Corinthians 2:5 ESV)*.

Ask for wisdom to get you through your trials, and God will direct your path. But do not do what most of us do and ask for advice, direction, or His meeting a need and then doubt His response, thinking you know better or failing to believe that He will provide. You will be free when you can put your complete trust in God to free you.

"Then you will know the truth, and the truth will set you free." *(John 8:32 NIV)*

15

Undeserved Grace

"Private Allen, you are hereby found guilty of failing to protect the compound, which resulted in fifteen deaths and seven wounded while under your guard. You will be sentenced to twenty years in federal prison for your actions."

I sat silently as I thought about the judge's words after three days of trial and intense deliberation by the jury. The rest of my life would be spent behind bars, all because I was too lazy to pick up a phone to verify the identities of the people entering the base. I did not hear the remainder of the judge's words as I contemplated what this would mean for me and my family. My daze was broken when I heard someone calling my name again.

"Allen, do you accept the offer presented to you?" asked the judge again with a slight hint of wetness in his eye.

"What offer? Sorry—I was lost in my thoughts." I was confused. I thought the time for deals was over.

"Your commander, JC, has offered to fulfill your sentence; all you have to do is accept what he's offering, and you will be free to go."

"What?" I looked over at JC as he made his way from the audience to sit beside me at the defendant's table. "You can't do that; it was my mistake. You don't deserve it."

JC responded. "Allen, I told you I would fight for you and die for you if necessary. I trained you to be a soldier, but my time here is done. I have bigger plans for you than to sit in prison for the rest of your life. Accept this offer and remember it as you fulfill your purpose in honor of me. "

"I will never forget what you've done for me," I said. "You changed my life and rescued me from my misguided ways. I thank you with all my heart and promise to remember your sacrifice as I live out the rest of my life."

With that, I was released from my restraints, and I watched as JC was pulled violently from the court with guards all around him. Not a single eye was dry as the judge banged the gavel down and said, "Court dismissed."

The Army of One

"Not guilty." Those are the words that every accused person hopes to hear when standing before their judge for a crime. Unfortunately, for many, this is not the case. When standing before the ultimate Judge in heaven, that is never the case, and we are all sentenced to death for our sins.

For all have sinned and fall short of the glory of God. *(Romans 3:23)*

For the wages of sin is death *(Romans 6:23)*

There would be no point in writing this book if this were the end of the story. But thankfully for us, these verses both have more to say:

...and are justified by his grace as a gift, through the redemption that is in Christ Jesus, whom God put forward as a propitiation by his blood, to be received by faith. This was to show God's righteousness, because in his divine forbearance he had passed over former sins. *(Romans 3:24–25 ESV)*

...but the free gift of God is eternal life in Christ Jesus our Lord. *(Romans 6:23 ESV)*

These verses are game changers as they are, but they make an even greater impact if you understand what the word propitiation means. Jesus did not just step in and ask God to forgive us. Death was a requirement; there were no ifs, ands, or buts about it. Someone had to pay. Jesus was that payment. But He also became the sacrifice for us, bearing God's wrath and turning it to favor on our behalf. Simply put, propitiation satisfies God's wrath against sin.

But if anyone does sin, we have an advocate with the Father, Jesus Christ the righteous. He is the propitiation for our sins, and not for ours only but also for the sins of the whole world. *(1 John 2:1-2 ESV)*

When Jesus came to this earth, He had one purpose—to shine the light on the darkness (sin) that plagues the world. Jesus states in John 12:46–48 *(ESV)*, **"I have come into the world as light, so that whoever believes in me may not remain in darkness. If** anyone hears my words and does not keep them, I do not judge him; for I did not come to judge the world but to save the world. The one who rejects me and does not receive my words has a judge; the word that I have spoken will judge him on the last day."

Jesus is the key to freedom from the great punishment we all deserve. Not only did He come to teach us how to live, but He also became the last sacrifice that will ever have to be made in atonement for our sins. Before Jesus, people had to undergo many sacrificial rituals to receive God's grace for their sins. Half the book of Leviticus discusses the requirements for sacrifice in detail. Blood was always the payment for sins. If it was not from the sinner himself but rather from the various animal offerings. That was a messy time and one full of faults. **"For if that first covenant had been faultless, there would have been no occasion to look for a second."** *(Hebrews 8:7 ESV)*.

Jesus was the change of all that. He became the ultimate sacrifice. By His blood alone, we would become forever pure in the eyes of God. **"After making purification for sins, he sat down at the right hand of the Majesty on high, having become as much superior to angels as the name he has inherited is more excellent than theirs."** *(Hebrews 1:3–4 ESV)*.

Before going on, I would like to offer an illustration. I have lived near many beautiful bodies of water throughout my life—from lakes and rivers to bays, the Gulf of Mexico, and the ocean. These bodies of water seem to capture our attention for their relative peacefulness compared to the busyness of the land in which we reside. People often sit and stare for hours at the vast span of nothingness that is these great bodies of water. But why do we do this?

A possible reason for this came to me one day when I first went paddle boarding on the bay. Before that outing, I saw only a three-mile-wide stretch of water extending far beyond what I could see. From the road, apart from the slight ripples of waves, this water was no more than a flat surface like the floor we walk on. But unlike the floor, this surface contained depths of unknown proportions that could contain many dangers hidden within. When I went paddle boarding that first time, I discovered that this vast bay was no more than waist-deep a third of the way out on both sides, as I later found out. Although I am sure it got much deeper toward the middle, the surface level of the water at that deeper point was the same as from where I was floating along.

Here is my point. What if the waterline, the calmness of the surface, was a representation of what God wishes for our lives—peaceful and without blemish? He desires to even the playing field of our lives by pouring out His blood to cover our deepest, darkest sins. Unfortunately, we are all far from peace and are stuck in pits of despair—some deeper than others.

We all dig deep holes for ourselves due to our sinful nature, which brings us farther beneath the water's surface. The deeper we go, the darker our lives become with the more potential for trouble, and the more likely we are to drown in our sorrows. But you see, when Jesus died for us, His blood came to cover our sins like the waters over our land. Since liquids will fill up deeper areas before the shallow, there is no chance that His blood will fail to cover even the deepest of sins. He will lift whoever believes in Him to the high ground, no matter how deep in sin we may have been.

He drew me up from the pit of destruction, out of the miry bog, and set my feet upon a rock, making my steps secure. *(Psalm 40:2 ESV)*

Remember how He flooded all the land in the days of Noah? If you stay beneath the surface of God's saving grace, you will surely drown. **"I sink in deep mire, where there is no foothold; I have come into deep waters, and the flood sweeps over me."** *(Psalm 69:2 ESV).*

But by your believing in Him, He will lift you to solid ground and make you a part of the mainland that supports your existence through His saving grace. Sometimes you may slide back under

Undeserved Grace

the surface depending on how solid a foundation you built, but God will always rescue you when you put your full faith in Him to do so.

When the high priests in the Old Testament performed their daily sacrifices, it was about the equivalent of pouring a bucket of water over their heads daily to cover sins as deep as the Grand Canyon. That "cleansing" may have hidden their sins for a short while, but it would eventually dry up as they continued digging a deeper hole of sin for themselves.

Because Jesus was over the high priest, His blood secured us **"eternal redemption. For if the blood of goats and bulls, and the sprinkling of defiled persons with the ashes of a heifer, sanctify for the purification of the flesh, how much more will the blood of Christ, who through the eternal Spirit offered himself without blemish to God, purify our conscience from dead works to serve the living God."** *(Hebrews 9:13-14 ESV).*

Remember that list in an earlier part of this book that indicated everything Jesus died for? Jesus's blood is enough to cover all sins from the fall of Adam and Eve to the sins of our unborn descendants.

Therefore, as one trespass led to condemnation for all men, so one act of righteousness leads to justification and life for all men. For as by the one man's disobedience the many were made sinners, so by the one man's obedience the many will be made righteous. *(Romans 5:18-19 ESV. See also Romans 5:12-21)*

Christ entered heaven and appeared before God on our behalf, every one of us. His sacrifice was made once and for all to sanctify us according to the Holy Spirit.

And every priest stands daily at his service, offering repeatedly the same sacrifices, which can never take away sins. But when Christ had offered for all time a single sacrifice for sins, he sat down at the right hand of God, waiting from that time until his enemies should be made a footstool for his feet. For by

a single offering he has perfected for all time those who are being sanctified. *(Hebrews 10:11–14 ESV)*

You should notice a couple of things about the previous passage. First, after just a single sacrifice by Jesus Himself, He rose to His rightful place in heaven to sit beside God. He did not sit because He just went through a horrible crucifixion, He did not sit because He just did the impossible and rose from the dead, and He did not sit because He was tired, lazy, or weak. He sat because His job was done. No more sacrifices had to be made to find favor in God's eyes. Our salvation was made eternal. All our debts from sin were paid, and our slates have been wiped clean. Through justification we were made righteous in the eyes of God and guaranteed a place in heaven if we choose to accept the offer of salvation.

God shows his love for us in that while we were still sinners, Christ died for us. Since, therefore, we have now been justified by his blood, much more shall we be saved by him from the wrath of God. *(Romans 5:8–9 ESV)*

But that is not all. Jesus will continue to **"reign until he has put all his enemies under his feet. The last enemy to be destroyed is death."** *(1 Corinthians 15:25–26 ESV)*. This means that God will rule once again over everyone and everything, regardless of their choice to follow Him.

The Life-Changing Choice

If you remember from an earlier part of this book, I stated that to receive this gift of God, all you had to do was believe. Although I still follow this view, there comes a catch. What does it mean to believe?

Before I answer, I think it is appropriate to understand why I am asking. One of the other major viewpoints in becoming a Christian is that you must believe and repent (or turn from) your sins to be saved. I both agree and disagree with this view. I disagree in that many people believe repentance means they must be sin-free and that you must try to make yourself good before God will even consider you as a child of His. This could not be farther from the truth, as it will never happen. We are not capable on our own. It is God who provides the means to change after the point of salvation through sanctification.

Repentance does not simply mean being sorry for your actions. It means that you recognize your past actions as sinful and wish to take the steps to change your ways going forward by following God's instructions for your life. In other words, it means changing your mind toward God.

Repentance is a major part of salvation, and without it, you likely never genuinely believed in the first place. Although it can be dangerous to judge if someone is a true believer, let me explain. If you believe that Jesus came to save us from our sins, wouldn't you think that you would start seeing at least some life-changing behavior? It will not usually happen overnight, but you should begin seeing some change in how you think about your sins.

As it is, I rejoice, not because you were grieved, but because you were grieved into repenting. For you felt a godly grief, so that you suffered no loss through us.

For godly grief produces a repentance that leads to salvation without regret, whereas worldly grief produces death. *(2 Corinthians 7:9–10 ESV)*

You do not have to have your life all figured out before becoming a Christian. God's purpose is to help you figure that out. But believing in Jesus involves far more than raising your hand in church and repeating some magical words. It is not what you say that grants you passage through the gates of heaven, but rather your change of heart.

Romans 12:1–2 *(ESV)* says, **"I appeal to you therefore, brothers, by the mercies of God, to present your bodies as a living sacrifice, holy and acceptable to God, which is your spiritual worship. Do not be conformed to this world, but be transformed** by the renewal of your mind, that by testing you may discern what is the will of God, what is good and acceptable and perfect."

We are to become "living sacrifices." This means that we are to submit ourselves to the one who paid for our lives and honor Him with our thoughts and actions. **"For if we go on sinning deliberately after receiving the knowledge of the truth, there no longer remains a sacrifice for sins, but a fearful expectation of judgment, and a fury of fire that will consume the adversaries."** *(Hebrews 10:26–27 ESV).*

Therefore, we must pay much closer attention to what we have heard, lest we drift away from it. *(Hebrews 2:1 ESV)*

It is not enough to go through the motions of becoming a Christian. If you still live according to the world, continuing to sin without the slightest hint of a changed heart and mind, then you likely never believed in the saving grace of God. You were obviously only after "fire insurance"—a way to continue your sinful lifestyle without facing the punishment that comes with it.

For when you were slaves of sin, you were free in regard to righteousness. But what fruit were you getting at that time from the things of which you are now ashamed? For the end of those things is death. But now that you have been set free from sin and have become slaves of God, the fruit you get leads to sanctification and its end, eternal life. *(Romans 6:20–22 ESV)*

A faithful Christian will undergo a sanctification process, a continual process of being made more holy. Although our sins will never completely go away while we are still on earth, our attitude toward them will change, some faster than others. This change in thoughts— repentance—is the difference between a believer and a non-believer who simply went through the motions in their efforts to be saved.

Wavering Belief

One of the most challenging things for many who claim to be Christian is overcoming the doubt that they may not be saved. When I used to evangelize on a college campus, I would ask professing Christians, "On a scale of 1 to 10, how sure are you that when you die, you will go to heaven?" For most of these Christians, their answer was 7. "Why not 10?" I would ask. The answer was often "Because I try to do good [read my Bible, go to church, pray], but sometimes I mess up and do things God probably won't forgive me for."

As we have established a few times in this book, salvation, or the lack thereof, has nothing to do with our actions or works for or against God. Our salvation depends entirely on whether we honestly believe in and accept the gift of Jesus. So why do we still doubt our salvation? A big part of this doubt stems from verses found in 1 John *(ESV)*.

If we say we have fellowship with Him while we walk in darkness, we lie and do not practice the truth. *(1:6)*

If we say we have no sin, we deceive ourselves, and the truth is not in us. *(1:8)*

If we say we have not sinned, we make Him a liar, and His Word is not in us. *(1:10)*

Whoever says "I know Him" but does not keep His commandments is a liar, and the truth is not in him. *(2:4)*

Whoever says he is in the light and hates his brother is still in darkness. *(2:9)*

Do not love the world or the things in the world. If anyone loves the world, the love of the Father is not in him. For all that is in the world—the desires of the flesh and the desires of the eyes and pride of life—is not from the Father but is from the world. *(2:15–16)*

According to these passages, if you still live in the world, have anger toward anyone, or believe you are not a sinner (or perhaps a lesser sinner than your peers), you are not saved. So are all Christians who continue to sin daily, have strife with their brothers, and still desire worldly things not saved? Maybe, maybe not. The difference is a matter of the heart and whether your decision to follow Christ was sincere. Jesus's death can pay for those sins, but only if you accept what He has made available to you.

The parable of the sower, found in Matthew 13, Mark 4, and Luke 8, describes the four responses people have when receiving the Word of God. Let us break it down using Luke 8:5–8 and 11–15 *(ESV)*:

"**A sower went out to sow his seed [spread the Word of God]. And as he sowed, some fell along the path and was trampled underfoot, and the birds of the air devoured it.**" *(v. 5)*

"**The ones along the path are those who have heard; then the devil comes and takes away the word from their hearts, so that they may not believe and be saved.**" *(v. 12)*

These are the ones who continue to refuse the truth given to them. The Word of God never enters their hearts, and they continue living in sin, never producing fruit.

Other seeds "**fell on the rock, and as it grew up, it withered away because it had no moisture**" *(v. 6)*. These are "**those who, when they hear the Word, receive it with joy. But these have no root; they believe for a while, and in time of testing fall away.**" *(v.13)*. This category of people is the first with questionable faith. They "believe" only when it fits their needs, sometimes picking and choosing which parts they want to believe in and which they don't. Because they did not establish a solid foundation or root system, they could not receive the living water that came from Jesus and, as a result, produced no fruit.

The third receiver of God's Word is like the seeds that "**fell among thorns, and the thorns grew up with it and choked it**" *(v. 7)*. These "**are those who hear, but as they go on their way they are choked by the cares and riches and pleasures of life, and their fruit does not mature.**" *(v. 14)*. Mark 4:19's version says, "**proves** unfruitful." When we allow life around us to overshadow God's Word, our spiritual journey gets snuffed out, resulting in a life that bears no fruit.

The final receivers of God's Word are those in which the seed **"fell into good soil and grew and yielded a hundredfold."** *(v. 8).* These **"are those who, hearing the Word, hold it fast in an honest and good heart, and bear fruit with patience."** *(v. 15).* This is the type of soil we should be striving for. As with any good garden, the fruit we bear requires a lot of work to be useful in God's kingdom, but it does produce fruit.

The success of your crop, your fruit, and your salvation greatly depends on properly preparing the soil or foundation where you live. This means repentance, turning from your old ways, and following Jesus. Jesus says, **"I am the light of the world. Whoever follows me will not walk in darkness but will have the light of life."** *(John 8:12 ESV).*

Just as crops require proper light to grow, we require the light of Jesus. **"If we walk in the light, as he is in the light, we have fellowship with one another, and the blood of Jesus his Son cleanses us from all sin."** *(1 John 1:7 ESV).*

We must also receive His living water and remove all the weeds or distractions that prevent us from growing in God. Jesus says, **"Remain in me, as I also remain in you. No branch can bear fruit by itself; it must remain in the vine. Neither can you bear fruit unless you remain in me."** (John 15:4 NIV).

After the Matthew 13 version of this parable, Jesus offered another: the parable of the weeds (Matthew 13:24–30). In this parable, a farmer planted good seeds. But an enemy scatted the seeds of weeds within the crop. As they grew, it became difficult to tell the difference between the two plants, so the gatherers were instructed to wait for them to fully develop so they could be distinguished from one another. The weeds would then be gathered and burned, and the wheat would then be harvested.

This parable illustrates that it can be difficult to tell the difference between true and false believers. So, while it can sometimes appear that someone who once believed has since walked away, I'm not sure if their belief was genuine. They might have believed in the idea of God, thinking of Him as some magic genie or good-luck charm, but was their trust fully in Him regardless of what life throws at them? Only God can truly answer this, as He can see the motivation behind our actions.

There's a chance that some who have walked away may be reunited with God in the afterlife, while others who appear to us to be devoted may be in for a rude awakening. Will God give them one last chance on judgment day? That's up to God. I'm sure He would know what people would do if they were taught correctly and wouldn't punish people for receiving misleading teaching. God's handling of salvation will be fair and just in accordance with His love for us. But we shouldn't put our trust in speculation; instead, we should strive to ensure that our hearts are aligned with God while here in the physical world.

If you find yourself doubting your salvation, read 1 John 3:19–21 *(ESV)*: **"By this we shall know that we are of the truth and reassure our heart before him; for whenever our heart condemns us, God is greater than our heart, and he knows everything. Beloved, if our heart does not condemn us, we have confidence before God."**

You will likely not feel any conviction for your sin if you are not a true believer. If you receive that conviction, God's grace can rectify that sin. You can rest assured and have joy, knowing you will never lose your salvation even when you fall into sin.

For the gifts and the calling of God are irrevocable. *(Romans 11:29 ESV)*

When we become a part of Jesus's flock—His sheep—we are secure under His protection for the rest of our lives. **"My sheep hear my voice, and I know them, and they follow me. I give them eternal life, and they will never perish, and no one will snatch** them out of my hand. My Father, who has given them to me, is greater than all, and no one is able to snatch them out of the Father's hand. I and the Father are one." *(John 10:27–30 ESV)*.

If there is any doubt whatsoever whether you have truly been saved, ask God to fill you with His Spirit. Turn from your sins and ask God to cultivate your life's soil so that you too may produce fruit for the kingdom of God.

Overcoming Doubt

There will be times in every Christian's life when we doubt our usefulness to God's army. Perhaps we messed up so badly that we feel ashamed and unworthy. Perhaps we just do not feel adequately trained. But as we established in the first chapter, God can and will use anyone, regardless of past actions or training. He prefers to use people without seemingly perfect backgrounds because then, both we and outside observers will have little choice but to recognize that a higher power, God, was behind our unlikely success.

God knows your heart and knows if it is for or against Him. If you accept Him as your leader, your teacher, and your Savior, He will use you. Assuming you genuinely believed when you accepted Christ, it is impossible to lose salvation. Some believe that salvation can be lost because they point to people who may have seemed active in the church at one point or held a leadership position but now have nothing to do with the church. However, these people are simply the ones who received the Word yet had no foundation or were overcome by the thorns of life. They most likely never had the saving belief to begin with. They simply went through the motions, fooling everyone, including themselves.

Hebrews 6:4–6 *(ESV)* says, **"For it is impossible, in the case of those who have once been enlightened, who have tasted the heavenly gift, and have shared in the Holy Spirit, and have tasted the goodness of the word of God and the powers of the age to**

The Army of One

come, and then have fallen away, to restore them again to repentance, since they are crucifying once again the Son of God to their own harm and holding him up to contempt."

This can be considered good or bad news, depending on how you view it. The bad news is you may not have ever been truly saved to begin with. The good news is you can still repent and turn toward God. Imagine the turmoil if salvation were determined by us yet followed the statement from Hebrews above. We would have to tell people they were no longer welcomed by God when they came back knocking on the church's door after a period of rebellion.

But even if we did achieve salvation, some Christians would still rebel.

Hebrews 6:10–12 *(ESV)* has an answer for that also: **"For God is not unjust so as to overlook your work and the love that you have shown for his name in serving the saints, as you still do. And we desire each one of you to show the same earnestness to have the full assurance of hope until the end, so that you may not be sluggish, but imitators of those who through faith and patience inherit the promises."**

The truth of the matter is that God doesn't accept flip-floppers. When Jesus says, **"No one can serve two masters, for either he will hate the one and love the other, or he will be devoted to the one and despise the other."** *(Matthew 6:24 ESV)*, He means we can't serve God on Sunday and seek pleasure from the world the rest of the week and expect God to work in us.

However, there is still hope for the genuine believer.

Galatians 2:19–21 *(NIV)* states: **"For through the law I died to the law so that I might live for God. I have been crucified with Christ and I no longer live, but Christ lives in me. The life I now live in the body, I live by faith in the Son of God, who loved me and gave himself for me. I do not set aside the grace of God, for if righteousness could be gained through the law, Christ died for nothing!"**

Share the Gospel

Now I would remind you, brothers, of the gospel I preached to you, which you received, in which you stand, and by which you are being saved, if you hold fast to the word I preached to you—unless you believed in vain. For I delivered to you as of first importance what I also received: that Christ died for our sins in accordance with the Scriptures, that he was buried, that he was raised on the third day in accordance with the Scriptures. *(1 Corinthians 15:1–4 ESV)*

Now that you have heard the gospel and learned what it means to be a Christian, it is time to share with others. As Christians, finding God is the ultimate goal for our lives. Teaching others how to find Him is a close second.

Through our actions and words, we are called to **"preach the word; be prepared in season and out of season; correct, rebuke and encourage—with great patience and careful instruction. For the time will come when people will not put up with sound doctrine. Instead, to suit their own desires, they will gather around them a great number of teachers to say what their itching ears want to hear. They will turn their ears away from the truth and turn aside to myths."** *(2 Timothy 4:2–4 NIV)*.

Sharing the Word of God is not all about getting up before a group of people to preach. The daily works you perform in God's name are often a greater testament than the words you preach. Anyone can preach about what to do, but if they do not put it into action themselves, even rightful teaching is useless to the one who professes it. Teaching or hearing the word without putting it into action and using what you learn is not enough.

But be doers of the word, and not hearers only, deceiving yourselves. For if anyone is a hearer of the word and not a doer, he is like a man who looks intently at his natural face in a mirror. For he looks at himself and goes away and at once forgets what he was like. But the one who looks into the perfect law, the law

of liberty, and perseveres, being no hearer who forgets but a doer who acts, he will be blessed in his doing. *(James 1:22–25 ESV)*

The gospel must be a daily part of our lives in which we live it without shame or embarrassment for our belief. We are entering a time when it is becoming increasingly unpopular to be called a Christian. Unfortunately, this may be in part due to many people fighting a battle under the Christian flag but with their own objectives in mind—meaning that the message of hope, peace, love, acceptance, and so forth has been replaced with messages of hate or intolerance.

We must work to ensure that the proper Christian message is preached. That often comes through how we interact with those around us and how we unashamedly share the only route to salvation.

Romans 1:16-17 *(NIV)* states, **"For I am not ashamed of the gospel, because it is the power of God that brings salvation to everyone who believes: first to the Jew, then to the Gentile. For in the gospel the righteousness of God is revealed—a righteousness that is by faith from first to last, just as it is written: "The righteous will live by faith."**

The gospel is not about scare tactics, such as saying all ____ are going to hell. The gospel should be a rescue mission: pulling people out of destructive ways, loving on them as God loves us despite our mistakes, and offering them the same gift of grace that freed us. It is not our job to save everyone we can. Nor is it our job to judge or condemn others for their actions. Our job is to "preach the good news, proclaiming the gospel to those we meet.

And he said to them, "Go into all the world and proclaim the gospel to the whole creation." *(Mark 16:15 ESV)*

"Go therefore and make disciples of all nations, baptizing them in the name of the Father and of the Son and of the Holy Spirit, teaching them to observe all that I have commanded you. And behold, I am with you always, to the end of the age." *(Matthew 28:19–20 ESV)*

Undeserved Grace

A disciple accepts and assists in spreading the doctrines of another. If God is calling out to you as in Isaiah 6:8 *(ESV)*, then your purpose has been defined:

And I heard the voice of the LORD saying, "Whom shall I send, and who will go for us?" Then I said, "Here am I! Send me."

No longer are you slaves to the struggles of your life. No longer will you have to worry about how you will provide or meet some needs. When we can learn to fully trust in God, even when things don't seem to be going the way we want, then there will be greater peace in our lives than we ever knew. But it comes with the responsibility to share.

"Everyone who calls on the name of the Lord will be saved." How then will they call on him in whom they have not believed? And how are they to believe in him of whom they have never heard? And how are they to hear without someone preaching? And how are they to preach unless they are sent? As it is written, "How beautiful are the feet of those who preach the good news!"
(Romans 10:13–15 ESV)

We must not show favoritism to those we talk to. We cannot judge based on appearances, past actions, or current beliefs. Everyone deserves to hear the gospel, a chance at freedom, and a chance for God to forgive them just as He has forgiven us.

My brothers and sisters, believers in our glorious Lord Jesus Christ must not show favoritism. Suppose a man comes into your meeting wearing a gold ring and fine clothes, and a poor man in filthy old clothes also comes in. If you show special attention to the man wearing fine clothes and say, "Here's a good seat for you," but say to the poor man, "You stand there" or "Sit on the floor by my feet," have you not discriminated among yourselves and become judges with evil thoughts?

Listen, my dear brothers and sisters: Has not God chosen those who are poor in the eyes of the world to be rich in faith and to inherit the kingdom he promised those who love him?

But you have dishonored the poor. Is it not the rich who are exploiting you? Are they not the ones who are dragging you into court? Are they not the ones who are blaspheming the noble name of him to whom you belong? *(James 2:1–7 NIV)*

Being a Christian means, you get to serve in God's army and complete the missions He set for every one of us. These are the works that come through faith. Jesus says in John 14:12 *(ESV)*, **"Truly, truly, I say to you, whoever believes in me will also do the works that I do; and greater works than these will he do, because I am going to the Father."**

We are called to work as Christians. Works are not what saves us but rather are a result of being saved. James 2:17–18, 24 *(ESV)* says, **"Faith by itself, if it does not have works, is dead. But someone will say, 'You have faith and I have works.' Show me your faith apart from your works, and I will show you my faith by my works. ... You see that a person is justified by works and not by faith alone."**

Even if you have a church on every corner or live in an area where most people call themselves Christians, that community may be largely dead because the people still choose the teachings of the world over the teachings of God. They talk the good talk but do not walk the walk. They did not perform the works God called them to. Whether or not they are saved is between them and God, but they are not doing their part in advancing the kingdom. Are you doing yours?

Service to God

"Choose this day whom you will serve ... But as for me and my house, we will serve the Lord." *(Joshua 24:15 ESV)*

Joshua 24:15 was directed to the Israelites after they took over the promised land. God has promised us numerous great things in this life, but many of them come with the expectations that we will obey the commands He set for us to the best of our ability.

The Israelites would maintain what they were given from God if they continued living under God's service. However, the moment they swayed from God's instructions, they served themselves through worldly desires influenced by the enemy. When they fell from God's service, God made it known, often resulting in the deaths of the offending party.

Jesus changed what desperately needed to be changed. It was too difficult to put ourselves in complete service to God and obey His commands completely. Death was imminent for even the most well-meaning of people. God wanted us free from this grasp of sin and destruction, so He sent His Son, Jesus.

For you were called to freedom, brothers. Only do not use your freedom as an opportunity for the flesh, but through love serve one another. *(Galatians 5:13 ESV)*

As stated before, your freedom through Christ is not a ticket to do what you want without consequence. You now have a set of responsibilities. These responsibilities depend on the gifts and callings that God has given you specifically.

I was called to write this book and perhaps others. My distraction by things of the world may be one reason I continue struggling so much. But I also believe that God will use my story of continuing to get back up when faced with challenges and that it may help those who need to hear it.

You see, I have two choices while going through my struggles. I can continue to sit and complain while allowing myself to get depressed, or I can turn back to God again despite distancing myself from Him as I have in the past. I chose to continue His mission to finish this book if it becomes the last thing I do. There were plenty of instances of depression and difficulties that tempted me to give up, but through my continual prayers to God, I am learning to trust in Him again and finish my mission at all costs.

Colossians 3:17, 23–24 *(ESV)* says, **"And whatever you do, in word or deed, do everything in the name of the Lord Jesus, giving** thanks to God the Father through him. ... **Whatever you do, work heartily, as for the Lord and not for men, knowing that from the Lord you will receive the inheritance as your reward. You are serving the Lord Christ."**

If you wash dishes, wash them as if you are serving God Himself. If you run a business, run that business as if God is your CEO. If you go to school, study diligently in preparation for your calling or callings from God. Including God in everything you do keeps you from preventable trouble and brings greater successes than you may have achieved on your own.

Show yourself in all respects to be a model of good works, and in your teaching show integrity, dignity, and sound speech that cannot be condemned, so that an opponent may be put to shame, having nothing evil to say about us. *(Titus 2:7–8 ESV)*

We all have a mission field, but not all of us are called to overseas missions. Who would attend to the lost people in your community if we were all busy in foreign nations? The salvation of your neighbors, co-workers, family, and every random person you encounter is just as important as those in distant countries. Our mission fields are often where we live, work, and play. If our actions are not always on point, the people we are supposed to witness to—the people God is trying to save—may instead turn their backs on God.

Our selfish desires may lead to eternal death, not just for ourselves but for those around us as well. Do you want to live with that on your conscience, knowing, as a believer in Christ who grants eternal life, that you did not do everything in your power to help influence that decision that could save someone?

I do not want to live with that on my heart, and I doubt you do either—yet most of us continue living selfishly. This is the biggest reason we must turn from our sins through repentance. Eyes will always be on us when we claim to follow God. Even if we had true belief and received salvation for ourselves, if our actions do not reflect that belief and we are viewed as hypocrites, we will have trouble fulfilling the missions set forth by God. If you tell yourself it is too late because you have already messed up, start now. You may have an uphill battle to climb, but it is never too late.

Remember the parable of the talents? God will trust us with either a little bit or a lot. How much depends on how much we know and follow His instructions. He will use you only if you are trusted with what He wants you to do. To be trusted, you must learn to follow Him.

Jesus says in John 15:14–15 *(ESV)*, **"You are my friends if you do what I command you. No longer do I call you servants, for the servant does not know what his master is doing; but I have called you friends, for all that I have heard from my Father I have made known to you."**

If you have felt distant from God, as I have many times in my journey to the finish line of life, you are likely trying to go through life without consulting your commander. We often wait until we are in trouble before reaching out to God, expecting Him to fix our mistakes so we can return to our sinful lives. Sometimes God will show His mercy, and sometimes, He will let us suffer some for our mistakes until we learn who is in control. He may help us quickly, or He may let us sit for some time until the lessons have time to sink in. Regardless of how God responds to your trials caused by sin, He would have much rather heard from you far before your time of need. To be close to God requires time with God. Between reading His Word and praying continually throughout your day, getting to know God and His commands for your life missions requires time, patience, and commitment to serving Him.

"But from there you will seek the Lord your God and you will find him, if you search after him with all your heart and with all your soul. When you are in tribulation, and all these things come upon you in the latter days, you will return to the Lord your God and obey his voice. For the Lord your God is a merciful God.

The Army of One

He will not leave you or destroy you or forget the covenant with your fathers that he swore to them." *(Deuteronomy 4:29–31 ESV)*

16

The War Is Won

Victory! The enemy has been defeated. We have won the war. Everywhere around us, the remaining enemy is bowing down in defeat. It was a long journey, and many souls were lost on both sides. Some will be honored, but many will not. Order and peace have been returned. All the pain and suffering was worth it as I look forward to a future without either. My commander called me to missions I never thought I could win, yet he led me through. As long as I trusted in his direction, I remained safe. His command kept me alive. His command set me free. I have nothing but thanks for his leadership.

"Blessed is the King who comes in the name of the Lord! Peace in heaven and glory in the highest!" *(Luke 19:38 ESV)*. Can you imagine a life without Satan's influence? No more sin, no more suffering, no more death. It is hard to imagine because we have lived with it all our lives, but that is what we can expect as children of the living God.

I declare to you, brothers and sisters, that flesh and blood cannot inherit the kingdom of God, nor does the perishable inherit the imperishable. Listen, I tell you a mystery: We will not all sleep, but we will all be changed—in a flash, in the twinkling of an eye, at the last trumpet. For the trumpet will sound, the dead will be raised imperishable, and we will be changed. For the perishable must clothe itself with the imperishable, and the mortal with immortality. When the perishable has been clothed with the imperishable, and the mortal with immortality, then the saying that is written will come true: "Death has been swallowed up in victory."

"**Where, O death, is your victory? Where, O death, is our sting?**" *(1 Corinthians 15:50–55 NIV)*

Are you ready for your new body, your new life, and your new future, living without fear or destruction? I am. God has come to change the world. Satan's power will be taken from him, and all will bow down to the coming of the King. **"God has highly exalted him and bestowed on him the name that is above every name, so that at the name of Jesus every knee should bow, in heaven and on earth and under the earth, and every tongue confess that Jesus Christ is Lord, to the glory of God the Father"** *(Philippians 2:9–11 ESV).*

Jesus's name will be exalted, lifted in praise, and worshiped through the end of time and beyond. Even those who failed to accept God's free gift will come to recognize Jesus as their king. There will be no other gods fighting for the title of ruler. Jesus will be the end of all tribulation, and for this, we will praise Him.

What Is Praise and Worship?

There is a common view that when Christians die, they find themselves a cloud and a harp and spend eternity singing to God. Since I have never been to heaven, I cannot say whether this claim is true, but I believe there will be much more, and praise will be a huge part. Contrary to the belief of many unbelievers, this opportunity to praise God for eternity will not be boring. I envision it being like the celebration of your favorite sports team winning its championship, only more extreme. Or perhaps it will be like the cheers and screams you hear at a concert of your favorite musician, only louder. Or maybe it will be like the extreme joy and happiness you get from the birth of a child and seeing them grow up, only way more intense. Whatever heaven is, it will be far beyond what we can imagine—and I promise it will not be boring.

So, what is praise and what is worship? For many in the church, praise and worship means singing. In some churches, this means hymns, while others may have more modern music. Some churches limit music to the organ, piano, or harp; others include drums, guitarists, or anything else that contributes to the music. Some churches have members who stand obediently in their place as they follow along with the music director; others have members who shout and dance in celebration. Whatever the case, is any one style better than the next? Is any style a more accurate representation of what it means to worship?

The answer is no. There are different styles for different people, and if the style brings people's attention to God and not the production or the people, then it is worship. Psalm 98: 4–6 *(ESV)* instructs us to **"Make a joyful noise to the Lord, all the earth; break forth into joyous song and sing praises! Sing praises to the Lord with the lyre, with the lyre and the sound of melody! With trumpets and the sound of the horn make a joyful noise before the King, the Lord!"**

Some people think it is wrong to have fun in church. They treat excitement and cheers as if they are sinful. But Psalm 150 and others encourage such behavior. Why wouldn't you shout for joy for the God who created the heavens and the earth? Why wouldn't you clap and cheer for the one who gave you the best gift of all—eternal life? Why wouldn't you celebrate your rebirth into the kingdom of God in every way you know how?

Psalm 150:3–6 *(ESV)* says, **"Praise Him with trumpet sound; praise Him with lute and harp! Praise Him with tambourine and dance; praise Him with strings and pipe! Praise Him with sounding cymbals; praise Him with loud clashing cymbals! Let everything that has breath praise the LORD! Praise the LORD!"**

Essentially, praise Him with everything you have—because if we remain silent, **"the very stones would cry out"** *(Luke 19:40 ESV)*. Do not let a bunch of stones outshine us in our worship of our God.

Praise and worship are not only about singing in church or elsewhere. In fact, praise and worship, although often thought of as synonymous, are two distinct things in which song and dance are only two representations. The dictionary describes praise as "to express approval of or admiration for" and "to extol or glorify." Worship is a "reverence for a deity or sacred object" or "the intense devotion to or esteem for a person or thing" and as a verb, "to love, admire, or esteem devotedly." None of these definitions mention singing at all. The fact is, God wants everything you do to be worship, and He wants the way you do it to be praiseworthy, knowing that God had a part in it.

Some people might be introverts or in a valley in their current walk, and shouting or dancing is not in their nature. But this does not mean you don't love the Lord as much as those who do those things. Even if you have to stand and praise silently, God will recognize it, and the more you can do so, even in the midst of struggles, the more you will grow and maintain your trust in God.

Finally, brothers, whatever is true, whatever is honorable, whatever is just, whatever is pure, whatever is lovely, whatever is commendable, if there is any excellence, if there is anything worthy of praise, think about these things. What you have learned and received and heard and seen in me—practice these things, and the God of peace will be with you. *(Philippians 4:8–9 ESV)*

Obey in everything those who are your earthly masters, not by way of eye-service, as people-pleasers, but with sincerity of heart, fearing the Lord. *(Colossians 3:22 ESV)*

Since therefore Christ suffered in the flesh, arm yourselves with the same way of thinking, for whoever has suffered in the flesh has ceased from sin, so as to live for the rest of the time in the flesh no longer for human passions but for the will of God. *(1 Peter 4:1–2 ESV)*

Above all, keep loving one another earnestly, since love covers a multitude of sins. Show hospitality to one another without grumbling. As each has received a gift, use it to serve one another, as good stewards of God's varied grace: whoever speaks, as one who speaks oracles of God; whoever serves, as

one who serves by the strength that God supplies—in order that in everything God may be glorified through Jesus Christ. *(1 Peter 4:8–11 ESV)*

God expects us to do as He commands. He expects us to use the gifts He has given us. He expects us to share in suffering as we strive to avoid a life of sin. He expects us to give everything we own to serve others as if we were serving Him directly. Our praise and our worship do not stop once we leave the church's doors. It is to be a part of our lifestyle every moment of every day. We should worship the Lord in everything we do and praise Him for all He does through us. Our worship will grow stronger the closer we get to God by knowing His Word. Worshiping without knowing who you are worshiping tends to be idolatry—an emotional attachment to the music or actions and not the worship recipient.

'**These people honor me with their lips, but their hearts are far from me. They worship me in vain; their teachings are merely human rules.**' *(Matthew 15:8–9 NIV)*

God desires the attention of your heart over a perfect musical production. This means that even if you cannot sing, your voice is still music to God's ears when your heart is aligned with Him.

Celebrating Victory

The war is won. All of God's soldiers line up in parade formation to celebrate the victory and honor those who lost their earthly lives fighting for Him. Some members of the opposing forces lined the side of the road, throwing rocks at us, trying in a last-ditch effort to distract us from the finish line. But we continue standing tall, looking forward to the end of the road, where we will break formation and celebrate the victory of our God.

The war we are fighting was determined long before the earth was created, and God had victory. He knew every battle we would face and whether we would win or lose. He knew the enemy's tactics to distract us and provided us with the means to get out if we so chose. He knew our weaknesses yet sent us into battles despite them just so His strength could be shown. He knew we would fail repeatedly, but He was always there to piece us back together in our brokenness.

He taught us how to love our enemies and bring peace to the hurting. He showed us how to eliminate our pride and trust in Him. He demonstrated undeserved mercy and forgiveness as no one else ever could. God pulled us through the impossible so that we could see His power and glory.

His love for us is unconditional, His forgiveness is limitless, and His ways are just. God is the ultimate example of all things good. Love, joy, peace, patience, kindness, goodness, faithfulness, gentleness, and self–control come from Him alone.

The race we are in is soon to be over. Have you done all you can to honor Him? God is waiting for you with arms open wide at the finish line, waiting to tell you, "Well done, good and faithful servant. You have fought the good fight and finished the race by keeping the faith."

He eagerly waits to award you the crown of righteousness as you complete your race, for He is the righteous judge who no longer sees sin in you. Your race was long and hard, but now your race is soon to be complete. Think back on all the trials that brought you to where you are today, and thank your God for the opportunity to serve in His army as you near the finish. I thank you for sticking with me on our journey together and pray we will one day celebrate our victories together when we meet up in heaven. Take care, and God bless you.

And the winner is ...
you!

Sinner's Prayer

Have mercy on me, O God, according to your unfailing love; according to your great compassion blot out my transgressions. Wash away all my iniquity and cleanse me from my sin.

For I know my transgressions, and my sin is always before me. Against you, you only, have I sinned and done what is evil in your sight; so you are right in your verdict and justified when you judge. Surely I was sinful at birth, sinful from the time my mother conceived me. Yet you desired faithfulness even in the womb; you taught me wisdom in that secret place.

Cleanse me with hyssop, and I will be clean; wash me, and I will be whiter than snow. Let me hear joy and gladness; let the bones you have crushed rejoice. Hide your face from my sins and blot out all my iniquity.

Create in me a pure heart, O God, and renew a steadfast spirit within me. Do not cast me from your presence or take your Holy Spirit from me. Restore to me the joy of your salvation and grant me a willing spirit, to sustain me. *(Psalm 51:1–12 NIV)*

The sinner's prayer is not about specific words you say but rather a sincere belief and faith in the one you are praying to. The passage above is just one example directly from the Bible.

But if you
Realize you are a sinner,
Recognize that Jesus died on the cross for you,
Repent of your sin,
and Receive Jesus into your life—
You will be saved.

VERSE INDEX

OLD TESTAMENT

GENESIS

Genesis 1:26 136

EXODUS

Exodus 20:12..............................18
Exodus 20:17..............................23

LEVITICUS

Leviticus 5:1 22

NUMBERS

Numbers 14:18........................138

DEUTERONOMY

Deuteronomy 4:29–31 243

JOSHUA

Joshua 24:15.............................239

FIRST SAMUEL

1 Samuel 16:7 96

FIRST KINGS

1 Kings 19:11–12 32

SECOND CHRONICLES

2 Chronicles 7:14......................123
2 Chronicles 20:17....................215

JOB

Job 1:8 176
Job 5:17–18.................................69
Job 14:5 31
Job 42:3 184

PSALM

Psalm 7:10 158
Psalm 16:11 34
Psalm 17:5 156
Psalm 18:30 157
Psalm 19:1–2..............................32
Psalm 25:4 33
Psalm 26:2–3 155
Psalm 32:3 189
Psalm 33:6, 9............................200
Psalm 34:17–20........................209
Psalm 37:23–24........................208
Psalm 39:4–6..............................31
Psalm 40:2 225
Psalm 41:5 55
Psalm 42:11 210
Psalm 46:1 212
Psalm 51:1–12..........................251
Psalm 66:10–12........................182
Psalm 69:2 225
Psalm 71:20 211
Psalm 73:26 195
Psalm 89:30–33..........................66
Psalm 98: 4–6............................246
Psalm 104:24–25........................32
Psalm 127:1 76
Psalm 139:13–14........................96
Psalm 139:23–24......................190
Psalm 150:3–6..........................246

PROVERBS

Proverbs 1:24–29 104
Proverbs 3:5–6.................92, 138
Proverbs 3:25–26 182
Proverbs 4:23 154
Proverbs 5:12–14 67
Proverbs 6:20–22 18
Proverbs 8:17..............................30
Proverbs 10:17............................66
Proverbs 11:2............................124
Proverbs 13:12............................29
Proverbs 14:16............................90
Proverbs 15:22............................90
Proverbs 16:2..............................25
Proverbs 16:9...................93, 142
Proverbs 27:17..........................106
Proverbs 29:23..........................124

ECCLESIASTES

Ecclesiastes 2:11..................5, 76
Ecclesiastes 4: 9–10, 12...........106
Ecclesiastes 7:16.........................94

ISAIAH

Isaiah 6:8..................................238
Isaiah 41:10 212
Isaiah 43:18 212

Isaiah 55:1–2, 6-7 5
Isaiah 56:2 17
Isaiah 61:7 212

JEREMIAH

Jeremiah 16:19–20 14
Jeremiah 17:5–9 169
Jeremiah 17:5,7 92
Jeremiah 29:11 92
Jeremiah 29:11-13 213
Jeremiah 30:17 210

EZEKIEL

Ezekiel 7:19 33
Ezekiel 28:12–19 173

DANIEL

Daniel 9:10 71

MICAH

Micah 7:19 211

HAGGAI

Haggai 1:5–6 5

MALACHI

Malachi 1:6 18

NEW TESTAMENT

MATTHEW

Matthew 4:8–9 165
Matthew 5:22 19
Matthew 5:22–24 72
Matthew 5:28 20
Matthew 5:44–48 116
Matthew 6:14–15 72
Matthew 6:20–21 154
Matthew 6:24 .... 10, 57, 235
Matthew 6:26 198
Matthew 6:33-34 210
Matthew 7:1–5 128
Matthew 7:13–14 32
Matthew 7:21–23 44
Matthew 10:20 145
Matthew 11:28–30 215
Matthew 12:6–8 16
Matthew 15:6–9 80
Matthew 15:8-9 248
Matthew 15:11 21
Matthew 16:24–25 57
Matthew 17:20 159
Matthew 18:3–4 36
Matthew 18:8–9 191
Matthew 18:15–17 131
Matthew 18:21–22 73
Matthew 22:37–39 .... 95, 139
Matthew 25:26–30 98
Matthew 28:19-20 237

MARK

Mark 2:27–28 16
Mark 8:35–36 11
Mark 10:21–31 78
Mark 16:15 237

LUKE

Luke 8:5–8,11-15 231
Luke 12:15 24
Luke 13:24 13
Luke 13:30 125
Luke 14:8–11 123
Luke 15:28-32 79
Luke 17:3–4 73
Luke 18:9–14 80
Luke 19:38 244
Luke 19:40 246
Luke 23:34 10

JOHN

John 1:1–5, 9–14 135
John 1:3 200
John 3:16 47
John 3:30 123
John 4:13–14 60
John 5:19–20 137
John 5:24 212
John 6:38 139
John 7:24 127
John 7:37–38 60
John 8:7 127
John 8:12 232
John 8:31–32 3
John 8:32 220
John 8:34 6
John 9:31 189
John 10:14–18 140
John 10:27–30 234
John 11:4 68
John 11:25–26 55
John 12:46-48 223
John 14:6 .... 12, 47, 81
John 14:12 239
John 14:16–17 144
John 14:17 153
John 14:26-27 142
John 15:1–6 56
John 15:4 232
John 15:5 141
John 15:14–15 242
John 16:7–11 143
John 16:33 56

ACTS

Acts 13:22 211
Acts 13:38–39 25
Acts 20:28 84

ROMANS

Romans 1:16-17 237
Romans 2:1–3 128
Romans 2:8–9 26

Romans 3:10 154
Romans 3:23-25 223
Romans 4:4—5 11
Romans 4:6—8 12
Romans 4:20—22 219
Romans 5:1—5 217
Romans 5:8 71
Romans 5:8—9 227
Romans 5:18-19 226
Romans 6:5—7 110
Romans 6:9—11 50
Romans 6:15—16 25
Romans 6:20—22 229
Romans 6:23 .... 12, 48, 223
Romans 7:14—18 214
Romans 7:21—23, 8:1—2 214
Romans 8:4—5 144
Romans 8:14—16 145
Romans 8:26 144
Romans 8:28 210
Romans 10:9 47
Romans 10:13-15 238
Romans 11:29 233
Romans 12:1—2 228
Romans 12:3 94
Romans 12:4—5 108
Romans 12:6—8 101
Romans 12:9—10 116
Romans 12:12 210
Romans 12:16 94
Romans 14:1, 4, 13 131
Romans 14:5—6 17
Romans 15:1—6 112
Romans 16:17—18 198

FIRST CORINTHIANS

1 Corinthians 1:26—31 126
1 Corinthians 2:5 220
1 Corinthians 3:1—3 36
1 Corinthians 4:7 94
1 Corinthians 9:24—27 120
1 Corinthians 10:13 26
1 Corinthians 10: 23—24 95
1 Corinthians 11:18—19 199
1 Corinthians 12:4—7 100
1 Corinthians 12:8—11 101
1 Corinthians 12:12—27 109
1 Corinthians 12:28—31 101
1 Corinthians 13:1—3 117
1 Corinthians 13:4—8 113
1 Corinthians 15:1—4 236
1 Corinthians 15:3—7, 12-23 49
1 Corinthians 15:21—22 48
1 Corinthians 15:25—26 227
1 Corinthians 15:42—44 57
1 Corinthians 15:50 55
1 Corinthians 15:50—55 245
1 Corinthians 16:13—14 149

SECOND CORINTHIANS

2 Corinthians 1:21—22 145
2 Corinthians 3:4—5 195
2 Corinthians 4: 8—10 212
2 Corinthians 4:17—18 184

2 Corinthians 5:21 48
2 Corinthians 7:9-10 228
2 Corinthians 9:10—11 106
2 Corinthians 10:3-5 164
2 Corinthians 10:3—6 216
2 Corinthians 12:9—10 214
2 Corinthians 12:10 195
2 Corinthians 13:5—9 181

GALATIANS

Galatians 1:10 95
Galatians 1:10—12 38
Galatians 2:19—21 235
Galatians 3:19 25
Galatians 4:8 14
Galatians 5:1 54
Galatians 5:13 240
Galatians 5:13—14 26
Galatians 5:16—21 37
Galatians 5:17 146
Galatians 5:22—23 37
Galatians 6:3—4 195

EPHESIANS

Ephesians 1:3—10 35
Ephesians 1:7 188
Ephesians 2:1—3 34
Ephesians 2:8—9 .... 71, 157
Ephesians 4:1—6 109
Ephesians 4:15—16 109
Ephesians 4:18 204
Ephesians 4:22 13
Ephesians 4:22—24 190
Ephesians 4:28 22
Ephesians 6:10—18 149
Ephesians 6:16 158

PHILIPPIANS

Philippians 1:6 124
Philippians 2:1—4 114
Philippians 2:3—4 95
Philippians 2:9—11 245
Philippians 3:12—16 120
Philippians 3:13—14 219
Philippians 4:6—7 168
Philippians 4:8—9 247
Philippians 4:11—13 93
Philippians 4:19 93

COLOSSIANS

Colossians 1:13—14 38
Colossians 1:15—20 139
Colossians 1:16 55
Colossians 2:8 204
Colossians 2:16—17 17
Colossians 3:12—14 155
Colossians 3:12—17 115
Colossians 3:17, 23—24 240
Colossians 3:22 247
Colossians 3:23—24 .... 93, 219

First Thessalonians

1 Thessalonians 5:8–15 112
1 Thessalonians 5:16-19 170

Second Thessalonians

2 Thessalonians 1:4 160
2 Thessalonians 1:9 50
2 Thessalonians 3:3 215

First Timothy

1 Timothy 1:12 216
1 Timothy 1:15–16 35
1 Timothy 2:3–6 35
1 Timothy 2:5–6 142
1 Timothy 4:12–16 84
1 Timothy 6:3–5, 20-21   23
1 Timothy 6:6–10 24
1 Timothy 6:17–19 59

Second Timothy

2 Timothy 1:7 170
2 Timothy 1:8–10 29
2 Timothy 2:3–4 216
2 Timothy 2:21 157
2 Timothy 2:22 155
2 Timothy 3:16–17 .... 25, 165
2 Timothy 4:2–4 236

Titus

Titus 2:7–8 241
Titus 2:11–14 115
Titus 3:3 6
Titus 3:3–7 215
Titus 3:9 199

Hebrews

Hebrews 1:3–4 224
Hebrews 2:1 229
Hebrews 4:9–11 17
Hebrews 4:12 165
Hebrews 4:15–16 178
Hebrews 4:16 163
Hebrews 5:11–14 122
Hebrews 5:12–6:2 36
Hebrews 6:4–6 234
Hebrews 6:10–12 235
Hebrews 8:7 224
Hebrews 9:13–14 226
Hebrews 9:14,22 189
Hebrews 10:11–14 227
Hebrews 10:17 6
Hebrews 10:24–25 112
Hebrews 10:26–27 229
Hebrews 11:1 .... 114, 157
Hebrews 11:6 161
Hebrews 12:1–2 120
Hebrews 12:5–11 66
Hebrews 13:4 20
Hebrews 13:5 24

James

James 1:2–4 .... 70, 217
James 1:2–12 179
James 1:5–8 220
James 1:13–15 174
James 1:19 178
James 1:22-25 237
James 2:1–7 239
James 2:10 11
James 2:14–17, 26 160
James 2:17–18, 24 239
James 4:6 123
James 4:7 216
James 4:11–12 131
James 4:17 25
James 5:4 21
James 5:19–20 30

First Peter

1 Peter 1:6–9 181
1 Peter 1:14–15 122
1 Peter 2:1–3 36
1 Peter 2:15–17 204
1 Peter 3:15 156
1 Peter 4:1–2 247
1 Peter 4:1–6 31
1 Peter 4:8–11 248
1 Peter 4:10–11 101
1 Peter 4:12–13 217
1 Peter 5:8 176
1 Peter 5:9 162

Second Peter

2 Peter 1:5–7 114
2 Peter 2:9 211

First John

1 John 1:6–10 190
1 John 1:6,8,10; 2:4,9,15-16   230
1 John 1:7 232
1 John 1:9 .... 71, 138
1 John 2:1-2 223
1 John 2:15-17 14
1 John 2:28 – 3:3 38
1 John 3:4, 8 10
1 John 3:10 11
1 John 3:15-16 19
1 John 3:16 19
1 John 3:16–18 113
1 John 3:19–21 233
1 John 4:7–8 113
1 John 4:20 116
1 John 5:16 131

Revelation

Revelation 3:20 35
Revelation 16:10–11 50
Revelation 20:10 50
Revelation 21:4 51
Revelation 22:18–19 152

ABOUT THE AUTHOR

Jon is a Christian author who uses his written word to reach audiences around the globe. He credits his work to God and is often inspired by his life circumstances and observations from others. Jon considers his work to be personal lessons from God, that he feels led to share with anyone else who may need to hear it too. Although Jon has experienced many struggles in life, he keeps pushing forward knowing that God will use him if he is faithful.

FIND ME ON GOODREADS

Connect to stay up to date and see other books by author.

Please consider leaving a review on Goodreads and Amazon to help me reach more readers.

www.ingramcontent.com/pod-product-compliance
Lightning Source LLC
Chambersburg PA
CBHW050857160426
43194CB00011B/2191